"LaBerge's book conveys the technique dreamers can use to revolutionize their inner dreamworld. Written with exceptional clarity, packed with new material, the book weaves a spell for the reader. I highly recommend this fascinating work."

DR. PATRICIA GARFIELD
Author of *Creative Dreaming*

"Lucid dreaming is typically a rare occurrence, but LaBerge demonstrates that it can be induced by anybody who sincerely wants to awaken to their dreams."

WILLIS HARMAN, PH.D. AND
HOWARD RHEINGOLD
Authors of *Higher Creativity*

"Stephen LaBerge has proven scientifically that people can be fully conscious in their dreams while remaining asleep and dreaming at the same time. LaBerge's book provides advice and techniques showing how to become a lucid dreamer and how to make practical use of the state for stimulating personal growth...and facilitating creative problem solving. A provocative and eminently readable book, rich with ideas and insights."

DR. ROBERT E. ORNSTEIN
Author of *The Psychology of Consciousness*

Also by Stephen LaBerge
Published by Ballantine Books:

EXPLORING THE WORLD OF LUCID DREAMING
  (with Howard Rheingold)

LUCID DREAMING

Stephen LaBerge, Ph.D.

Foreword by
Robert Ornstein, Ph.D.

BALLANTINE BOOKS • NEW YORK

Library of Congress Catalog Card Number: 85-4691

ISBN 0-345-33355-1

This edition published by arrangement with
Jeremy P. Tarcher, Inc.

The author would like to thank the following authors and publishers for their permission to reprints material:

Man and Time by J. B. Priestly. Copyright © 1964 Aldus Books, London.
Life After Life by Raymond Moody. Copyright © 1977.
"The Precious Jewel," by Idries Shah from *Thinkers of the East.* Copyright © 1971 by Idries Shah.

Manufactured in the United States of America

First Ballantine Books Edition: July 1986

23 22 21 20 19 18 17 16 15

To my parents

Contents

Foreword by Robert Ornstein, Ph.D.   xi
1. Awake in Your Dreams   1
2. The Origins and History of Lucid Dreaming   21
3. The New World of Lucid Dreaming   42
4. Exploring the Dream World:
   Lucid Dreamers in the Laboratory   78
5. The Experience of Lucid Dreaming   100
6. Learning Lucid Dreaming   138
7. The Practical Dreamer:
   Applications of Lucid Dreaming   167
8. Dreaming: Function and Meaning   197
9. Dreaming, Illusion, and Reality   227
10. Dreaming, Death, and Transcendence   253
    Epilogue: Alive in Your Life   273
    Notes   283
    Index   297

Acknowledgments

"Originality," it has been said, "is merely unconscious plagiarism." Because the ideas in this book de-
rive from so many sources, I have not always been able
to remember whom to credit. My apologies to those not
explicitly cited, and my thanks to all.

Daniel Goleman and Robert Eckhardt provided early
encouragement for the writing of this book. The Holmes
Center for Research in Holistic Healing and the Mon-
teverde Foundation graciously awarded me grants.

I wish to thank Dr. William Dement who provided
laboratory space at the Stanford Sleep Research Center
for my experiments, and Dr. Lynn Nagel for his crucial
assistance at the beginning of our work. I also wish to
thank my research assistants for their help, and all of
the Oneironauts who participated in our lucid dream
project, especially Dr. Beverly Kedzierski.

A number of individuals have my gratitude for reading and commenting upon various drafts of the manuscript; they include Lorna Catford, Henry Greenberg,
Dorothy Marie Jones, Lynne Levitan, Robert Ornstein,
Howard Rhinegold and Jon Singer. I am also indebted

to Jeremy Tarcher for sage advice, and to Hank Stine and Laurie LaBerge who heroically edited the entire manuscript.

Finally, I am grateful to L. P. for only she knows how much.

Foreword

Stephen LaBerge has done something unusual: he has shown that what was once thought to be impossible in the realm of consciousness is in fact possible. He has proven scientifically that people can be fully conscious while remaining asleep and dreaming at the same time. How he has done this makes a fascinating story told in the first section of this book.

LaBerge's proof is important because it shows, once again, that the possibilities of human consciousness are greater than we had thought. Many scientists had believed that dreams were in their very nature "irrational" and "unconscious." From this perspective, lucid dreaming was beyond the pale.

Incorrect conceptions frequently act as barriers to understanding, thereby concealing possibilities from view. To give a parallel example, it was once considered impossible to run a mile in less than four minutes. In fact, this idea seemed to form a real barrier for many runners until one man succeeded. Soon after this conceptual barrier was broken, many others found themselves able to run four–minute miles. We seem to attempt only what we assume to be possible.

The same principle holds for consciousness, and LaBerge's demonstration of the possibility of conscious and deliberate action in the dream state may serve to inspire others to do the same.

For readers interested in developing the skill of lucid dreaming, LaBerge's book provides not only inspiration, but also advice and techniques showing how to become a lucid dreamer and how to make practical use of the state for stimulating personal growth, enhancing self-confidence, promoting mental and perhaps also physical health, and facilitating creative problem solving.

Dr. LaBerge has written a provocative and eminently readable book. Readers of the last section of *Lucid Dreaming* especially will be richly rewarded with ideas and insights that forbid, in the words of William James, "a premature closing of our accounts with reality." The author has shown that lucid dreaming—as much as any other activity—if followed with an open and sensitive mind, can lead to a more unified understanding of consciousness.

Robert E. Ornstein, Ph.D.

1

~~~~~~~~~~~~~

Awake in Your Dreams

As I wandered through a high-vaulted corridor deep within a mighty citadel, I paused to admire the magnificent architecture. Somehow the contemplation of these majestic surroundings stimulated the realization that I was *dreaming!* In the light of my lucid consciousness, the already impressive splendor of the castle appeared even more of a marvel, and with great excitement I began to explore the imaginary reality of my "castle in the air." Walking down the hall, I could feel the cold hardness of the stones beneath my feet and hear the echo of my steps. Every element of this enchanting spectacle seemed real—in spite of the fact that I remained perfectly aware it was all a dream!

Fantastic as it may sound, I was in full possession of my waking faculties while dreaming and soundly asleep: I could think as clearly as ever, freely remember details of my waking life, and act deliberately upon conscious reflection. Yet none of this diminished the vividness of my dream. Paradox or no, I was awake in my dream!

~ 1 ~

Finding myself before two diverging passageways in the castle, I exercised my free will, choosing to take the right-hand one, and shortly came upon a stairway. Curious about where it might lead, I descended the flight of steps and found myself near the top of an enormous subterranean vault. From where I stood at the foot of the stairs, the floor of the cavern sloped steeply down, fading in the distance into darkness. Several hundred yards below I could see what appeared to be a fountain surrounded by marble statuary. The idea of bathing in these symbolically renewing waters captured my fancy, and I proceeded at once down the hillside. Not on foot, however, for whenever I want to get somewhere in my dreams, I fly. As soon as I landed beside the pool, I was at once startled by the discovery that what from above had seemed merely an inanimate statue now appeared unmistakably and ominously alive. Towering above the fountain stood a huge and intimidating genie, the Guardian of the Spring, as I somehow immediately knew. All my instincts cried out "Flee!" But I remembered that this terrifying sight was only a dream. Emboldened by the thought, I cast aside fear and flew not away, but straight up to the apparition. As is the way of dreams, no sooner was I within reach than we had somehow become of *equal* size and I was able to look him in the eyes, face to face. Realizing that my fear had created his terrible appearance, I resolved to embrace what I had been eager to reject, and with open arms and heart I took both his hands in mine. As the dream slowly faded, the genie's power seemed to flow into me, and I awoke filled with vibrant energy. I felt like I was ready for anything.

The dream I have just recounted is a sample of a little-explored and fascinating world of inner experiences. Being "awake in your dreams" provides the opportunity for unique and compelling adventures rarely surpassed elsewhere in life. That alone ought to be more than enough to spark the interest of the adventurous in lucid dreaming, as this remarkable phenomenon of dreaming while being fully conscious that you are dreaming is called. Yet adventure may prove to be the least important of a variety of reasons you might find it rewarding to cultivate the skill of lucid dreaming. (It *is* learnable, as you will see in Chapter 6.) For example, lucid dreaming has considerable potential for promoting personal growth and self-development, enhancing self-confidence, improving mental and physical health, facilitating creative problem-solving, and helping you to progress on the path to self-mastery.

The foregoing list may strike some as extravagant, but I believe there is substantial evidence supporting these claims. The particulars will be dealt with in due course, but first it may be helpful to take a more general approach. All of these applications of lucid dreaming sleep under the same blanket: They each possess, to a greater or lesser extent, the potential for improving the quality of your life and enhancing your sense of well-being by enriching, broadening, and even radically transforming the varieties of experience open to you as a human being.

The suggestion that lucid dreams could improve the quality of your life applies to both your everyday and everynight life. One reason for this is that whatever wisdom you acquire in your lucid dreams seems to remain at your disposal to help you live your waking life. Moreover, the reverse is equally true: You can remember the lessons you have learned in waking life in your lucid dreams. Unfortunately, neither is usually the case for the ordinary dreamer, who experiences a lack of connection between dreams and waking life. Typically, non-lucid dreamers suffer from a state-specific form of amnesia, so that while awake they remember their dreams only with difficulty, and while asleep they recall their waking lives through a carnival mirror, darkly and distortedly, or not at all. You might conceivably ask, Is this so bad? Why should it matter whether we live two lives or one? By way of an answer, I would offer an analogy: Suppose the odd and even days of the months were for some reason so unrelated for you that on any given day you could only remember thoughts and actions from *half* (the even or the odd, as the case might be) of your past. I leave it to you: Would this be so bad? In lucid dreams, however, the veil of amnesia is lifted, and with the help of memory, lucidity builds a bridge between the two worlds of day and night.

A skeptic might object that this analogy is misleading. After all, the odd and even days of waking life are equally valuable, but what is the world of dreams able to offer that compares to the world of waking reality? Is a bridge between our waking and dream worlds worth the trouble? Specifically, what sort of return could you expect on the time and energy needed to seriously cultivate dreams in general and lucid dreams in particular?

A number of answers could be given. One line of argument might start from Freud's conception of the dream as the *Via Regia,* or royal road to the unconscious mind. Anyone interested in personal growth can hardly afford to ignore the insights derived from a study of his or her own dreams. And to reap the fullest harvest from the dream state requires lucidity. In a word, dreams are a must for those interested in self-development.

Mental health aside, what else does the world of dreams have to offer? The answer that springs first to mind is "physical health." For one thing, the distinction between "mental" and "physical" is not always easy to make, and is in fact based on outdated philosophies. The more modern, "systems" view sees health as a matter of integration of the whole person. "Integration," here refers to the coordinated functioning of the human biosystem as a unit. For *Homo sapiens,* this involves interactions among at least three levels of organization: the biological, the psychological, and the sociological. The intuitive appeal of this conception of health seems clear enough as it is. Still, it seems even more sensible if one considers some of the synonyms of *health,* such as *wholesome, sound,* and *hale:* all share the root meaning of integration or wholeness.

I stress the concept of wholeness at this point because it will help you appreciate the emphasis I place on self-integration later in this chapter. Also, it sets the stage for presenting the fact that psychological events of the dream can indeed affect biological functioning of the body, as the experiments at Stanford University have shown. Considering that most diseases have at least a partial psychosomatic component, there may even be reason to believe that lucid dreams can be used to facilitate the healing of psychosomatic syndromes.

One more application of lucid dreaming should be mentioned: creative problem solving and decision making. In the course of history, dreams have frequently been credited as an important source of creativity in a wide range of human endeavors, including literature, science, engineering, painting, music, cinema, and even sports. Among the first creative dreamers to come to mind is Robert Louis Stevenson, who attributed many of his writings to dreams, including *The Strange Case of Dr. Jekyll and Mr. Hyde;* an even more famous example is Samuel Taylor Coleridge and his opium-dream poem, "Kubla Khan." Among scientists, we may cite the nineteenth-century German chemist Friedrich August Kekulé's dream discovery of the structure of the benzene molecule, and Otto Loewi's dream-inspired experiment demonstrating the chemical mediation of nerve impulses, which won him the Nobel prize for physiology in 1938. In the field of engineering, there are several instances of inventions revealed in dreams, including Elias Howe's sewing machine. Painters also attribute some of their works to dreams; William Blake and Paul Klee provide two of the best-documented cases. Likewise, among composers, we find that quite a number—including Mozart, Beethoven, Wagner, Tartini, and Saint-Saens—

have credited dreams as a source of inspiration. As for cinema, there are many instances of dream-inspired films— to cite a few at random, Alain Resnais's *Last Year at Marienbad,* Ingmar Bergman's *Hour of the Wolf,* and Judith Guest's screenplay for *Ordinary People.* Finally, the famous golfer, Jack Nicklaus, claims to have made a discovery in a dream that improved his game by ten strokes— overnight! These examples will have served their purpose if you are now willing to accept the premise that people have not infrequently received creative ideas in dreams.

Up until now, we have had little or no control over the occurrence of creative dreams. But at this point, it seems well within the realm of possibility that the fantastic and heretofore unruly creativity of the dream state might be brought within our conscious control by means of lucid dreaming. Kekule's words on the occasion of presenting his dream discovery to his colleagues are worth repeating: "Gentlemen"—to which I hasten to add, "and ladies"— "let us learn to dream."

Let us turn now from such possibly prosaic applications of lucid dreaming to what is perhaps its most sublime potentiality. Suppose I were to tell you that hidden within your dreams there is a precious jewel, a treasure of incalculable value if you were to find it. But to find it, you must first master the power of being awake in your dreams. The reason why is easily explained. If you had lost something, say the key to your house, would you sooner find it searching with your eyes open or closed? What is obvious in regard to your outer vision applies, I believe, analogously to your inner vision.

In most of our dreams, our inner eye of reflection is shut and we sleep within our sleep. We are usually unconscious that what we are doing is dreaming. There are profound possibilities inherent in the dream state, but it is difficult to take advantage of them if we fail to recognize them until after we awaken. Fortunately, while this condition of ignorance is usually the rule, it is not the only rule. The exception takes place when we "awaken" within our dreams—without disturbing or ending the dream state—and learn to recognize that we are dreaming while the dream is still happening. During such lucid dreams we become and remain fully conscious of the fact that we are dreaming— and therefore that we are asleep. Thus we are, in a sense, simultaneously both "awake" and "asleep."

Asleep but conscious? Conscious yet dreaming? Phrases such as these may seem at first glance to embody the very essence of self-contradiction. However, this paradox is only an apparent one. It is resolved by realizing that "asleep" and "conscious" refer, here, to two entirely different domains. I say that lucid dreamers are asleep in regard to the physical world because they are not in conscious sensory contact with it; likewise, they are awake to the inner worlds of their dreams because they are in conscious contact with them. It is in this precise sense that I speak of being "awake in your dreams."

While I am clarifying terms, I have been speaking of the lucid dreamer as "conscious." What exactly does this mean? In general terms, you are acting consciously if you know what you are doing while you are doing it, and are able to spell it out explicitly. So if, you can say to yourself while dreaming that "what I am doing just now is *dreaming,*" you are, in fact, conscious.

Most of our behavior, whether waking or dreaming, is relatively unconscious, because consciousness is limited— in the sense that we can only focus our attention on one thing, or at most a few things, at a time. We cannot, therefore, be conscious of everything around us at any given time. But still we tend to be less conscious than we could be, and this is because "paying attention" requires mental effort. Under normal circumstances we only take the trouble to be as conscious of any aspect of our current experiential world as we need to be. More precisely, we tend to focus attention only where we believe it is necessary for achieving our current goals.

Under most ordinary circumstances, our lives are so predictably arranged that unconscious habits are adequate to get us where we want to go. Thus, for example, if you habitually drive to work, you do so with very little attention focused on what you are doing. Occasionally you have found yourself driving to work on "automatic pilot," only to awaken from your reverie to the realization that you were not, in fact, intending to go to work at all! Habit was driving you to work; *you* actually may have wanted to go out and buy a book about (why not?) lucid dreams! But once you became conscious that your automatic behavior was not serving your intended goal, you were able to change deliberately course in order to arrive at the bookstore.

This illustrates the special usefulness of conscious, deliberate action: it gives you more flexible and creative responses to unexpected, non-routine situations. Consciousness confers the same advantages on the dream state as it does on the waking state. As a consequence, while awake in your dreams you are in a unique position to respond creatively to the unexpected situations you can encounter there. This quality of flexible control, which is characteristic of lucid dreams, brings within reach a remarkable range of possibilities—from indulging your boldest fantasies to fulfilling your highest spiritual aspirations.

Consciousness brings the lucid dreamer other gifts besides the capacity for deliberate action. The lucid dreamer is also generally able to think clearly and to remember past experience and intentions. Lucid dreamers can usually recall any particular plans they may have previously made regarding what they would like to do in their dreams. This opens up a whole new approach to the scientific study of dreams and consciousness, as will be described shortly. But for the average lucid dreamer, it means being able to face one's fears in dreams, or to explore new realms of experience, or to work on some particular problem within the dream.

This new dimension in dreaming can be likened to seeing things in living color when before you saw only the lifeless shades between black and white. The impact of the sudden emergence of lucidity can be profound. A hint of it might be conveyed to readers who have seen *The Wizard of Oz*. Who could forget Dorothy's reaction when she unexpectedly found herself transported from the black-and-white world of Kansas to the spectacular color of the Land of Oz? The lucid dreamer would certainly agree with the conclusion the astonished Dorothy shared with her canine companion upon arriving over the rainbow: "Toto, I don't think we're in Kansas anymore!" This cinematic example suggests something of the excitement and exhilaration that seems especially characteristic of a dreamer's first experience of full lucidity. However, this feeling has not altogether disappeared from my own lucid dreams even after the nearly nine hundred such experiences I have recorded since 1977.

The impact resulting from the emergence of lucidity is probably proportional to the clarity and completeness of the dreamer's change of consciousness. There are degrees of lucidity, and the common experience of awakening from a nightmare after realizing it was "only a dream" is typical of the lower ranges (or why escape from what is "only a dream"?), and is usually accompanied by no greater feeling than relative relief. But the full-blown lucid dream, in which the dreamer stays in the dream for a period extended enough to allow the experience of wonder, can be associated with an electrifying sensation of rebirth and the discovery of a new world of experience.

First-time lucid dreamers are often overwhelmed by the realization that they have never before experienced their dreams with all their being, and now they are utterly awake

in their sleep! This is how one lucid dreamer described the
expanded sense of aliveness brought by the lightning flash
of lucidity: he felt himself possessed of a sense of freedom
"as never before"; the dream was suffused with such vital
animation that "the darkness itself seemed alive." At this
point, a thought presented itself with such undeniable force
that he was driven to declare: "I have never been awake
before."

This is an extreme, but by no means uncharacteristic,
instance of the overwhelming impact the emergence of lucidity sometimes brings. To take another example, let us
consider one young woman's first lucid dream. On the night
before it took place, she had read a short piece by Scott
Sparrow, entitled "Lucid Dreaming as an Evolutionary
Process." The article described the ordinary dream state as
"a level where man is still a child" and compared the
development of lucid dreaming to the earlier development
of consciousness in primitive humanity, making repeated
references to the "infantile ego" and stressing the importance of "taking responsibility" for our disowned conflicts
and especially for the immature aspects of our personalities. Evidently these ideas made a profound impression on
her mind—both conscious and unconscious—for she went
to bed with a strong desire to give lucidity a try, and sometime after dawn, dreamed that she "seemed to be responsible for a baby which was very messy and sitting on a
pot." (Shades of "taking responsibility" for the "infantile
ego"!) She went looking for a bathroom in order to clean
up the baby "without being noticed." As she picked up
the baby, she distinctly felt "that it should be older and
better trained." When she looked more closely at the
child's face, she found it full of wisdom, and suddenly she
knew that she was dreaming. Excitedly, she "tried to remember the advice in the article," but the only thought
that came to mind was a phrase of her own: "Ultimate
Experience." Leaving behind the concerns dealt with in

her bedtime reading, she felt herself taken over by a "bliss-ful sensation . . . of blending and melting with colors and light" that continued to unfold, "opening up into a total 'orgasm.' " Afterward, she "gently floated into waking consciousness" and was left with "a feeling of bubbling joy" that persisted for a week or more.[1]

The carry-over of positive feelings into the waking state shown in this example is an important feature of lucid dreaming. Dreams, remembered or not, can color our mood for a good part of the day. Just as the negative aftereffect of "bad" dreams can cause us to feel as if we got up "on the wrong side of the bed," the positive feelings of a good dream can give us an emotional uplift, helping us to start the day with confidence and vigor. This is all the more true of an inspirational lucid dream: As a result of such expe-riences, lucid dreamers may be motivated to try out new behaviors leading to psychological growth and positive changes in their waking lives. Since we are free to try out untested behaviors in our lucid dreams without fear of harming ourselves or others, the lucid dream state provides a uniquely secure environment for personal (as well as sci-entific) experimentation—a laboratory as well as a play-ground for developing new ways of living.

Fully lucid dreams produce an effect on the dreamer's thinking that is no less profound than the emotional impact associated with the emergence of lucidity. To understand why this impact is so powerful, it is first necessary to con-sider the way in which ordinary dreamers experience being in the dream world. Non-lucid dreamers perceive them-selves as being contained within the experiential world of their dreams. Whether they play starring roles or are only pawns in the dream game, they are still contained in a dream that they take for external reality. As long as they perceive themselves contained in this world, they are sen-tenced to a virtual prison with walls no less impenetrable for the fact that they are made of delusion.

In contrast, lucid dreamers realize that they themselves contain, and thus transcend, the entire dream world and all of its contents, because they know that their imaginations have created the dream. So the transition to lucidity turns dreamers' worlds upside down. Rather than seeing themselves as a mere part of the whole, they see themselves as the *container* rather than the *contents*. Thus they freely pass through dream prison walls that only seemed impenetrable, and venture forth into the larger world of the mind.

Although lucid dreamers normally continue to take the leading role in their dream plays, they no longer fully identify with the part they are playing. They are in the dream, but not altogether of it. This detached but not uninterested frame of mind allows them to confront otherwise fearful nightmares and anxieties, and by resolving inner conflicts, furthers psychological development toward self-integration and inner harmony.

One of my own experiences can serve as an example of how the awareness that you are dreaming can help you overcome anxieties and move toward harmony. I dreamed that I was in the middle of a classroom riot; a furious mob was raging about, throwing chairs and trading punches. A huge, repulsive barbarian with a pockmarked face, the Goliath among them, had me hopelessly locked in an iron grip from which I was desperately trying to free myself. At this point, I recognized I was dreaming, and remembering what I had learned from handling similar situations previously, I immediately stopped struggling. As soon as I realized the struggle was a dream, I knew that as a matter of principle, the conflict was with myself. It was clear that this repulsive barbarian was a dream personification of something I wanted to deny and set myself apart from. Perhaps it was merely a representation of someone, or some quality in another, that I disliked. But since whatever it was touched me closely and deeply enough to cause me to have this dream, I knew that the way to inner harmony lay in accepting whatever I might find in myself—even the odious barbarian—as part of myself. Doing so invariably resolved my dream conflicts and brought me closer to my goal of self-integration. My experience had shown me that, in the dream world at least, the best and perhaps only ultimately effective way to bring hate and conflict to an end was to love my enemies as myself.

When I attained lucidity in this particular dream and stopped fighting (with myself, I assumed) I was absolutely certain about the proper course of action. I knew only love could truly resolve my inner conflict, and I tried to feel loving as I stood face to face with my ogre. At first I failed utterly, feeling only revulsion and disgust for the ogre. He was simply too ugly to love: that was my visceral reaction. But I tried to ignore the image and seek love within my own heart. Finding it, I looked my ogre in the eyes, trusting my intuition to supply the right things to say. Beautiful words of acceptance flowed out of me, and as they did, he melted into me. As for the riot, it had vanished without a trace. The dream was over, and I awoke feeling wonderfully calm.

Up to this point, I have mentioned only possibilities. At present only one area of application for lucid dreaming has been established to any degree; this is lucid dreaming as a tool for scientific research on the psychophysiological nature of the dream state, which provides a model for a powerful approach to research on human consciousness as well. For several years now, at the Stanford University Sleep Laboratory, we have been using lucid dreaming as a tool to study mind-body relationships. For the first time in history, we have been able to receive on-the-scene reports from the dream world as dream events happen (or, I should say, seem to happen). At Stanford and elsewhere, lucid dreamers in laboratories have been able to signal to observers while remaining physiologically asleep.

Such messages from the dream world prove beyond any

reasonable doubt that lucid dreams normally occur exclusively during the "rapid eye movement" (REM) stage of sleep. This remarkable brain state has also been called "paradoxical sleep" since the late 1950s, when experiments revealed it to be a much more active state than the traditional view of sleep as a passive condition of withdrawal from the world would allow. The active REM periods normally last ten to thirty minutes and recur every sixty to ninety minutes throughout the night (about four to five times per night). They alternate cyclically with relatively quiet phases of sleep, referred to as "non-REM," "quiet sleep," and a variety of other names.

All normal people go through this pattern of quiet sleep, active sleep, quiet sleep, and so on throughout their sleeping lives. Experiments have shown that during REM sleep, everybody dreams, every night—whether they remember anything or not. During the four or five REM periods you will pass through tonight, your dreaming brain will in most cases be considerably more active than it is right now—unless you happen to be reading this book while jogging, making love, or drowning! In spite of REM's paradoxical and unexpected properties, all the experts agree (for once!) that it is a *bona fide* form of genuine sleep.

The same cannot be said quite yet for lucid dreaming, and indeed this phenomenon would seem to qualify as the strangest paradox yet to emerge from paradoxical sleep. What makes lucid dreaming so paradoxical is that lucid dreamers, while being completely out of sensory contact and therefore fully asleep to the outer world, are at the same time fully conscious of their dreams and as much (or nearly so) in possession of their mental faculties as when awake. They seem to qualify, then, as being fully awake to the inner worlds of their dreams. Among the majority of professional sleep researchers, such a notion seemed so difficult to credit, before our unequivocal proof to the contrary at Stanford, that it was generally assumed that accounts of so-called lucid dreaming resulted from the waking fantasies of overly imaginative minds. To most sleep and dream researchers, it seemed that such things as lucid dreams did not—could not—take place during sleep at all. And if lucid dreams, whatever they were, were not a phenomenon of sleep, then they became someone else's problem, outside the scope of sleep research, and that was that. Philosophers have also tended to find anecdotes of lucid dreaming problematic and even absurd, and this is one of the reasons that the mere existence of lucid dreams is conceptually important. The proven fact of lucid dreaming effectively challenges a number of conventionally held misconceptions about dreaming, consciousness, and reality.

"Dreams are a reservoir of knowledge and experience," writes Tarthang Tulku, a contemporary Tibetan teacher, "yet they are often overlooked as a vehicle for exploring reality."[2]

Among such vehicles, lucid dreaming is a flying carpet. In the course of lucid dream explorations, a number of unexpected findings have been brought to light that may provide the keys to unlocking previously impenetrable mysteries of the world—such as why dreams seem real.

The fact is, dreams seem so completely real that they regularly deceive us into an unquestioning acceptance of their reality for as long as we sleep. Why is this? People have tended in the past to consider dreams as much more deeply related to fantasy than to actuality. But if dreams are nothing more than imagination, we ought to be able to recognize them for what they are, as easily as we are able to distinguish daydreams from actual perceptions, or memories of such perceptions from the originals. Perhaps we "ought" to be able to be lucid in our dreams without effort, but the fact is we aren't. If a valid argument leads to false conclusions, one or more of its premises must be wrong. In this case, the false premise seems to be the presumption linking dreaming more closely to imagination than to perception. Indeed, a series of our experiments provides evidence that, from the point of view of both dreamers and their brains (and to a lesser extent, bodies), dreaming of doing something is more like actually doing it than like imagining it. This, I would suggest, is why dreams seem so real to us.

What is it about dreams that grants them honorary reality? The answer is partly that dreams—lucid ones particularly—are not, as they have been sometimes supposed, "children of an idle brain," but rather of an extremely active one. As a result, dreams can produce as great an impact on the dreamer's brain as waking experience; correspondingly, dreams feel experientially real, or "more real than real"—while they last. For example, sexual encounters—including orgasm—during lucid dreams are reported to seem vividly real and gratifyingly pleasurable. Accordingly, our laboratory studies have revealed that sexual lucid dreams show physiological changes remarkably similar to those that accompany actual sexual activity (see Chapter 4). From these findings, we can see that dream content produces real and substantial effects on our brains and bodies, and that we probably ought to take dreams (our own in particular) more seriously than we in the contemporary Western world generally do.

As I suggested earlier, within the unexplored depths of your unconscious mind there may be untold riches; if this is so, as an ancient tradition testifies, among them is a treasure of incalculable value. It is said that if you were to find this most precious jewel, your experience of living would be transformed "beyond your wildest dreams." I trust it is obvious that we are not talking here of riches of the sort you can deposit in your bank. As the alchemical saying puts it, "Our gold is not the gold of the vulgar." As it happens, the hidden "treasure," or "jewel," or "gold" of which we have been speaking is sometimes

identified by various spiritual traditions as finding out the
secret of who you really are. In this regard, the Sufi master
Tariqavi has written that when you meet yourself, "you
come into a permanent endowment and bequest of knowledge that is like no other experience on earth."[3]

The Tibetan Buddhists, since the eighth century at least,
have laid particular value on lucid dreaming as a path to
self-discovery. Tarthang Tulku has written that "realizing
while dreaming that a dream is a dream can be of great
benefit." For example, "we can use our dream experiences
to develop a more flexible attitude," and "we can learn to
change ourselves as well." As a result of practicing lucid
dreaming, "our experiences in waking life become more
vivid and varied. . . . This kind of awareness, based on
dream practice, can help create an inner balance" that not
only "nourishes the mind in a way that nurtures the whole
living organism" but "illuminates previously unseen facets
of the mind and lights the way for us to explore ever-new
dimensions of reality."[4]

There is a famous story in which someone explains that
he has been looking for the key he lost *inside* his house
outside under a streetlamp, "because there's more light
there." Thus people look for the precious jewel of which
I have spoken (or, in the terms of the story, the key to their
real identities) in the wrong place—outside in the world.
There may be more light out there, but the key is to be
found inside their houses (that is, their inner worlds)—
though not easily, if they search for it groping about in the
dark. With the light of lucidity illuminating some of the
darkness of your unconscious mind, why shouldn't it be
easier to find your lost key? In other words, with the light
of your consciousness illuminating the unconscious darkness of your dream world, shouldn't it be easier to find the
treasures there?

Richard Wagner would probably have been delighted to
discover the existence of lucid dreams, for they make pos-

sible the achievement of a goal the celebrated musician set for the future over a hundred years ago: making the unconscious conscious. Wagner's aspiration has been shared by a number of illustrious individuals since then, including the father of modern dream psychology, Sigmund Freud. Freud's motto and psychoanalytic battle cry was *"Wo Es war, soll Ich werden!"* In English, this may be rendered as "where it [the unconscious mind, or the id] was, I [the conscious mind or ego] shall be." On this point, Carl Jung, the most famous of Freud's rebellious disciples, agreed with the master, viewing the goal of psychotherapy as a state of "completed individuation" uniting the opposing conscious and unconscious poles of personality. Recently, a follower of Jung's school explicitly made the connection we have been considering, proposing that the culmination of the individuation process "leads to the lucid dream state in which man's conscious and unconscious minds are made finally one."[5]

However intriguing these accounts of lucid dreams and their possible applications may sound, if *you* rarely or never have had lucid dreams, this fact might understandably dampen your enthusiasm. Indeed, lucid dreams are quite uncommon events for most of us. Most people have experienced lucid dreaming at least once in their lives—for some it may have been only a fleeting glimpse—yet for all but a few of us, lucid dreams occur so infrequently as to call into question the usefulness of this undeniably interesting state of consciousness. *If* this situation were to prove not only usual but unalterable as well, the widespread application of lucid dreaming would remain an impossible dream. *If* lucid dreaming were to remain nothing more than an insignificant exception to the general rule of unconsciousness in dreams, lucid dreams would be doomed to remain a mere curiosity, of theoretical interest only to dream experts and philosophers.

Fortunately, it now seems possible for ordinary dreamers

to learn to have lucid dreams much more frequently than would normally occur by chance. Thanks largely to recently developed techniques, you can probably learn to have them whenever and as often as you like—if you are willing to practice. The fact that lucid dreaming is indeed a learnable skill keeps alive the hope that the lucid dreaming state may prove to have wide applications along the lines we have been tracing.

We have been considering a number of the reasons you might find developing the ability of lucid dreaming worthwhile. Almost all of them depend upon your having a desire to go further in your life. This may take the form of longing for a richer, wider range of experience, looking for a challenge, or wanting to discover who you really are. Possibly you have developed, as Baudelaire put it, "a taste for the infinite." Or perhaps you have your heart set upon the discovery and actualization of hidden talents. You may feel your life is empty of meaning, or that you are out of touch with yourself. Perhaps you want to reconcile or heal some division you feel within yourself. You might suffer from terrifying nightmares and yearn to sleep peacefully, without fear; perhaps you feel lost, inadequate, or depressed—or simply curious to explore the adventures of the dream world.

Even if you are otherwise completely satisfied with the quality of your life, there remains a final and perhaps ultimately convincing argument why lucid dreaming might merit your interest. How do you feel about the meager—to put it as politely as possible—*quantity* of your life? Do you think that life is all too brief? Yes, it seems undeniable. But now add the fact that you have to sleep through a third of it! To the extent that sleep is for us a relative form of nonexistence, the sleeping portion of our lives belongs not to us but to the night, and the gloomy situation we have been contemplating seems darker still.

But, like everything else, night has a bright side too.

Every night we are resurrected from the grave of sleep by the miracle of dreams. Everyone dreams. It is not "to sleep, perchance to dream," but rather "to sleep is to dream, perchance to remember." It can be estimated that in the course of our lives, we enter our dream worlds half a million times. This state of affairs presents us all with a challenge: as we neglect or cultivate the world of our dreams, so will this realm become a wasteland or a garden. As we sow, so shall we reap our dreams. With the universe of experience thus open to you, if you must sleep through a third of your life, as it seems you must, are you willing to sleep through your dreams too?

2

The Origins and History of Lucid Dreaming

"For often," wrote Aristotle, "when one is asleep, there is something in consciousness which declares that what then presents itself is but a dream."[1] From this we see that among philosophically inclined Athenians of the fourth century B.C., lucid dreaming was a familiar experience. The same may well be true for the fortieth century B.C., since it seems likely that people have been having occasional lucid dreams as long as they have possessed a word for "dream." However, it is not until the fourth century A.D. that we find a written account of a lucid dream.

The earliest lucid dream report in Western history is preserved in a letter written in 415 A.D. by St. Augustine. While arguing for the possibility of having experiences after death when the physical senses no longer function, Augustine quoted the dream of Gennadius, a physician of Carthage. Gennadius, who suffered from doubts as to whether there was an afterlife, dreamed that a youth "of remarkable appearance and commanding presence accosted him with

the order: 'Follow me!' '' Obediently following the angelic
youth, Gennadius came to a city where he heard singing
"so exquisitely sweet as to surpass anything he had ever
heard." Inquiring what the music was, he was informed
that "it is the hymn of the blessed and the holy." Thereupon Gennadius awoke and thought of his experience as
"only a dream." The next night, he dreamed again of the
youth, who inquired whether Gennadius recognized him.
When Gennadius replied, "Certainly!" the young man
questioned where he had made his acquaintance. Gennadius's memory "failed him not as to the proper reply,"
and he recounted the events of the previous dream. The
youth thereupon inquired whether these events had taken
place in sleep or wakefulness. To Gennadius's reply, "In
sleep," the youth pursued what had become a Socratic in-
terrogation, declaring, "You remember it well; it is true
that you saw these things in sleep, but I would have you
know that even now you are seeing in sleep."

Gennadius thus became conscious that he was dreaming.
The dream—now lucid—continued with the youth asking:
"Where is your body now?" To Gennadius's proper response, "in my bed," the dream inquisitor pursued his
argument: "Do you know that the eyes in this body of
yours are now bound and closed, and that with these eyes
you are seeing nothing?" Gennadius replied, "I know it."
At this the dream teacher reached the conclusion of his
argument, demanding, "What then are the eyes with which
you see me?" Gennadius, unable to solve this puzzle, remained silent, and the dream catechist thereupon "un-
folded to him what he was endeavoring to teach him by
these questions," triumphantly exclaiming, "As while you
are asleep and lying on your bed these eyes of your body
are now unemployed and doing nothing, and yet you have
eyes with which you behold me, and enjoy this vision, so,
after your death, while your bodily eyes shall be wholly
inactive, there shall be in you a life by which you shall

still live, and a faculty of perception by which you shall still perceive. Beware, therefore, after this of harboring doubts as to whether the life of man shall continue after death."[2]

St. Augustine tells us that the dreamer's doubts were thereby completely removed. The force of the argument (though not of the lucid dream) is diminished, it must be admitted, by the fact that the reassuring youth was himself no more able than Gennadius to explain the nature of the eyes with which we see in dreams. In spite of the clarity of Aristotle's arguments to the contrary, to Gennadius and most of his contemporaries, seeing was still believing. Dreaming of seeing something implied that the something was no mere image but an object existing somewhere outside the dreamer. Equally, for the prescientific mind, seeing something in a dream implied the actual existence of dream eyes with which to see, and by the same reasoning, a dream body with which to be—presumably analogous to the corresponding physical organs of sense and consciousness, and to the physical body. At the same time, since this second or dream body seemed to do quite well while the physical body was minding its own business asleep, it was easy to conclude that the two bodies were in fact independent of each other.

We have uncovered nothing so far to prepare us for the amazing development, several centuries later, of a remarkably sophisticated dream technique. On the "rooftop of the world," as early as the eighth century A.D., the Tibetan Buddhists were practicing a form of yoga designed to maintain full waking consciousness during the dream state. With these dream yogis of Tibet, we find for the first time a people who possess an experientially based and unequivocal understanding of dreams as solely the mental creation of the dreamer. This is a concept fully at the level of our most recent scientific and psychological findings.

In many ways, these masters seem to have gone beyond

anything known to Western psychology today. For example, according to an ancient manual for would-be yogis, it is claimed that the practice of certain dream control techniques leads to the capacity to dream any imaginable experience. But these dream yogis evidently set their sights far above the pursuit of any trivial pleasures that might result from such a power. For the Tibetan yogis, the lucid dream represented an opportunity to experiment with, and realize the subjective nature of the dream state and, by extension, waking experience as well. Such a realization was regarded as of the profoundest possible significance. Through the practice of lucid dreaming,

> the *Yogin* is taught to realize that matter, or form in its dimensional aspects, large or small, and its numerical aspects, of plurality and unity, is entirely subject to one's will when the mental powers have been efficiently developed by *yoga*. In other words, the *yogin* learns by actual experience, resulting from psychic experimentation, that the character of any dream can be changed or transformed by willing that it shall be. A step further and he learns that form, in the dream-state, and all the multitudinous content of dreams, are merely playthings of mind, and, therefore, as unstable as mirage. A further step leads him to the knowledge that the essential nature of form and of all things perceived by the senses in the waking-state are equally as unreal as their reflexes in the dream-state, both states alike being *sangsaric*. The final step leads to the Great Realization, that nothing within the *Sangsara* is or can be other than unreal like dreams.[3]

Readers who find that this explanation itself needs an explanation will find their needs satisfied in Chapter 10, when we return to the topic.

Similar practices were evidently being carried out in India at about the same time. Although Tantra was primarily an oral tradition, handed down from teacher to disciple, there is a tenth-century Tantric text that alludes to methods for retaining consciousness while falling asleep. However, the techniques are so obscurely described as to be of little use to the uninitiated. For example, the yogi is said to attain mastery of dreams by means of the "intermediate state," as a result of making himself "profoundly contemplative" and then placing himself "at the junction between waking and sleeping."[4]

Several centuries later, during the flowering of Islamic civilization, came the next references to lucid dreaming. In the twelfth century, the famous Spanish Sufi, Ibn El-Arabi, known in the Arab world as "the Greatest Master," is reported to have asserted that "a person must control his thoughts in a dream. The training of this alertness . . . will produce great benefits for the individual. Everyone should apply himself to the attainment of this ability of such great value."[5]

A century later, St. Thomas Aquinas mentioned lucid dreaming in passing, citing Aristotle's supposition that the senses may occasionally show relatively little diminishment during sleep. Aquinas asserted that this happens especially "towards the end of sleep, in sober men and those who are gifted with a strong imagination." He went on to explain that in this case, " . . . not only does the imagination retain its freedom, but also the common sense is partly freed; so that sometimes while asleep a man may judge that what he sees is a dream, discerning, as it were, between things and their images."[6] We here have evidence that medieval Europe knew of lucid dreaming. But the fact that dreams were generally held in disrepute during the Middle Ages, considered more frequently the inventions of demons than of God, suggests that public discussion of lucid dreaming might have resulted in a private audience with the local Inquisition.

With the nineteenth century came the recognition that

there is more to the brain than we are normally aware of: beyond the limited circle of light bounding our conscious mind is the vast darkness of our unconscious mind. Conscious knowledge, what we know that we know and can explicitly spell out, is a small part of the mind. Most of our knowledge is unconscious—tacit, implicit, and difficult to verbalize. The very ground upon which consciousness stands is the unconscious mind; mental processes such as consciously directed thinking develop from the far older structures of unconscious thinking, upon which they depend.

Dreams, in the nineteenth century, were no longer seen as deriving from the underworld of the dead or the supernatural domain of the gods: we now knew that the world of dreams was the underworld of the human mind—the unconscious. The door was open for psychologists and physiologists to begin the scientific study of dreams.

Many scientists took up the challenge of exploring the unconscious mind through studying dreams. However, our concern here is not with those scientists, but with the few who went still further, accepting Richard Wagner's call to make the unconscious conscious, and explored lucid dreaming.

The greatest pioneer among these was the Marquis d'Hervey de Saint-Denys. By day a professor of Chinese literature and language, by night he was an industrious and dedicated experimenter who recorded his dreams from the time he was thirteen years old. Sigmund Freud, who coincidentally was born on Saint-Denys' thirty-fourth birthday, described him as "the most energetic opponent of those who seek to depreciate psychical functioning in dreams."[7]

In his remarkable book, *Dreams and How to Guide Them*, first published in 1867 and recently translated into English in abridged form,[8] the Marquis documented more than twenty years of dream research. Unfortunately, the original edition never seems to have been widely available; Freud mentioned having been unable to obtain a copy "in spite of all efforts,"[9] with the regrettable consequence that the founder of psychoanalysis never gained more than the most superficial acquaintance with the possibilities of lucid dreaming or dream control.

In the first part of his book, Saint-Denys described the sequential development of his ability to control his dreams: first, increasing his dream recall; next, becoming aware that he was dreaming; then, learning to awaken at will; and finally, being able, to a certain extent, to direct his dream dramas. The second part of *Dreams and How to Guide Them* reviewed earlier dream theories and presented his own ideas, based on extensive self-experimentation. A notion of the Marquis' approach can be gained from the following extract:

I fell asleep. I could see clearly all the little objects which decorate my study. My attention alighted on a porcelain tray, in which I keep my pencils and pens, and which has some very unusual decoration on it. . . . I suddenly thought: whenever I have seen this tray in waking life, it has always been in one piece. What if I were to break it in my dream? How would my imagination represent the broken tray? I immediately broke it in pieces. I picked up the pieces and examined them closely. I observed the sharp edges of the lines of breakage, and the jagged cracks which split the decorative figures in several places. I had seldom had such a vivid dream.[10]

Many of Saint-Denys' experiments can be faulted for failing to allow for expectation. As my research at Stanford has shown, expectation seems to be one of the most important determinants of what happens in dreams, lucid or otherwise. Thus, if you carry out dream experiments expecting a particular result, you will very likely get exactly the result you want—and this is the trap into which the Marquis sometimes fell. However, this criticism leaves untouched what is probably his most important contribution to the field: the demonstration that it is possible to learn to dream consciously.

Not everyone who has made the effort to learn this skill has had such success. Frederic W. H. Myers, a classical scholar at Cambridge and one of the founders of the Society for Psychical Research, complained that by "mere painstaking effort" he succeeded on only three nights out of three thousand in realizing that he was dreaming. Although Myers attributed his small gains to his "poor endowments" as a dreamer, he may serve as a reminder that what is needed is not "painstaking effort" but *effective* effort. In an 1887 article on automatic writing and other psychic phenomena, Myers briefly digressed to explain that

> I have long thought that we are too indolent in regard to our dreams; that we neglect precious occasions of experiment for want of a little resolute direction of the will. . . . We should constantly represent to ourselves what points we should like to notice and test in dreams; and then when going to sleep we should impress upon our minds that we are going to try an experiment—that we are going to carry into our dreams enough of our waking self to tell us that they *are* dreams, and to prompt us to psychological inquiry.

Myers then quoted a "curious dream" of his own, hoping that "its paltry commonplaceness may perhaps avert the suspicion that it has been touched up for recital":

> I was, I thought, standing in my study; but I observed that the furniture had not its usual distinctness—that everything was blurred and somehow evaded a direct gaze. It struck me that this must be because I was

dreaming. This was a great delight to me, as giving the opportunity of experimentation. I made a strong effort to keep calm, knowing the risk of waking. I wanted most of all to see and speak to somebody, to see whether they were like the real persons, and how they behaved. I remembered that my wife and children were away at the time (which was true), and I did not reason to the effect that they might be present in a dream, though absent from home in reality. I therefore wished to see one of the servants; but I was afraid to ring the bell, lest the shock would wake me. I very cautiously walked downstairs—after calculating that I should be more sure to find someone in pantry or kitchen than in a work-room, where I first thought of going. As I walked downstairs I looked carefully at the stair-carpet, to see whether I could visualise better in dream than in waking life. I found that this was *not* so; the dream carpet was not like what I knew it in truth to be; rather, it was a thin, ragged carpet, apparently vaguely generalised from memories of seaside lodgings. I reached the pantry door, and here again I had to stop and calm myself. The door opened and a servant appeared—quite unlike any of my own. This all I can say, for the excitement of perceiving that I had created a new personage woke me with a shock. The dream was very clear in my mind; I was thoroughly awake; I perceived its great interest to me and I stamped it on my mind—I venture to say—almost exactly as I tell it here.[11]

Before leaving the nineteenth century, let us consider a miscellany of brief references that will fill in our picture of the climate surrounding lucid dreaming at the time. These are mostly little more than testimonials for or against the existence of lucid dreams. Then, as always, there were those who considered the notion of being awake in your dreams an impossible chimera.

Among theses skeptics, two of the foremost were the French psychologist Alfred Maury and the English psychologist Havelock Ellis. Although a pioneer in the scientific investigation of dreams, Maury was evidently personally unacquainted with the phenomenon of lucid dreaming and was quoted as saying that "these dreams could not be dreams." Ellis, of even greater renown than Maury, declared his disbelief in lucid dreams by stating, "I do not believe that such a thing is really possible, though it has been borne witness to by many philosophers and others from Aristotle . . . onwards." Neither of these psychologists bothered to waste more words than I have quoted here on a subject they considered only a curiosity.

On the other hand, Ernst Mach of the University of Vienna footnoted his discussion of what he considered the characteristic inertness of attention in dreams with the following qualification: "The intellect often sleeps only in part . . . we reflect, in the dream-state, concerning dreams, recognize them as such by their eccentricities, but are immediately pacified again." The eminent psychologist showed his personal acquaintance with lucid dreams, recounting in the same note that "at a time when much engrossed with the subject of space-sensation, I dreamed of a walk in the woods. Suddenly I noticed the defective perspective displacement of the trees, and by this recognized I was dreaming. The missing displacements, however, were immediately supplied."[12]

Finally, there is a brief mention of lucid dreaming by one of the most famous philosophers of the nineteenth century: Friedrich Nietzsche. While arguing that we use dreams to train ourselves to live, Nietzsche explained that "the whole 'Divine Comedy' of life, and the Inferno [pass before the dreamer] not merely . . . like pictures on the wall—for he lives and suffers in these scenes—and yet not without" the philosopher added in apparent reference to lucid dreaming, "that fleeting sensation of appearance. And perhaps many a one will, like myself, recollect having sometimes called out cheeringly and not without success amid the dangers and terrors of dream life: 'It is a dream! I will dream on!' "[13] Thus we see that Nietzsche, the "prophet of the modern age," had lucid dreams. He was also considered the prophet of psychoanalysis by the founder of the movement, Freud himself, and as it happens, died in 1900, the same year that gave birth to Sigmund Freud's masterwork—*Die Traumdeutung*.

The first edition of Freud's *The Interpretation of Dreams*, made no overt reference to lucid dreaming at all. However, Freud added a note to the second edition in 1909, that " . . . there are some people who are quite clearly aware during the night that they are asleep and dreaming and who thus seem to possess the faculty of consciously directing their dreams. If, for instance, a dreamer of this kind is dissatisfied with the turn taken by a dream, he can break it off without waking up and start it again in another direction—just as a popular dramatist may under pressure give his play a happier ending."[14]

Freud makes another mention of lucid dreaming, one that I believe tells us much more about the man who sat behind the couch than about lucid dreams: "Or another time, if his dream had led him into a sexually exciting situation, he can think to himself, 'I won't go on with this dream any further and exhaust myself with an emission; I'll hold back for a real situation instead.' "[15] Of course, the subject of Freud's remarks—the unnamed dreamer of the 1909 edition—could readily be identified by psychoanalytical methods as Freud himself. On the basis of this interpretation, the supposition presents itself that Freud had lucid dreams upon occasion, and under pressure from his moralistic superego was compelled to give his dream play a more acceptably upright, though not happier, ending. The fear of exhausting oneself was even then an unconvincing rationalization. Nineteenth-century prudishness and guilt over enjoying even sexual fantasies appears to offer a more plausible explanation for Freud's holding back from the dream fulfillment of a wish. In spite of his unrestrained intellectual curiosity about sex, Freud was still a Victorian. The attitudes revealed by this passage could be interpreted to explain why his view of the dream world was relatively sterile.

In all his subsequent writings, Freud had but a single paragraph to add to what he had already said about lucid dreaming, and that was in his dream book's fourth edition in 1914: "The Marquis d'Hervey de Saint-Denys . . . claimed to have acquired the power of accelerating the course of his dreams just as he pleased, and of giving them any direction he chose. It seems as though in his case the wish to sleep had given place to another preconscious wish, namely to observe his dreams and enjoy them. Sleep is just as compatible with a wish of this sort as it is with a mental reservation to wake up if some particular condition is fulfilled (e.g. in the case of a nursing mother or wet-nurse)."[16] If we accept Freud's analysis we must infer that unlike Saint-Denys, Freud apparently did not wish to enjoy his dreams, since he seems to have become lucid in so few of them, perhaps because enjoyment of almost any kind would have provoked guilt. So, if we are to apply psychoanalytic theory to its founder, we may surmise that Freud slept with his own particular sort of mental reservation: to wake up immediately if he realized he was dreaming and was consequently in danger of compromising his rigid morality.

To Frederik Willems van Eeden, a Dutch psychiatrist and well-known author, we owe the term "lucid dreams," and the first serious research into lucid dreaming. Van Eeden kept a diary of his own dreams for many years, noting with particular care those cases in which he was fast asleep and yet had "full recollection of [his] day-life, and could act voluntarily." Although interested in all aspects of dreaming, van Eeden found that these lucid dreams aroused his "keenest interest." At first he veiled his observations in a novel called *The Bride of Dreams,* because, as he later admitted, the fictional guise allowed him "to freely deal with delicate matters."

In 1913 van Eeden presented a paper to the Society for Psychical Research reporting on 352 of his lucid dreams, collected between 1898 and 1912. "In these lucid dreams," he declared, "the re-integration of the psychic functions is so complete that the sleeper reaches a state of perfect awareness and is able to direct his attention, and to attempt different acts of free volition. Yet the sleep, as I am confidently to state, is undisturbed, deep, and refreshing."[17]

By a curious coincidence, van Eeden's first lucid dream was quite similar to Ernst Mach's experience quoted earlier. "I obtained my first glimpse of this lucidity," wrote van Eeden, " . . . in the following way. I dreamt that I was floating through a landscape with bare trees, knowing that it was April, and I remarked that the perspective of the branches and twigs changed quite naturally. Then I made the reflection, during sleep, that my fancy would never be able to invent or to make an image as intricate as the perspective movement of little twigs seen in floating by."[18]

Van Eeden, like Saint-Denys, whom he quotes, took an experimental approach to his dreams, as is illustrated by the following report:

On Sept. 9, 1904, I dreamt that I stood at a table before a window. On the table were different objects. I was perfectly well aware that I was dreaming and I considered what sorts of experiments I could make. I began by trying to break glass, by beating it with a stone. I put a small goblet of glass on two stones and struck it with another stone. Yet it would not break. Then I took a fine claret-glass from the table and struck it with my fist, with all my might, at the same time reflecting how dangerous it would be to do this in waking life; yet the glass remained whole. But lo! when I looked at it again after some time, it was broken.[19]

"It broke all right," van Eeden continued with a charming phrase, "but a little too late, like an actor who misses his cue." He explained that "this gave me a very curious impression of being in a *fake-world*, cleverly imitated, but with small failures. I took the broken glass and threw it out of the window, in order to observe whether I could hear the *tinkling*. I heard the noise all right and I even saw two dogs run away from it quite naturally. I thought what a good imitation this comedy-world was."[20]

At about the same time van Eeden was carrying out his investigations in the Netherlands, the French biologist Yves Delage was engaged in a similar study of his own lucid dreams. Delage characterized his lucid dreams in the following terms:

> I say to myself: here I am in a situation which may be troublesome or pleasant, but I know very well that it is completely unreal. From this point of my dream, knowing that I cannot run any risk, I allow scenes to unfold themselves before me. I adopt the attitude of an interested spectator, watching an accident or catastrophe which cannot affect him. I think: over there are waiting for me people who want to kill me; I then try to run away; but suddenly, I realize that I am dreaming and I say to myself: since I have nothing to fear I am going to meet my enemies, I will defy them, I will even strike them *in order to see what will happen*. However, although I am sure enough of the illusory character of the situation to adopt a course of action which would be unwise in real life, I have to overcome an instinctive feeling of fear. Several times, I have in this way thrown myself on purpose into some danger in order to see what would come of it.[21]

This lucid dream could easily be taken for one of Saint-Denys' reports; the two Frenchmen seemed to have had similarly rational and experimental approaches to their lucid dreams.

On the other side of the English Channel, Mrs. Mary Arnold-Forster was also exploring the world of dreams. From her own experience she reached a conclusion that it would be well to remember even today: "There are dreams and dreams, and we must get rid of the assumption that they all resemble each other."[22] A few of the dreams described in her book were lucid; what is of relevance here is her description of how she, too, learned to recognize that her frightening dreams were "only dreams." She also seems to have had success with teaching this method to children, a practice surely deserving wider application. It does not appear, however, that Arnold-Forster developed her consciousness in dreams very extensively, perhaps due to the fact that of earlier published accounts, she seems to have known only Myers' and was unacquainted with such much more informative sources as Saint-Denys and van Eeden.

At about the same time, Hugh Calloway, a compatriot of Mrs. Arnold-Forster, undertook much more extensive experimentation with lucid dreams and closely related states. Publishing his occultist writings under the pen name of Oliver Fox, he apparently discovered lucid dreaming completely on his own, developing a high degree of proficiency in it. In the summer of 1902, when he was a sixteen-year-old student of science and electrical engineering in London, he dreamed a lucid dream which he said marked "the real beginning" of his research. "I dreamed," he wrote,

> that I was standing on the pavement outside my home. The sun was rising behind the Roman wall, and the waters of Bletchingden Bay were sparkling in the morning light. I could see the tall trees at the corner of the road and the top of the old grey tower beyond the Forty

Steps. In the magic of the early sunshine the scene was beautiful enough even then.

Now the pavement was not of the ordinary type, but consisted of small, bluish-grey rectangular stones, with their long sides at right-angles to the white curb. I was about to enter the house when, on glancing casually at these stones, my attention became riveted by a passing strange phenomenon, so extraordinary that I could not believe my eyes—they had seemingly all changed their position in the night, and the long sides were now parallel to the curb!

Then the solution flashed upon me: though this glorious summer morning seemed as real as real could be, I was *dreaming!*

With the realization of this fact, the quality of the dream changed in a manner very difficult to convey to one who has not had this experience.

Instantly, the vividness of life increased a hundredfold. Never had sea and sky and trees shone with such glamourous beauty; even the commonplace houses seemed alive and mystically beautiful. Never had I felt so absolutely well, so clear-brained, so inexpressibly *free!* The sensation was exquisite beyond words; but it lasted only a few minutes and I awoke.[23]

Fox called his lucid dreams Dreams of Knowledge, "for one had in [them] the *knowledge* that one was really dreaming." He pictured himself in his Dreams of Knowledge "free as air, secure in the consciousness of my true condition and the knowledge that I could always wake if danger threatened, moving like a little god through the glorious scenery of the Dream World."[24]

A Russian philosopher, Piotr D. Ouspensky, wishing "to verify a rather fantastic idea," which he says occurred to him as an adolescent, asked himself, *"Was it not possible to preserve consciousness in dreams,* that is, to know while dreaming that one is asleep and *to think consciously* as we think when awake?"[25] The answer Ouspensky decided upon, as others had before him, was yes. His main interest in lucid dreaming, or "half-dream states" as he called them, was simply to observe the formation and transformation of ordinary dreams. He claimed:

> The fact is that in 'half-dream states' I was having all the dreams I usually had. But I was fully conscious, I could see and understand how these dreams were created, what they were built from, what was their cause, and in general what was cause and what was effect. Further, I saw that in 'half-dream states' I had a certain control over dreams. I could create them and could see what I wanted to see, although this was not always too successful and must not be understood too literally. Usually I only gave the first impetus, and after that the dreams developed as it were of their own accord, sometimes greatly astonishing me by the unexpected and strange turns they took.[26]

Here is Ouspensky's description of one of his half-dream states:

> I remember once seeing myself in a large empty room without windows. Besides myself there was in the room only a small black kitten. 'I am dreaming,' I say to myself. 'How can I know whether I am really asleep or not? Suppose I try this way. Let this black kitten be transformed into a large white dog. In a waking state it is impossible and if it comes off it will mean that I am asleep.' I say this to myself and immediately the black kitten becomes transformed into a large white dog. At the same time the opposite wall disappears, disclosing a mountain landscape with a river like a ribbon receding into the distance.
> 'This is curious,' I say to myself; 'I did not order this landscape. Where did it come from?' Some faint recollection begins to stir in me, a recollection of having seen this landscape somewhere and of its being some-

how connected with the white dog. But I feel that if I let myself go into it I shall forget the most important thing that I have to remember, namely, *that I am asleep and am conscious of myself. . . .*[27]

In a 1936 article, "Dreams in Which the Dreamer Knows He is Asleep" in the *Journal of Abnormal Psychology,* Alward Embury Brown reported on "almost a hundred" of his own lucid dream experiences. The article showed that he was familiar with most of the earlier writings, with the significant exception of Saint-Denys. Apart from testifying to "the very existence of the phenomenon," Brown was chiefly concerned with countering the position taken by some skeptics among his psychologist colleagues—that lucid dreaming was nothing more than "daydreaming." In any case, Brown demonstrated the difference between the two states on several occasions, by daydreaming (imagining) during his lucid dreams. He also introduced a valuable and subsequently widely used criterion for deciding whether or not one is dreaming: jumping into the air and testing the sensation of gravity. Significantly, Brown's is one of only two papers devoted to the topic of lucid dreaming to be found in the mainstream of scientific psychology, up to the past few years.

The second of those articles appeared in a German psychology journal two years later. The author, Dr. Harold von Moers-Messmer, reported and commented on twenty-two of the lucid dreams he had between 1934 and 1938. That Moers-Messmer possessed an unusually logical mind can be seen from the following report:

From the top of a rather low and unfamiliar hill, I look out across a wide plain towards the horizon. It crosses my mind that I have no idea what time of year it is. I check the sun's position. It appears almost straight above me with its usual brightness. This is surprising, as it occurs to me that it is now autumn, and the sun was much lower only a short time ago. I think it over: The sun is now perpendicular to the equator, so here it has to appear at an angle of approximately 45 degrees. So if my shadow does not correspond to my own height, I must be dreaming. I examine it: It is about 30 centimeters long. It takes considerable effort for me to believe this almost blindingly bright landscape and all of its features to be only an illusion.[28]

Whenever Moers-Messmer found himself awake within his dreams he made use of the opportunity to satisfy his scientific curiosity, carrying out a variety of experiments in his lucid dreams. After his "indestructable intellectualism" had emerged in a lucid dream, he continued:

. . . it suddenly gets dark. After a little while, it grows light again. After some consideration, the word that I have long borne in mind occurs to me: "Magic!" I find myself in a city, on a large, relatively uncrowded street. Next to one of the houses I see nearby an entrance gate; the doors are closed, and flanked to right and left by two wide, jutting pillars. These are composed of five squared-stone blocks piled on top of each other, upon which there is projecting relief work in the shape of garlands. I cry out, "This will all grow much larger!" At first nothing happens, even while I fixedly imagine that the gateway is larger than the way I see it. All at once, a great number of little pieces of stone come crumbling out of the second highest block on the left, which is set in slightly towards the inside. More and more keep coming, mixed with sand and larger stones, until there is nothing left of the block, while on the ground there now lies a whole pile of rubble. Through the open space that has thus resulted, I can see a gray wall towards the back.[29]

The preceding illustrates Moers-Messmer's use of key

words ("magic," in the example above) to remind him of what he wanted to do in his dreams. In another lucid dream, he wished to test whether people really speak in dreams:

> . . . I am in a large street, with people passing by. I repeatedly feel that I want to address myself to someone, but I always hesitate at the last moment. Finally I gather up all my courage, and say to a male personage who is just passing by, "You're a monkey." I chose this particular phrase in order to provoke him into a harsh reply. He remains standing there and looks at me. It is so uncomfortable for me that I would have most liked to have apologized. Then I hear his voice saying, "I've been waiting for that; you've been weighing it over in your mind for a long time." Whether I even saw him speaking, I do not recall. He continues speaking with the intonations of a preacher; however, I realize that I will soon have forgotten everything. I therefore grab for my notebook and pull it out of my pocket. Then I realize the absurdity of my intentions, and I throw it aside.[30]

Ten years later, Nathan Rapport, an American psychiatrist, extolled the delights of lucid dreaming in an article entitled "Pleasant Dreams!" According to Rapport, "the nature of dreams may be studied best on those rare occasions when one is aware that he is dreaming," and I fully agree. His method for lucid-dream induction is similar to that used by Ouspensky: "While in bed awaiting sleep, the experimenter interrupts his thoughts every few minutes with an effort to recall the mental item vanishing before each intrusion by that inquisitive attention." This habit of introspection is cultivated until it continues into sleep itself. Rapport's enthusiasm for lucid dreaming is clearly conveyed by the terms in which he concluded his article:

As to the mysterious glories all too seldom remembered

from dreams—why attempt to describe them? Those magical fantasies, the weird but lovely gardens, these luminous grandeurs; *they are enjoyed only by the dreamer who observes them with active interest, peeping with appreciative wakeful mind, grateful for glories surpassing those the most accomplished talents can devise in reality.* The fascinating beauty found in dreams amply rewards their study. But there is a higher call. The study and cure of the mind out of touch with reality can be aided by attention to dreams. And when secrets are wrested from the mystery of life, many of them will have been discovered in pleasant dreams.[31]

Although lucid dreaming has been known since antiquity, it was not until the nineteenth century that people in the West seemed to realize the phenomenon merited—and was accessible to—careful study. One can see a parallel with electricity: The Greeks knew of it, but for thousands of years no one regarded it as more than a curiosity. The scientific study of electricity gave rise to remarkable technological developments and an astonishing variety of unexpected applications; one of the most unexpected of these, as we shall see in the next chapter, was the scientific study of lucid dreaming.

3

~~~~~~~~~~~~~~~~~~~~~~~~~~~~~~~~

The New World of
Lucid Dreaming

Scientific Studies of
Sleep and Dreaming

In spite of humanity's perennial fascination with dreaming, the dream did not become a topic of widespread scientific inquiry until the second half of the twentieth century. One of the reasons for this is that scientific interest in dreaming had to await experimental psychology's nineteenth-century birth and twentieth-century development. Another factor was technological: until a short time ago, the scientific instruments for probing the dream world had not yet been invented. The sophisticated electronic instruments of modern sleep and dream research detect, measure, and record the minute electrical potentials associated with all biological functioning. Scientists are now able to discern certain changes in bioelectrical potentials emanating from the dreaming brain which accompany (and perhaps generate) the psychological events experienced by the dreamer. A little background information and history will help you to understand and appreciate how this miracle is accomplished.

The beginning of the electronic age can be traced back to the eighteenth century and the Italian physiologist Luigi Galvani's discovery of "animal electricity" in one of the most famous experiments in the history of science. Galvani was astonished to observe that when he brought a freshly dissected frog's leg into contact with two different kinds of metal, the dead leg jumped as if it were alive. Moreover, when Galvani connected wires from the frog's leg to devices capable of detecting electrical potentials, he found that electricity was indeed being generated. Galvani theorized that the nerves in the leg were the source of the electricity, and further speculated that all animal tissue gave rise to "animal electricity" as a result of the vital processes in living creatures. As it happened, Alessandro Volta, an Italian physicist, proved Galvani wrong about the source of the electricity that made his frog's leg twitch. Volta showed that the electrical potential (or voltage, so named in the physicist's honor) was produced by the copper and iron wires in contact with the wet tissue—a primitive battery, in other words, powerful enough to stimulate muscle reflex action. (Galvani was later partially vindicated when it was discovered that muscle and nerve cell activity produced minute variations in electrical charge: animal electricity!)

By the middle of the nineteenth century, scientific understanding of electricity and magnetism had progressed sufficiently to allow quantitative measurement of the electrical activity of neurons anywhere in the nervous system. When one end of a peripheral nerve was effectively stimulated, it was invariably found to transmit an electrical impulse to its other end. Richard Caton of Liverpool University reasoned that what was the case for reflexes of the peripheral nervous system (that is, sensory and motor nerves outside the central nervous system) ought to be the case also for the central nervous system (the nerves in the brain and spinal chord). Thus if one were to measure the electrical potentials of a brain, they should show variation mirroring the sensory stimulation impinging on the brain.

At this time, the brain was generally thought to be nothing more than a chain of reflexes, an organ acting entirely in response to external stimuli and doing nothing by itself—speaking, as it were, only when spoken to. If such a brain were not a *tabula rasa*, it was only because the senses had written on its slate. In 1875, Caton attempted to measure the brain's hypothetical evoked response to sensory stimuli. He administered anesthesia to a dog and surgically exposed the surface (cortex) of its brain. But when Caton connected electrodes to the dog's cortex, he received a shock—and not an electrical one. Since the anesthesized dog was receiving no sensory stimulation, Caton expected its brain to show no physiological variation. But instead of the expected steady potential, the dog's brain showed what seemed to be a continuously changing, rapidly fluctuating electrical potential. The evidence clearly indicated that the brain was no mere stimulus/response automaton: its neutral state was not rest, but activity. At least, this was the case for "man's best friend."

The recording of the brain activity of human volunteers had to await the development of an alternative experimental procedure—one not requiring surgery to expose the cerebral cortex. The bioelectrical potentials of the brain are extremely weak, on the order of millivolts or less. (A millivolt is a thousandth of a volt; for comparison, the voltage produced by an ordinary flashlight battery is 1500 millivolts.) Clearly, the brain's electrical potentials are minute enough even when measured on the surface of the cortex. But they are many times weaker when measured from the scalp, due to the electrical resistance presented by the intervening layers, especially the skull. Even the most sensitive instruments available in the nineteenth century were not sensitive enough to record brain waves with amplitudes on the order of microvolts (millionths of a volt). The invention of the vacuum tube amplifier in the early twentieth century provided the enormous degrees of amplification necessary for the job (and at the same time also made possible high-fidelity recording, radio, and television).

Hans Berger, a German neuropsychiatrist, was able, with the aid of this new invention, to record the electrical activity of the human brain through the skull and scalp of human volunteers. Berger was just as surprised by what he found as Caton had been fifty years before. Berger had been expecting to observe the same random fluctuations as had been recorded from the brains of many other animals—rabbits, dogs, cats, and monkeys. But his human subjects showed strikingly rhythmical oscillations. Berger called the record of these brain waves the electroencephalogram (EEG) and reported that when subjects were allowed to shut their eyes, lie back, and relax, their brainwaves showed very regular oscillations repeating about ten times per second. This was the famous "alpha rhythm" (so named by its discoverer), indicating a state of relaxation (as well as meditation). Berger found that its frequency (number of waves per second) fell within the range of eight to twelve per second, and the alpha rhythm disappeared when the subject received an unexpected stimulus, such as a handclap. At last science was in possession of a window promising a clear view of the mind.

It is interesting to note that Berger's observations were at first met with considerable skepticism in the scientific community. Most electrophysiologists felt Berger's alpha rhythm was merely the result of some sort of measurement error rather than a genuine product of brain activity. The experts had two reasons to be dubious. In the first place they believed the only kind of electrical activity the brain could give rise to was the ''spike potentials'' associated with firing of nerve cells. Secondly, the very regularity of Berger's alleged alpha rhythm seemed to mark it as deriving from some malfunctioning equipment rather than the human brain—nature is seldom so tidy. After being replicated by scientists at Cambridge University, Berger's basic findings gained general acceptance, and the science of electroencephalography began to grow in earnest. Among Berger's pioneer explorations into the relation of the state of consciousness and the brain was the first EEG recording of sleep.

Berger's initial observation that the EEG shows consistent changes at sleep onset was extended by a series of studies at Harvard University in the 1930s.[1] The Harvard group classified waking and sleeping EEGs into five stages, and made observations suggesting that dreaming occurred during the lighter stages of sleep. A similar series of investigations at the University of Chicago during the same period studied variations in the mental activity reported by subjects awakened from various stages of sleep, concluding that dreaming seldom occurred during the deepest phase of sleep.[2] These studies suggested the possibility that the study of dreaming might be made more objective and scientific if there were some way to be sure whether or not a given person actually dreamed, and if so, when. However, it was several decades before this possibility was pursued.

In the late 1940s, it was discovered that stimulating a network of nerves in the brain stem called the reticular formation led to cortical activation. For example, stimulation of the reticular formation caused sleeping cats to awaken; conversely, its destruction resulted in a state of permanent coma. Since sensory input is the major source of activation of the reticular formation, it was theorized that sleep might involve processes that somehow inhibited neuronal activity in the reticular system. Sleep onset could be due to the decreased reticular activity, as a passive result of diminished sensory input.

The view of sleep onset as a passive process has obvious merit: isn't it easier for almost anyone to fall asleep in a quiet, dark room than in a noisy, brightly illuminated one? But the theory of sleep as a mere passive result of decreased sensory input also has obvious limitations: After all, no matter how dark and quiet the room is, if you don't *feel* sleepy, you are likely to remain awake. On the other hand, if you have been awake long enough, you will be able to sleep anywhere, even standing up at a rock concert! Obviously, sleep onset cannot be explained by this theory alone. It was, therefore, not surprising when evidence was later found for the existence of *active* sleep-inducing (hypnogenic) centers in the brain stem, forebrain and other areas, where electrical or neurochemical stimulation leads to sleep.

This was essentially the point scientific knowledge on the biology of sleep and dreaming had reached by the late 1940s. Sleep was viewed as one end of a continuum of arousal. At the other end of this continuum was wakefulness ranging in degrees from relaxation, through attentiveness and vigilant alertness, reaching the extreme of mania or panic. Where you were on this spectrum of arousal depended upon the degree of activity in your reticular formation. In this view, sleep was a unitary phenomenon; the deepest and shallowest stages differed only in their degrees of arousal. Dreaming, having been found to occur more frequently in the lighter stages of sleep, was regarded as the confused meanderings of a partially awake, and therefore partially functioning, mind. As for the onset of sleep, this was thought to be a passive process caused by decreased sensory input, resulting in diminishing activity of the reticular system until the lower levels of arousal associated with sleep were reached. As it turns out, this old view of sleep and dreams has been largely superseded by the new views created by the dramatic developments of the 1950s.

Dreaming and REM Sleep

In 1952, Eugene Aserinsky, then a graduate student working under Nathaniel Kleitman at the University of Chicago, made a serendipitous observation while studying the sleep patterns of infants. Aserinsky noticed that periods of eye movement and other indications of activity seemed to alternate regularly with periods of comparatively quiet sleep. These recurring periods of rapid eye movement, or REM, could be easily observed by means of electrodes taped next to the subject's eyes—the resulting record being called an electro-oculogram or EOG. Simultaneous polygraphic recording of the EEG and EOG showed the periods of REM activity to be accompanied by readings indicating light sleep. Furthermore, when subjects (adults in this case) were awakened from these REM (pronounced to rhyme with "them") periods, they almost always reported vivid dreams; in contrast, they reported dreams only a fifth as often when awakened from other phases of sleep (collectively referred to as "non-REM sleep," or NREM).[3]

Science finally appeared to have the key to dreams in hand—or at least the key to such puzzles as how often and how long we dream, and whether there are people who never dream, or only people who never remember their dreams.

Among those working in Kleitman's laboratories was a second-year medical student named William C. Dement, who, after finishing medical school, earned a Ph.D. in physiology under Kleitman. For his doctoral dissertation, Dement carried out an extensive program of experiments designed to further elucidate the relation of REM sleep (the term, incidentally, was coined by Dement) to dreaming. Dement's pioneering investigation revealed a number of the basic characteristics of REM dreams. Among these results was the discovery of a direct relationship between the amount of REM sleep allowed before subjects were awakened and the length of their subsequent dream reports: The longer the REM time before awakening, the longer the dreams. This provided the first (although indirect) evidence for a correspondence between physical time and dream time. Dement also presented evidence for a rather precise correspondence between the direction of eye movements and the direction of dream gaze changes reported upon awakening. The suggestion that REMs are the result of the dreamer looking about in his dreams has since generated considerable controversy.

I will only note in passing that in the last 30 years, thousands of sleep and dream studies have resulted from the groundbreaking work of Aserinsky, Dement, and Kleitman.

The Psychophysiological Approach to Dream Research

Why did the study of dreaming become scientifically respectable and the subject of widespread interest after the discovery of REM sleep? This question was answered in a paper by Johan Stoyva and Joe Kamiya entitled "Electrophysiological Studies of Dreaming as the Prototype of a New Strategy in the Study of Consciousness." The studies of dreaming referred to in the title are those correlating electrophysiological measurements with subjective reports. According to Stoyva and Kamiya, this is an instance of "converging operations," in which the agreement of objective measurements and subjective reports provides a degree of validation for a hypothetical (because not publicly observable) mental state.

Since the subject's report is the most direct account available concerning his mental processes, scientists would naturally like to make use of it. However, there is a problem. Heraclitus called the senses bad witnesses, and of these bad witnesses, the "introspective sense" seems to be the most unreliable. Given that the only "eyewitness" to dreaming is this introspective sense, we need a means of corroborating its testimony. Concurrent physiological measurements could sometimes provide the necessary circumstantial evidence to validate the subjective report.

The Stages of Sleep

In 1957 Dement and Kleitman introduced a new set of criteria for classifying sleep stages that subsequently gained wide acceptance. However, because of certain ambiguities in the application of some of the criteria, disagreements arose between different groups of researchers about the precise scoring of the sleep stages. This meant that the results of studies from one laboratory could not necessarily be compared to studies elsewhere.

To remove what was becoming a serious impediment to growth in the field, the UCLA Brain Information Service sponsored a project to develop an absolutely unambiguous manual for sleep-stage scoring. A committee refined Dement and Kleitman's original criteria to the currently universally accepted formulations described in *A Manual of Standardized Terminology, Techniques and Scoring System for Sleep Stages of Human Subjects*. The manual's precision established a high degree of agreement between different laboratories regarding the measurement and scoring of sleep.

According to the *Manual*, standard sleep-stage scoring requires the simultaneous recording of three parameters: brain waves (EEG), eye movements (EOG), and muscle tension (EMG). All of this is ordinarily recorded on a polygraph machine, which takes a form much like the standard "lie-detector" polygraphs: tracings in ink of several channels of physiological data on a continuously moving strip of paper. When a subject spends the night in a dream laboratory, the machine uses up over a thousand feet of paper! The following is a synopsis of what this record might reveal to the trained eye of the dream researcher, and of what you might experience during a typical night of sleep.

As you lie in bed relaxed but awake, preparing to sleep, your EEG will probably exhibit Berger's alpha rhythm almost continuously; your EOG may show occasional blinking and isolated rapid eye movements; and finally, your EMG will probably indicate a moderate degree of muscle tension. If, on the contrary, you were for any reason particularly tense, you might show little or no alpha rhythm and very high muscle tension. Whether you are relaxed or aroused, terrified or calm is of no concern to the *Manual;* as long as you are awake, your state is termed "Stage W." Surprisingly, in spite of being "awake" in both subjective and physiological terms, subjects not infrequently recount vivid reveries when asked for reports of their mental activity during Stage W.

After lying in bed for a few minutes in a quiet, darkened room you would likely become drowsy. Your subjective sensation of drowsiness is objectively registered by a change in your brain waves: Your formerly continuous alpha rhythm gradually breaks up into progressively shorter trains of regular alpha waves and is replaced by low-voltage mixed-frequency EEG activity. When less than half of an epoch (usually 30 seconds) is occupied by continuous alpha rhythm, sleep onset is considered to have occurred and Stage 1 sleep is scored. At this point, your EOG would reveal slowly drifting eye movements (SEMs); your muscle tone might decrease or remain the same. If you were awake at this point, you might well report "hypnagogic" (leading into sleep) imagery, which can be extremely vivid and bizarre, as the following report suggests: "I was observing the inside of a pleural [chest] cavity. There were small people in it, like in a room. The people were hairy, like monkeys. The walls of the pleural cavity are made of ice and slippery. In the mid-part there is an ivory bench with people sitting on it. Some people are throwing balls of cheese against the inner side of the chest wall."[4]

Beyond the seemingly meaningless distortions of the preceding report, Stage 1 hypnagogic imagery can also take on a uniquely archetypal character and significance, as illustrated by another subject's experience: "I saw the huge torso of a man," she reported, "rising out of the depths of a profoundly dark-blue sea. I knew, somehow, that he was a god. Between his shoulders, in place of a head, he had a large golden disc engraved with ancient designs. It reminded me of the high art of the Incas. He continued to rise out of the sea. The rays of light streaming out from behind him told me the sun was setting. People, clothed in dark garments, were diving into his face—the golden disc. I knew they were dead, and it seemed to me they were being 'redeemed' by this action. This image was very significant for me, yet I did not know exactly why."

Stage 1 is a very light stage of sleep, described by most subjects as "drowsiness" or "drifting off to sleep." Normally, it lasts only a few minutes before further EEG changes occur, defining another sleep stage.

As you descend deeper into sleep, Stage 2 occurs. The EEG is marked by the appearance of relatively high-amplitude slow waves called "K-complexes" as well as 12–14 Hz (the standard unit for frequency is the Hertz, abbreviated to Hz)[5] rhythms called "sleep spindles." Your EOG would generally indicate little eye movement, and the EMG would show somewhat decreased muscle tone. Reports of mental activity from this stage of sleep are likely to be less bizarre and more realistic than those from Stage 1. Nevertheless, during Stage 2 sleep and particularly later in the night, you might report lengthy and vivid dreams, especially if you are a light sleeper.

At this point, high-amplitude slow waves gradually begin to appear in your EEG. When at least twenty percent of an epoch is occupied by these "delta" waves (1–2 Hz), Stage 3 sleep is defined. Usually, this slow wave activity increases until it completely dominates the appearance of the EEG. When the proportion of delta EEG activity exceeds fifty percent of an epoch, Stage 3 becomes Stage 4, the "deepest" stage of sleep. During stages 3 and 4, often collectively referred to as "delta sleep," your EOG channel would show no eye movements, but only the brain's delta waves. Muscle tone is normally low, although it can be remarkably high, as when sleep-walking or sleep-talking occurs. Recall of mental activity on arousal from delta sleep is generally very poor and fragmentary, and more thought-like than dreamlike.

After about an hour and a half, the progression of sleep stages is reversed, and you cycle back through Stage 3 and Stage 2 to Stage 1 again. But by the time the EEG reveals you have crossed the border to Stage 1 again, your EMG would show virtually no activity at all, indicating your muscle tone has reached its lowest possible level. Your EOG now discloses the occurrence of rapid eye movements, at first only a few at a time, but later in dramatic profusion. You are, of course, now in "dreaming"—or REM—sleep. This state has also been referred to as "paradoxical sleep," "ascending Stage 1 REM," and most recently, "active sleep," in contrast to which NREM sleep is called "quiet sleep." In the dream lab, eighty to ninety percent of all awakenings from REM sleep yield recall of vivid and sometimes extremely detailed dreams.

After a period of REM sleep lasting perhaps five to fifteen minutes, you typically go through the preceding cycle again, vividly dreaming three or four more times during the remainder of the night, with two major modifications. One is that decreasing amounts of slow-wave EEG activity (stages 3 and 4, or delta sleep) occur in each successive cycle. Later in the night, perhaps after the second or third REM period, no delta sleep appears at all, only NREM Stage 2 and REM.

The other modification of the sleep cycle is that as the night proceeds, successive REM periods tend to increase in length—up to a point. While the first REM period commonly lasts less than ten minutes, later REM periods often last thirty or forty minutes; an hour or more is not uncommon late in the sleep cycle. At the same time REM periods are getting longer, the intervals between them tend to decrease in length, from the approximately ninety minutes characteristic of the first part of the night to as little as twenty or thirty minutes in the late morning.

All of these details may be beginning to sound unnecessarily technical and perhaps of interest only to academics or specialists. Not so. The fact that REM periods get longer and closer together as the night progresses has the greatest practical significance for dreamers: In a night when you get seven hours of sleep, fifty percent of your dreaming time will fall in the last two hours. If you can afford to sleep an extra hour, it will be almost all dreaming time. So if you want to cultivate your dream life, you will have to find a way to sleep late—at least on weekends.

The New World of Lucid Dreaming

Although scientific interest in the study of dreams underwent an unprecedented period of rapid growth that started in the 1950s, this peaked in the mid-1960s and declined thereafter. However, at the same time scientific interest in dreaming was beginning to wane, popular interest in dreams, especially lucid dreams, began to wax. Most recently, we have seen a renewal of scientific interest in the dream state, as indicated by the first laboratory studies of lucid dreaming and by an extremely rapid, almost explosive, growth in scientific attention to the phenomenon. How did all this come about?

A number of factors have contributed to the birth of the science of lucid dreams. The psychophysiological dream research of the 1950s and 1960s was undoubtedly important, providing as it did the basic methodology for the laboratory studies of lucid dreaming destined to follow in the late 1970s and beyond. But it is as if the earlier research merely prepared the ground for what was to come later. Other events were more responsible for planting the seeds of interest in lucid dreaming that have recently begun to yield an abundant harvest.

One of the most important of these events was the publication in 1968 of a book entitled *Lucid Dreams*, by Celia Green, an English parapsychologist. The book was based upon the published accounts we have already largely reviewed as well as upon case material collected by the Institute of Psychophysical Research, which Green directs. The Institute's activities, it should be noted, are not actually in the field of psychophysiology, but in the field of parapsychology. Green's interest in lucid dreaming connects with an English tradition in parapsychology going back to Frederic W. H. Myers and the founding of the Society for Psychical Research in the nineteenth century.

However, it is important to understand the context in which most scientists put *Lucid Dreams* as a result of its author's professional identification. A decade later, Green could still assert, not without truth, that ''lucid dreams are not studied except by those with an interest in parapsychology.''[6] I am afraid that one of the reasons more conventional scientists remained uninclined to study lucid dreams was exactly because parapsychologists *were* interested in the topic, giving lucid dreams the unwarranted reputation of being somehow related to ghosts, telepathy, flying saucers, and other topics regarded by traditional science as superstitious nonsense.

Whatever the reason, the time was evidently simply not yet ripe for the scientific study of lucid dreams. Even as recently as 1976, Green made the following eloquent appeal:

> In the case of lucid dreaming, one might think that the paradoxical nature of the phenomenon would make a thorough investigation of it particularly interesting. It might be thought that it would be interesting to discover what the neurophysiological state of a person was when their mind was in a state of rational activity although they were physically asleep. If this state should turn out to be exactly the same as that of a person who was asleep and dreaming in the ordinary manner, this would be strange and interesting. If it should turn out to be different, the nature of the differences might shed light on the true nature of sleep and the true nature of rational mental functioning.[7]

Green's book represented the most extensive review of the available literature on the topic, and was also quite scholarly in its treatment of the subject. In spite of this, it had a cool reception in academic circles; ironically, its dry analytical style was probably a major factor limiting its popular success. Nevertheless, the book appears to have stimulated an interest in lucid dreaming in a number of individuals who were to play prominent roles in the development of the field.

In the United States, Charles Tart's 1969 book *Altered States of Consciousness* probably generated even more widespread interest in lucid dreams than Green's less well-known book. Tart's anthology reprinted thirty-five scientific papers on a variety of subjects, including the hypnagogic state, dream consciousness, hypnosis, meditation, and psychedelic drugs. These were all very topical issues during the late 1960s, and the book generated widespread interest. It was undoubtedly influential for many young scientists developing an interest in the rich research possibilities presented by altered states of consciousness. I was certainly one of these, and I could not have failed to notice the words with which Tart introduced the volume: "Whenever I speak on the topic of dreams," he wrote, "I mention a very unusual sort of dream, the 'lucid' dream in which the dreamer knows he is dreaming and feels fully conscious in the dream itself." Aside from briefly introducing the topic and testifying to having had a few lucid dreams himself, Tart reprinted van Eeden's classic paper "A Study of Dreams." He thereby did a whole generation of future lucid dreamers a valuable service by making this work available, and provided for many (including myself) their first acquaintance with both the term and concept of "lucid dreams."

Ann Faraday's popular books had a great impact on the public awareness of dream consciousness in the early 1970s. Faraday, a psychotherapist and former sleep researcher, treated lucid dreaming in unreservedly positive terms. "This remarkable state of consciousness," she wrote, "is in my view one of the most exciting frontiers of human experience. . . ." Faraday believed that lucid dreams were occasioned by a movement toward self-integration in waking life, and stated that ". . . one of the most thrilling rewards of playing the dream game is that this type of consciousness, with its feeling of 'other worldliness,' begins to manifest itself much more frequently as self-awareness grows through dream work."[8]

Probably only one other author has influenced public

opinion regarding dreaming as much as—and perhaps even more than—Ann Faraday. I am referring to Patricia Garfield, whose 1974 book, *Creative Dreaming,* contains a wonderful collection of tools for lucid dream work as well as a great deal of fascinating information, including a survey of approaches to dream control in a variety of cultures. Garfield also gives an account of her development of fairly frequent (approximately weekly) experiences of lucid dreaming that I found personally valuable. Her pioneering efforts at learning lucid dreaming were some of the inspirations that helped me when I was attempting to do the same. As for *Creative Dreaming,* I would venture to say, without fear of contradiction, that it was inestimably influential in stimulating the current revolution in lucid dream work.

There is one more author whose books have contributed significantly to the development of contemporary interest in lucid dreaming, and that is Carlos Castaneda. Whether his entertaining and immensely popular works are ''fictional nonfiction'' or ''nonfiction fiction,'' as various defenders and detractors have claimed, is a controversial question. However, several of his books mention an unusual state of consciousness that bears a definite resemblance to lucid dreaming. Castaneda refers to this state as *''dreaming.''* Incidentally, I am perhaps not alone in wondering how the distinction between ''dreaming'' and *''dreaming''* was maintained in the original conversations, since italics are rather more difficult to achieve with the spoken word than with the written. Maybe the explanation is that ''Carlos'' and ''don Juan'' never felt it necessary to talk about ''ordinary'' dreaming at all. The broad appeal of his books provided many people with their first introduction to the concept of lucid dreaming, so perhaps it doesn't much matter how Castaneda set his type.

Whenever I lecture on the topic of lucid dreaming, someone always brings up the topic of Carlos Castaneda, usually mentioning the famous incident in *Journey to Ixtlán* in which the character "don Juan" teaches the character "Carlos" to find his hand in a dream, ostensibly as a means of stabilizing *dreaming*. Since "Carlos" is consistently presented as a bumbling idiot, learning to find his hand anywhere at all may be considered an improvement. But for most other would-be lucid dreamers, remembering to find your hand might be useful as a lucidity cue, but once you are lucid, there are a number of more interesting things to do.

What, my audience further wants to know, do I think of the Castaneda books? I generally reply that we owe Castaneda a debt of gratitude because his "tales of power" have served to inspire so many readers to explore their inner worlds and to open their minds to the possibilities of alternate realities. That is the good news. As for the bad, the weight of evidence seems to contradict the notion that these books are "nonfiction," as their author claims. For example, an ethnobotanist has argued that based on the flora and fauna Carlos claims to have encountered in the Sonoran desert, it would not be outrageous to conclude that Castaneda, the anthropologist, has never been there. In any case, the desert that Castaneda, the author, describes is apparently not the one he claims it is.[9] Similarly, based on Carlos's account of the world of *dreaming*, I am led to wonder whether he has ever really been there either.[10]

The seminal contributions of Green, Tart, Garfield, Faraday, and Castaneda during the late 1960s and early 1970s combined to produce a highly favorable climate for the development of widespread interest in lucid dreaming, not only among the general public, but among graduate students and others in training to become experimental psychologists and researchers. But in order to understand the difficulties that had to be overcome before lucid dreaming became scientifically acceptable, we must also find out how the topic was viewed from the establishment side of the wall.

In the academic world, the reigning attitude regarding lucid dreams starkly contrasted with the attitudes we have just surveyed, and can be summarized in a single word: skepticism. Among professional sleep and dream researchers, the orthodox view seemed to be that there was something philosophically objectionable about the very notion of lucid dreaming. Because of the philosophical nature of this skepticism, it would be informative to consider first what the philosophers of the time had to say on the topic.

The most influential philosophical writing on dreaming since the 1950s is probably Norman Malcolm's monograph *Dreaming*,[11] a book containing quite a number of remarkably provocative assertions. Professor Malcolm, an analytic philosopher, promises at the outset to challenge common sense and the generally accepted view that dreams are experiences we have during sleep and may or may not later recall upon awakening. On the contrary, he claims, what is ordinarily meant by a "dream" is not in fact an "experience during sleep" at all. Instead, examination of the common usage of the word "dreams" indicates that it refers only to the curious stories people tell upon awakening from sleep. If you want to know what we call the experiences we have during sleep later reported as "dreams," Malcolm will only tell you that we don't call them anything and it would be nonsense to do otherwise. Why? Because, he claims, what we mean by "sleep" is not a condition in which we are experiencing anything at all. Writing in the heyday of psychophysiological dream research, the philosopher audaciously dismisses as "irrelevant" the findings of that entire field.

Finally, as a corollary to the notion that being "asleep" means experiencing nothing whatsoever, Professor Malcolm concludes that the statement "I am asleep" is meaningless. Moreover, he demonstrates (to his own satisfaction) that "the idea that someone might reason, judge, imagine or have impressions, presentations, illusions or hallucinations, while asleep, is a meaningless idea. . . ."[12] Having established the impossibility of making judgements in sleep, he reduces lucid dreaming to absurdity: "If 'I am dreaming' could express a judgement it would imply the judgement 'I am asleep,' and therefore the absurdity of the latter proves the absurdity of the former." Thus "the supposed judgement that one is dreaming" is "unintelligible" and "an inherently absurd form of words."[13]

These curious conclusions illustrate that a valid argument can lead to an absurdly false conclusion if the premises upon which it is based happen to be wrong. In Malcolm's case, he has erred on two of his assumptions. The first is his misunderstanding of the everyday use of the term *dream*. We do use it in reference to stories or dream reports, but also in reference to the experiences we are reporting. Second, there are more varieties of being "asleep" than the hypothetical condition in which we are experiencing nothing at all. Dreams themselves provide an obvious example, but also there is sleepwalking and "fitful" sleep. I realize that the arguments I have offered would seem somehow deficient to Malcolm, but there is a simpler refutation of his views that will be obvious enough to you if you have ever had a lucid dream.

Common sense may well cry, Enough! Can't we dispense with philosophy entirely and get on with the dream? No, because "having no philosophy" is itself a naive philosophy likely to obscure one's vision. Scientists, including sleep and dream researchers, tend to think of themselves as "philosophy-free," but this doesn't mean it is so. Moreover, untested philosophical assumptions have until recently blocked the scientific study and acceptance of lucid dreaming. Up until the past few years, most dream experts considered lucid dreaming impossible on essentially philosophical grounds: it just didn't seem to be the sort of thing that could happen during what *they* meant by "sleep" and "dreaming." Five or ten years ago, the orthodox view re-

garding "lucid dreams" was essentially identical to the
orthodox view of a century ago as expressed by Alfred
Maury, that "these dreams could not be dreams."

Among sleep (as opposed to dream) researchers, those
whose studies were exclusively physiological had no more
to say about lucid dreaming than about any other form of
mental activity. On the other hand, most of those using
psychophysiological methods (considering the dreamer's
subjective report in association with physiological recordings) either ignored, or at most footnoted and dismissed,
anecdotes of lucid dreaming as too irrelevant or inconse-
quential to merit further investigation. What was the reason
for this rather ostrich-like behavior? I believe there were at
least two contributing factors, present in varying propor-
tions from one case to another. One of the factors, and I
think the major one, we have already mentioned: the "philosophical" climate of the time made lucid dreaming an
awkward notion because of the generally held set of theoretical assumptions about the nature of the dream state.
There was also the Freudian conception of the dream as a
seething cauldron of irrationality and primitive impulses.
This was not the sort of place to expect rational waking
thought, much less consciousness—a suspect concept anyway in a psychology ruled by dogmatic behaviorism for
the past fifty or sixty years. Thus, through the lenses of
mainstream psychology's accepted assumptions, lucid
dreaming appeared as quite distorted or ghostly—that is to
say, nearly nonexistent. Lucidity was the ghost in the
dream!

The second factor is the result of a rather common and
readily observable human tendency: the inclination to "pass
the buck." How many times have you heard someone say,
"It's not my problem" or "It's not my responsibility?" If
reports of lucid dreaming actually derived from, say, waking fantasies, then sleep and dream researchers could say
without qualm, "It's not my problem," and get back to

their own interesting problems without further delay. As for lucid dreams, someone else was going to have to worry about them, whatever they might prove to be.

As for the footnotes (and the first two references are literally that), here is a sample: Ernest Hartmann of Tufts University called lucid dreaming an occasional exception to the usual acceptance by the dreamer of the bizarre and even the impossible in dreams, and hazarded the impression that "such events are not typical parts of dreaming thought, but rather brief partial arousals."[14] Arousals, whether "partial" or "brief," meant waking states, and if this were so, lucid dreams would logically belong in someone else's field. On the other coast, Ralph Berger of the University of California at Santa Cruz noted the same exception: "Occasionally, the dreamer may 'realize' during dreaming that he is dreaming. But there have not been any experiments to determine whether or not these instances are accompanied by momentary physiological awakenings. . . ."[15] Again, here is the suspicion that lucid dreaming ought to belong to studies of waking rather than sleep.

In 1978 a well-known sleep and dream researcher, Allan Rechtschaffen of the University of Chicago, published an influential paper entitled "The single mindedness and isolation of dreams."[16] This essay appears to have made, as he said himself, "perhaps too much of" nonreflectiveness as an almost constant attribute of dreams. Dr. Rechtschaffen treated lucid dreaming as a rare exception (which it is in our time and culture) that only shows how characteristic nonreflectiveness is of dreams. Rechtschaffen demonstrated his theoretical willingness to consider lucid dreaming as a legitimate phenomenon of sleep and dreams, by recording one or two self-reported lucid dreamers for a few nights in his laboratory. Unfortunately, his subjects produced no lucid dreams on those nights and his study of lucid dreaming went no further.

Not all sleep and dream researchers seemed to regard

lucid dreaming with skepticism or virtual indifference. In 1975, while considering "some fanciful implications of the reality of dreaming," Dr. William C. Dement of Stanford University gave the impression that he regarded dream control as an intriguing, though unlikely, possibility. Dement also raised the possibility of lucid dreaming, wondering whether a person " . . . with the appropriate training or instructions," could "enter the dream knowing that it was a dream and knowing his task was to examine it."[17] Five years later, Dement found out that the answer to his question was "yes," as the reader shall soon see.

The picture presented by these few references shows that as recently as 1978, although most contemporary psychophysiological dream researchers had heard reports or at least rumors of lucid dreaming, they did not consider it to be of any special significance, or a legitimate phenomenon of sleep. If pressed to explain how lucid dreams happened to occur, they would usually cite a French paper published in 1973 by Schwartz and Lefebvre.[18] This study of patients with various sleep disorders revealed that they exhibited an unexpectedly high number of intrusions of wakefulness and partial arousals within their REM periods. Schwartz and Lefebvre proposed that these partial arousals, which they called "microawakenings," might somehow provide a physiological basis for lucid dreaming. Although the paper has been criticized for the fact that no direct evidence in support of this hypothesis was presented, and because its conclusions were based entirely on the abnormal sleep patterns of a few subjects, this explanation seemed to be generally accepted until very recently. It was not until 1981 that the "microawakening" theory of lucid dreaming was successfully challenged, and the majority of the membership of the Association for the Psychophysiological Study of Sleep (APSS) came to accept lucid dreams as the legitimate offspring of paradoxical sleep.

Most scientific fields have professional organizations under whose auspices researchers present their results to be considered and critiqued. In the case of sleep and dream research, the international forum for scientific research is the APSS, founded in 1960.[19] Nearly every professional sleep and dream researcher in the Western world belongs to it. At the annual convention of the APSS, sleep and dream researchers report the results of their work to their professional colleagues, who subject the findings to the critical evaluation which plays such a crucial role in the scientific process.

When Patricia Garfield enthusiastically sang the wonders of lucid dreaming to the fifteenth annual meeting of the APSS, in 1975, the response was somewhat mixed. Some dream researchers were intrigued and even excited by her reported successes with dreaming about particular topics, and especially by her claim to have voluntarily increased her frequency of lucid dreams. Most members, however, were skeptical. While amateur dreamers everywhere were buying her book, *Creative Dreaming*, the professionals were not; at least they weren't buying the idea of dream lucidity and control.

Scientists tend to follow a rule of thumb derived from the Marquis de Laplace, a French mathematician and astronomer of the eighteenth century. In matters of scientific judgement, Laplace held to the principle that "the weight of the evidence must be in proportion to the strangeness of the fact." In other words, he was willing to accept a hypothetical finding on the basis of relatively little evidence if the finding was consistent with other previously demonstrated results. However, if a claim were made that seemingly contradicted a body of accepted observations or theories, he would admit it to the body of scientific findings only after extensive evidence and the most rigorous proof.

To most dream researchers in 1975, lucid dreaming seemed so strange as to barely merit consideration, to say nothing of granting it the status of fact. Why was this?

Following Laplace's principle, of the correspondingly weighty evidence required by the strangeness of the fact, there was none at all! That is, none but the fact that some people claimed to have lucid dreams sometimes, and also to be able to exercise a considerable degree of control over them. Anecdotes, however, carry very little weight in experimental science.

Adding to the negative side of the balance were the results of an experimental study David Foulkes presented at the next meeting of the APSS, in which he attempted to demonstrate that college students could dream about a topic of their own choice. Unfortunately, the students—all of whom had professed interest in dream control as described in Garfield's book—were unable to dream reliably about a preselected topic, and an apparently careful follow-up study yielded the same result.[20]

These studies considerably dampened whatever little enthusiasm there had been for Patricia Garfield and *Creative Dreaming*. Although dream lucidity per se was not tested in any of the studies, its plausibility seemed to suffer in equal measure—perhaps a case of guilt by association, or a result of Garfield losing credibility.

Things began to look up in 1978, when at the eighteenth annual meeting of the APSS, held in Palo Alto, a group of Canadian researchers reported a degree of success while "searching for lucid dreams"[21] in the sleep laboratory. Two monitored subjects had reported one and two lucid dreams after awakening from REM periods. Unfortunately, no proof was given that the lucid dreams had actually occurred *during* the REM periods preceding the awakenings and reports. Consequently there was no way to know whether the lucid dreams had taken place during REM, as opposed to NREM, sleep or even before rather than during or after the awakenings. The subjects themselves were somewhat uncertain about just when their lucid dreams had taken place. The most they could say was that they had the "impression'' their lucid dreams had taken place shortly before they awoke and reported them. But this was too weak an argument to persuade anyone even moderately skeptical of lucid dreams that they took place during sleep. The Canadian study was further undercut by the fact that its conclusions were based upon a total of no more than three alleged lucid dreams reported by only two subjects. The APSS did not seem particularly impressed, to say nothing of convinced. Certainly, ''the weight of the evidence'' was not yet in proportion to ''the strangeness of the fact.'' One indication that this was the case was the publication later that year of Rechtschaffen's paper mentioned earlier. This widely cited and influential work, published in the first issue of *Sleep*, the new journal of the APSS, attempted to provide a theoretical basis for why lucid dreaming was unlikely. While stopping short of proving lucid dreams impossible (à la Norman Malcolm), Rechtschaffen made them seem peculiar aberrations.

It was at this point that I entered the picture. But before I describe my own scientific encounters with the APSS, I need to put my lucid dream research in context, and explain how I became involved with lucid dreaming in the first place. I have had occasional lucid dreams since I was five years old, and over the years developed a strong interest in the subject. I came across Celia Green's book in the fall of 1976, while browsing through the Palo Alto Public Library. Until that point, I had only been acquainted with Frederik van Eeden and Tibetan yoga. I was excited to discover that van Eeden was not the only lucid dreamer in Western history. But even more important for me was the realization that if others had learned to have lucid dreams, then nothing prevented me from doing the same. Just reading about the topic had resulted in several lucid dreams for me, and before long, in February of 1977, I began my efforts in earnest, starting a journal that seven years later contained nearly nine hundred lucid dream reports.

From the very beginning, I had been interested in the possibility, first raised by Charles Tart, of communication from the lucid dream to the outside world, *while* the dream was happening.[22] The problem was, since most of the dreamer's body is paralyzed during REM sleep, how could the dreamer send such a message? What might the lucid dreamer be able to do within the dream that could be observed or measured by scientists? A plan suggested itself to me. There is one obvious exception to this muscular paralysis, since eye movements are in no way inhibited during REM sleep. After all, it is the occurrence of rapid eye movements that gives this stage of sleep its name.

Earlier dream studies had shown that there is sometimes a precise correspondence between the direction of dreamers' observable eye movements and the direction they are looking in their dreams.[23] In one remarkable example, a subject was awakened from REM sleep after making a series of about two dozen regular horizontal eye movements. He reported that in his dream he had been watching a Ping-Pong game, and just before being awakened he had been following a long volley with his dream gaze.

I knew that lucid dreamers could freely look in any direction they wished while in a lucid dream, because I had done this myself. It occurred to me that by moving my (dream) eyes in a recognizable pattern, I might be able to send a signal to the outside world when I was having a lucid dream. I tried this out in the first lucid dream that I recorded: I moved my dream gaze up, down, up, down, up, to the count of five. As far as I knew at the time, this was the first signal deliberately transmitted from the dream world. The only trouble, of course, is that there was no one in the outside world to record it!

What I needed was a dream lab. I knew Stanford University had an excellent one under the direction of the sleep and dream research pioneer, Dr. William C. Dement. I made inquiries in the summer of 1977 and found a researcher, Dr. Lynn Nagel, at the Stanford University Sleep Research Center who was very interested in the prospects of studying lucid dreams in the laboratory.

In September of the same year, I applied to Stanford University, proposing to study lucid dreams as part of a Ph.D. program in psychophysiology. My proposal was approved, and in the fall of 1977 I started my work on lucid dreams. Serving on my faculty committee were professors Karl Pribram and Roger Shepard from psychology, Julian Davidson from physiology, and Vincent Zarcone Jr. and William Dement from psychiatry. Since Lynn Nagel was not a member of the Stanford faculty, our relationship was entirely unofficial. However, Lynn was my *de facto* principal advisor and collaborator on my dissertation research.

Lynn and I didn't waste any time getting me into the sleep lab. On my first night we had, unfortunately, decided to see if it would be helpful to awaken me at the beginning of each REM period in order to remind me to dream lucidly when I went back to sleep. It is clear in hindsight that this was *not* a good idea, since the result was very little REM sleep. It was not very helpful being reminded to dream lucidly when doing so prevented me from dreaming at all!

Worse than that was what happened in my first dream. The Stanford sleep lab has its windows boarded up to allow for time-isolation studies. I felt a little claustrophobic because of this, and apparently, by way of compensation, had the following dream. It seemed as if I had awoken at dawn and was witnessing an exquisitely beautiful sunrise through the *picture window* next to my bed. But before I had time to be more than startled by this anomaly, I was awakened by Lynn's voice reminding me to have a lucid dream.

We decided that next time we would let me have more of a chance—both to sleep and to have lucid dreams. We scheduled our next recording night for a month later—the next available opening—which happened to be Friday the 13th of January, 1978. Every time I had a lucid dream (at

home) while waiting for the fateful date, I would suggest
to myself that I would do it again in the lab. Finally the
night arrived, and Lynn hooked me up and watched the
polygraph recording while I slept. I had been hoping that
Friday the 13th would prove to be my lucky night, and that
turned out to be the case.

I slept very well indeed, and after seven and a half hours
in bed had my first lucid dream in the lab. A moment
before, I had been dreaming—but then I suddenly realized
that I must be asleep because I couldn't see, feel, or hear
anything. I recalled with delight that I was sleeping in the
laboratory. The image of what seemed to be the instruction
booklet for a vacuum cleaner or some such appliance floated
by. It struck me as mere flotsam on the stream of consciousness, but as I focused on it and tried to read the
writing, the image gradually stabilized and I had the sensation of opening my (dream) eyes. Then my hands appeared, with the rest of my dream body, and I was looking
at the booklet in bed. My dream room was a reasonably
good copy of the room in which I was actually asleep.
Since I now had a dream body I decided to do the eye
movements that we had agreed upon as a signal. I moved
my finger in a vertical line in front of me, following it with
my eyes. But I had become very excited over being able
to do this at last, and the thought disrupted my dream so
that it faded a few seconds later.

Afterward, we observed two large eye movements on the
polygraph record just before I awakened from a thirteen-
minute REM period. Here, finally, was objective evidence
that at least one lucid dream had taken place during what
was clearly REM sleep! I sent a note to the 1979 meeting
of the APSS in Tokyo mentioning this and other evidence
suggesting that lucid dreams are associated with REM
sleep.[24] Of course, I did not expect anyone to be convinced
of the reality of lucid dreaming by this brief summary. But

I wanted to share our results with other dream researchers as quickly as possible.

Our early success was not easy to repeat. The next six nights I spent in the sleep lab yielded no lucid dreams. I had not yet developed MILD (Mnemonic Induction of Lucid Dreams), the method that allowed me to induce lucid dreams on command, which I describe in Chapter 6. After I had become proficient at MILD we tried again, and in September of 1979 I had two more lucid dreams at the Stanford sleep lab. I was still having many more lucid dreams at home than at the lab, which was probably due to the fact that I was more relaxed about it at home. So we arranged to install a polygraph at my home for six weeks. During this Christmas vacation, I successfully captured another dozen lucid dreams, and again, my eye movement signals showed them all to have taken place during REM sleep.

By 1980, word was getting around about our interest in lucid dreaming, and several other lucid dreamers volunteered to try signaling lucid dreams in the lab. Roy Smith, a resident in psychiatry, was the first to succeed; his lucid dreams also took place in REM sleep. Two women, Beverly Kedzierski, a computer scientist, and Laurie Cook, a dancer, completed our initial group of lucid-dream subjects. We referred to ourselves as *oneironauts,* (pronounced "oh-nigh-ro-knots"), a word I coined from the Greek roots, meaning explorers of the inner world of dreams. The results of these first experiments formed the major part of my Ph.D. dissertation, *Lucid Dreaming: An Exploratory Study of Consciousness during Sleep.*

Let us return now to the APSS and the story of my efforts to publish this new method of communication from the dream state and proof that lucid dreaming can occur during unequivocal sleep.

It was too late for Lynn Nagel and me to present our results to the 1980 APSS meeting. Instead, we submitted a brief report of our preliminary findings for publication in the journal *Science* in March 1980, entitled "Lucid dreaming verified by volitional communication during REM sleep." We were excited about our discoveries and eagerly awaited the response.

Two months later we received a reply from *Science*. The editors of scientific journals base their decisions largely upon the opinions of anonymous reviewers, specialists in the relevant area. One of our two reviewers had written, "This is an excellent report, giving a new discovery validating lucid dreaming under laboratory conditions. The implications of lucid dreaming are interesting and important, and a major new field of research could flow from this discovery. The report is very clearly and concisely written, and I give it my highest recommendation for publication."

The second reviewer's response was, however, a polar opposite. Viewing our paper in the light of Rechtschaffen's work, this reviewer found it impossibly " . . . difficult to imagine subjects simultaneously both dreaming their dreams and signaling them to others," as was said of another study. It seemed he was basically unable to accept, on what were essentially philosophical grounds, that our results were possible. Consequently he managed to come up with a number of "interpretive problems"—all possible explanations of how we might have arrived at our obviously mistaken conclusions. Naturally, he did not recommend publication, and the editor deferred to his judgement.

In September, we submitted a revision of our paper to *Science,* having extended our original study with twice as many lucid dreamers and observations and having clarified the points the second reviewer had found problematic. But the paper was rejected again, on the basis of what were once more inherently philosophical objections. The problem seemed to be that our reviewers—presumably members of the APSS—simply did not believe lucid dreaming was really possible.

Hoping for a fresh consideration, we sent the paper to *Nature,* the British equivalent of *Science.* However, it was returned unreviewed. According to the editors of *Nature,* the topic of lucid dreaming was "not of sufficient general interest" to merit consideration! To make a long story short, after six months we finally did get our paper published in a psychological journal, *Perceptual and Motor Skills.*

I have emphasized at some length the initial difficulties we encountered, in order to bring a certain fact into clear relief: as late as 1980, dream researchers in general, and members of the APSS in particular, were nearly unanimous in rejecting lucid dreaming as a *bona fide* phenomenon of sleep—REM or otherwise. Lucid dreams were evidently still viewed as aberrant chimeras, brief daydreamlike intrusions of wakefulness into disturbed sleep; but not in any case as something sleep researchers need concern themselves with.

In June 1981, the same month our article appeared, I presented four papers on lucid dreaming to the twenty-first annual APSS meeting in Hyannis Port, Massachusetts. Happily, by now, our data were strong enough to convince even the most skeptical that lucid dreaming was a *bona fide* phenomenon of unambiguous REM sleep. For lucid dreaming, the weight of the evidence was finally in proportion to the strangeness of the fact.

After all the resistance we had encountered, I was at first surprised and then gratified to observe the positive response my presentations received. Several scientists told me in private that before seeing our data they had believed lucid dreaming impossible, but were now compelled to change their minds. Among these were some who had previously expressed their disbelief in print; I was greatly encouraged to see these signs of sincerity and openness to new ideas, and gained a lasting respect for these scientists. Such openness is regrettably not always the rule in science—no more, for that matter, than it is in any other area of human endeavor.

But this does illustrate something about how science works, when it works properly. "Science" is really a community of scientists who adhere to a common set of standards of verification. As such, science tends to be conservative—to resist the new perhaps too zealously, and hold perhaps too tenaciously to the accepted. The philosopher Thomas Kuhn has suggested that new theories in science do not replace old ones until the supporters of the old die off! I had feared this might be the case with the APSS and lucid dreaming, and was pleasantly surprised to find myself mistaken.

Lucid dreaming, once associated in the minds of many scientists with the occult and parapsychology, had become an accepted part of mainstream science and as such, a legitimate topic for research. This was an important step toward broader exploration and the development of a science of lucid dreaming.

Robert K. Merton of Columbia University, one of the foremost theorists of science, has shown that almost all major scientific ideas are arrived at more than once, and frequently nearly simultaneously, by researchers working "independently." This is because all scientists working in a field draw upon the same set of previously established findings and stand, in Newton's phrase, on the shoulders of the same giants. Since they are reasoning, as it were, from the same premises, it is to be expected that they are likely to arrive at the same conclusions.

Probably the most famous example of independent discovery in science occurred in 1858, when, after twenty years of work, Charles Darwin was finally preparing for publication his epochal book on the theory of evolution, the *Origin of Species*. Imagine Darwin's astonishment when he received a letter from a virtually unknown biologist named Alfred Russell Wallace. While recovering from malaria in Malaya, Wallace had independently worked out the theory of natural selection in a form almost identical to Darwin's, as proven by a manuscript enclosed with the letter. So Darwin was not the first to develop a theory of evolution based on natural selection; Wallace had undeniable priority. However, priority is not always the most important issue; Darwin's work had the meticulous detail necessary to convince the scientific community. As Wallace himself stated with astuteness no less than generosity, in a subsequent letter to Darwin, " . . . my paper would never have convinced anybody or been noticed as more than an ingenious speculation, whereas your book has revolutionalized the study of Natural History, and carried away the best men of the present age." Wallace was not merely being modest. History shows that his work played no significant part in the scientific acceptance of the theory of evolution, and it is to Darwin's work alone that we owe this revolution in our thinking.

I have dwelt on this example at some length, because I believe it bears a definite resemblance to the circumstances surrounding the acceptance of lucid dreaming over a century later. History does indeed repeat itself, sometimes on a greater scale and sometimes on a lesser. In this case, we are clearly dealing with the lesser scale, but bearing in mind Darwin and Wallace should help to put the events into perspective. When, in the fall of 1980, an article entitled "Insight into Lucid Dreams" was called to my attention, I was as astonished as Darwin must have been when he first read of Wallace's work. The article, published in *Nursing Mirror*, a little-known British magazine, described work that was remarkably similar to my own. The author, Keith Hearne, a talented British parapsychologist, outlined a brief account of his Ph.D. dissertation study carried out at Hull and Liverpool universities with the help of a proficient lucid dreamer. I later learned that Hearne's subject had been Alan Worsley, an extremely dedicated explorer of lucid dreams. Over the course of a year, Worsley had spent forty-five nights in a sleep lab while Hearne monitored him. During these nights, Worsley had eight lucid dreams, in each of which he marked the EOG with eye-movement signals whenever he realized he was dreaming.

At first the similarity between our work at Stanford and theirs at Liverpool seemed uncanny. Upon reflection, however, I realized that the idea of validating lucid dreams by eye movement signaling would be relatively obvious to anyone familiar with recent psychophysiological dream research and the possibilities of lucid dreaming. Viewed in this light, independent discovery no longer appeared uncanny or even unexpected.

The only odd thing about it was that Hearne finished his dissertation fully two years before I did. Yet, in spite of having made the most extensive review of the literature on lucid dreaming available in English, I had heard not so much as a rumor of Hearne and Worsley until after I completed my dissertation in 1980. One might have thought that Hearne would have been eager to share his findings with the scientific community. But evidently not. I understand from Worsley that Hearne "wanted to make a few discoveries first," before publishing.[25] In any case, it appears that as late as 1980 he was swearing to secrecy those few professionals who knew about his work. But whatever the explanation, six years after completing his dissertation, Hearne still has not published an account of his original study in any peer-reviewed scientific journal.

As a result of Hearne's reticence, or maybe just by accident, we at Stanford knew nothing of the English work until late 1980. By then, our own more extensive studies had gone considerably beyond Hearne's earlier dissertation work, and consequently his pioneering research only confirmed what we already knew. Had the results of the Liverpool experiments been available to us several years earlier, we could have built on what would have been

Hearne's tremendous contribution to the field. But that isn't what happened. As a result, Hearne's pioneering study appears to have played a relatively minor role in the scientific acceptance of lucid dreaming. Having said that, I want to add that there seems little doubt that Keith Hearne is an innovative and energetic investigator from whom we may hope for new developments in the years to come. As for Alan Worsley, he has gone on to collaborate with other research groups in England, carrying out some intriguing experiments both in the laboratory and at home.[26] Whatever else he may do, however, Worsley deserves the credit for being the first person, as far as I know, to successfully send a deliberate message from the dream world.

We have followed the story of lucid dreaming in the laboratory up to the point of its acceptance by the scientific world at the beginning of this decade. Since then, there has been a veritable explosion of public and scientific interest in lucid dreams. Dozens of papers on the topic have been published in the past few years, and the number of researchers in the area has been rapidly accelerating. All of this contributes to the impression of a highly exciting field of exploration that is unfolding *now:* the new world of lucid dreaming.

4

Exploring the Dream World: Lucid Dreamers in the Laboratory

Mapping Out the Dream World

The relationship between the dream world and the physical world has had a fascination for humanity that probably pre-dates recorded history by many thousands of years. But like such questions as "Why is the sky blue?" or "What is on the other side of the moon?" the solution to the dream reality problem had to await the technological developments of the very recent past. Some progress had been achieved by the psychophysiological approach to dream research, but as long as the subjects were non-lucid dreamers, this method continued to have significant limitations.

If researchers were interested, for example, in whether reported changes in the direction of a dreamer's gaze were accompanied by corresponding physical movements of the eyes, they would have to approach the problem something like this: First, they would arrange to measure the dreamer's eye movements, easy enough with an EOG. Next they would have to observe the dreamer's eye movements during REM periods, waiting—and here is the problem—until by chance the dreamer made a sufficiently distinct and regular sequence of eye movements. Only very rarely would there be an unusual pattern that could be definitely linked to dream eye movements the subject could identify, as in the Ping-Pong dream of Chapter 3. In the thousands of sleep and dream studies conducted over the past several decades, instances as striking as this can be counted on one hand. In any case, if an experimenter were to design a study looking for this sort of event, it would take a great deal of waiting before the subject—by chance—did what the experimenter wanted.

Let us take another example that shows this approach is limited by more than just the experimenter's patience. Suppose our researcher were interested in whether or not the dreamer's brain shows shifts in activity (as measured by EEG) dependent upon particular mental tasks, such as singing or counting. In the waking state, singing activates the right cerebral hemisphere of most right-handers, while counting activates the left. Could our researcher ever reasonably expect to find a case in which the non-lucid dreamer "just happened" to sing and count in the same dream? How could anyone know exactly when the dreamer was doing what?

The main problem with this version of the psychophysiological approach to dream research is that as long as dreamers are non-lucid, the researcher simply has no way of being sure they will dream what the researcher needs them to for the particular experiment. This is really little better than a shot-in-the-dark approach, and dream researchers have quite understandably been showing less and less interest in it as the years, and miles of polygraph paper, have rolled by with few results to show for it. As a result of these difficulties, some dream scientists have even been calling for the complete abandonment of the psycho-physiological approach in favor of purely psychological studies. David Foulkes, an influential dream researcher, has written that " . . . psychophysiological correlation research now appears to offer such a low rate of return for effort expended as not to be a wise place for dream psychology to continue to commit much of its limited resources." This assessment seems justified as long as it refers only to the traditional practice of psychophysiological research, using non-lucid subjects. The use of lucid dreamers, however, solves the basic deficiencies of the old approach and allows the researcher to complete his designed experiments successfully. It well may be the answer to revitalizing the psychophysiological method.

The fact that lucid dreamers know they are asleep, can remember to perform previously agreed-upon actions, and can signal to the waking world, makes possible an entirely new approach to dream research. These specially trained oneironauts can carry out all kinds of experimental tasks, functioning both as subjects and experimenters in the dream state. For the first time, sleepers can signal the exact time of particular dream events, thus allowing for the convenient testing of otherwise untestable hypotheses. A researcher can ask a subject to perform any chosen action within the dream, and the lucid dreamer can carry these directions out. This signaling also allows a clear mapping of mind/body relationships.

Our studies at Stanford cover considerable ground, showing the relationship between physiological changes in lucid dreamers' bodies and a variety of actions carried out by their "dream" bodies within the dreams. Our investigations addressed a range of relationships: between estimated dream time and actual time; between dream action, including eye movements, speech, and breathing, and corresponding muscle action; between dreamed singing and

counting, and relative activation of the left and right cerebral hemispheres of the brain; and between dreamed sexual
activity and changes in a variety of genital and nongenital
physiological measures.

Dream Time

How fast can we dream a dream and how long do dreams
take? These are questions that have intrigued humanity for
centuries. The traditional answer has been that dreams take
very little or no time at all. There is, for example, the story
of Mohammed's Night Journey. The Prophet is said to have
overturned a pitcher of water just before leaving (via flying
horse) on a tour of the seven heavens, in the course of
which he met and conversed with the seven prophets, numerous angels, and God himself. Having taken in all the
sights of paradise, the Prophet returned to his bed to find
that the water had not yet run out of the pitcher he had
overturned.

Likewise, the nineteenth-century pioneer of dream research, Alfred Maury, recalled late in his life a dream he had
had many years earlier, in which he somehow had gotten
mixed up with the French Revolution. After witnessing a
number of scenes of murder, he was himself brought before
the revolutionary tribunal. After a long trial in which he saw
Robespierre, Marat, and other heroes of the revolution, he
was sentenced to death and led to the place of execution in
the midst of the usual jeering mob. Waiting his turn among
the condemned, he watched the quick and grisly work of the
guillotine. Then his turn came and he mounted the scaffold.
The executioner tied him to the board and tipped it into place.
The blade fell . . . and at this critical point, Maury awoke
in terror, only to find his head still attached to his body. He
realized almost at once what had happened: the headboard

had fallen on his neck. He concluded that his lengthy dream must have been initiated by the impact of the headboard on his neck, and that the entire dream must have taken place in the briefest instant! (If you suppose that these are only the beliefs of centuries gone by, note that as recently as 1981 a well-respected dream researcher published a paper supporting the view that dreams take place during the brief time of awakening.[1])

While dreams undoubtedly do occasionally occur in this fashion, evidence suggests that dreams normally take the same amount of time the actions would take in real life. In one study, Dement and Kleitman awakened five subjects at either five or fifteen minutes after the beginning of their REM periods, and asked them to decide which amount of time had elapsed. Four of the five subjects were consistently able to choose the correct time. The same study showed that dreams reported after fifteen minutes of REM sleep were longer than those following five minutes of REM. Such reports appear to contradict the notion of instantaneous dreaming. However, they do not prove that dream time is the same as "real time," but only indicate that they are generally proportional to one another.

However, subjective dream duration can be directly and easily measured by using lucid dreamers. Oneironauts are instructed to signal when they become lucid in their dream, and then to estimate an interval of, say, ten seconds by counting to ten in the dream. The lucid dreamer signals again to mark the end of the interval, which can then be directly measured on the polygraph record.

In our experiments,[2] we found that the average length of these estimated ten-second intervals was thirteen seconds, which was also the average estimation of a ten-second interval while subjects were awake. On one occasion, a star subject of ours, Beverly, even performed this experiment for a BBC television crew. She described her experience as follows:

By this point, fairly late in the morning, I was *very* determined to have the expected lucid dream: I felt especially motivated by all the filming crew being there, waiting for me to perform. So, when I found myself at the transition point between being awake and asleep I "made" it happen: my dream body began to float up in the air out of bed, a bed very much like the one that I knew my physical body was sleeping in. I waited until I was completely floating to be sure that I was really dreaming. But it seemed that I was being held back by something: my electrodes! However, I reasoned that these were only *dream* electrodes and I wasn't going to let my dream control *me!* At that point, I merely flew away not really caring about the "electrodes," which I presumed no longer existed. As I flew across the room, right through the wall, I signaled "left-right-left-right" to show that I was lucid. All of this so far took only a few seconds. I began estimating ten seconds, counting "one-thousand and one, one thousand and two . . ." as I passed through the wall into the lounge area. Everything looked very dark and I felt that I wasn't very deep into my sleep until I saw a weak reflection of my face in a mirror. When I stared at it the room became very clear and lifelike. Still counting, I decided that I'd like some action to report on later, so I grabbed a chair and playfully threw it into the air, watching it tumble and float. When I finished counting to ten, I signaled again. Next I was supposed to estimate ten seconds without counting, and this was when I got the idea that it would be interesting to fly to the polygraph room and actually watch a dream dramatization of my own signals being recorded. I needed to get there within ten seconds, so I flew right through the adjoining room, which was filled with boxes and chairs. For some reason, I let myself get caught up in avoiding stumbling on them, hoping to get to the polygraph before my next signal. In the distance, I heard a voice similar to mine doing the counting that I wasn't supposed to be doing! That puzzled me a little, but I found it intriguing. Just in time, I arrived at

the polygraph machine where several people were
crowded around watching. I announced, "Hey, everyone, I'm doing it *live!*" as I signaled for the third time,
seeing the polygraph pens flashing about wildly in my
dream.

As these experiments indicate, estimated time in dreams
seems very nearly equal to clock time—at least for lucid
dreams.

I am sure many readers will object, saying something
like "But I've had dreams in which I spent what seemed
like years or lifetimes." So have we all, but I believe this
seeming passage of time is accomplished in dreams the
same way it is in the movies or the theater. If we see
someone in a movie turning out the light at midnight, and
a few moments later see her turning off an alarm shortly
after dawn, we accept that seven or eight hours have passed
even though we "know" it has only been a few seconds.
I think the same kind of mechanism operates in dreams to
produce the sensation of extended passages of time. I have
no argument with this sense in which dream time may not
equal clock time. Nevertheless, the evidence of our lucid
dream experiments with time suggests that it takes just as
long to dream you are doing something as it does to actually do it.

This result ought not to surprise anyone. There are, after
all, definite psychophysiological limitations to how fast our
brains can process information. If I were to ask you if a
canary can sing, it would take you over a second to reply;
and if I were to ask you whether a canary can fly, it would
even take you a little longer. Why can't we answer such
obvious questions instantly? Because our brains need time
to search through our billions of memories to determine
whether or not the answer is in fact "obvious." This is
why we cannot do things instantaneously in our dreams:
our brains need time to dream them.

Breathing

We undertook an experiment to determine the extent to which lucid dreamers' patterns of breathing were paralleled by changes in their actual patterns of respiration.[3] The dream body obviously has no need to breathe. It is, after all, only a mental representation of the dreamer's physical body. And in waking life, although we breathe every second, we are for the most part unconscious of it. Normally we only become conscious of the process when something draws our attention to it—if we are not getting enough air, or if we wish to hold our breath for some reason.

Because we are seldom aware of our breathing while awake, we are seldom aware of it while dreaming. I first became aware of and interested in this problem at the age of five. At the time I was in the habit of dreaming a sort of serial dream on successive nights. In the dream serial, I was an undersea pirate, and on at least one occasion I worried for a moment about having been underwater for a *very* long time—much longer than I could hold my breath. But then I remembered with great relief that in "these dreams" I could breathe underwater. Or was it that I didn't need to breathe in dreams? I wasn't sure and wondered no more until almost thirty years later.

We were interested in the question of whether or not subjects holding their breath in dreams physically do so. Using the old methodolology of dream research, this would be a very difficult question to approach. But through the use of lucid dreaming, it was easy to answer. Three of our oneironauts agreed to join me in attempting to carry out (with our dream bodies) a previously agreed-upon pattern of breathing whenever we realized we were dreaming. We were to mark with an eye-movement signal the beginning and end of a five-second interval in which we would either breathe rapidly or hold our breath. The four of us spent two to three nights in the sleep lab while our respiration was monitored, along with the usual physiological measures used for determining sleep stages.

Altogether, the four of us reported having carried out the breathing task in twelve lucid dreams. The relevant polygraph records were given to an independent researcher to see if it was possible to determine whether particular instances were cases of rapid breathing or of breath-holding. The researcher was able to correctly identify every instance. Since the odds of doing this by chance are only 1 in 4096, we were able to conclude confidently that voluntary control of the mental image of respiration during lucid dreaming is reflected in corresponding changes in actual respiration.

This doesn't mean that every variation in breathing during REM sleep is releated to dream content. For instance, a respiratory pause on a polysomnogram wouldn't necessarily imply that the dreamer was holding his dream breath. But if the dreamer *was,* we would expect to see a pause in breathing on the record. Many factors, on a variety of levels of psychophysiological organization, contribute to the pattern of breathing when we are awake, and the same holds true when we are asleep. Some of these respiratory influences are physiological, some psychological; together they form the consciously experienced content of the dream.

All that we have demonstrated in our research is that respiratory content in a dreamer's consciousness appears to affect the sleeper's actual pattern of breathing. The results are not surprising when viewed in the proper light. The same relationship would probably hold true for walking, talking, or any other form of behavior, except for the fact that most of our muscles are paralyzed during REM sleep. The brain-stem system that accomplishes the general suppression of muscle tone during REM dreaming saves us from running around with our eyes closed in the middle of the night—a practice almost as hazardous now as it was for our ancestors back in the jungle. However, not all muscle groups are equally inhibited during REM sleep. For example, there is no way we can harm ourselves with eye movements; consequently the extraocular muscles are not inhibited at all during REM. Quite the contrary: they give the active state of sleep its common name. Another set of muscles is exempted from the general paralysis of REM sleep, but for a different reason: the respiratory muscles, and they are not inhibited for obvious reasons.

Singing and Counting

The brain is divided into two cerebral hemispheres, and for most people the left hemisphere shows increased activity during language use and analytical thinking, while the right shows increased activity during spatial tasks and holistic thinking. Though the degree of lateral specialization of the brain has been exaggerated in the popular press, numerous scientific studies have demonstrated reliable differences in brain-wave activity between the left and right hemispheres and these differences depend precisely upon which mental activities the subject is engaged in at the moment.

All of these studies were, of course, done while the subjects were awake. A question that has intrigued dream researchers is, would similar relationships hold during REM dreaming? Here again was a question that only lucid dreamers could answer. We decided to compare dreamed counting and dreamed singing—activities that are supposed to engage the left and right hemispheres respectively.[4] Why these particular tasks? The choice was a practical one. Unlike many other possible tasks, counting and singing required nothing more than a dream body with a functioning dream tongue—standard issue for an oneironaut!

I was the first to attempt the experiment. Early in the

night I spent at the lab, I awoke from a dream and practiced my memory method for inducing lucid dreams (MILD) before returning to sleep. Not long afterward, I awoke from another non-lucid dream and again tried MILD—with the same disappointing result. My third effort seemed to have failed as well. I was lying in bed awake for the fourth time that night, worrying and wondering what was wrong with me—was I losing my touch after all these years? Then, suddenly, I found myself flying high above a field. I realized at once—with great excitement—that *this* was the lucid dream I had been seeking! I made an eye-movement signal and began to sing:

> Row, row, row your boat
> Gently down the stream.
> Merrily, merrily, merrily, merrily,
> Life is but a dream.

Still flying high over the meadow, I made a second eye-movement signal and began to count slowly to ten. Upon finishing, I made a third eye-movement signal marking the completion of this experimental task. I was overjoyed at my success and turned a virtual cartwheel in midair. After a few seconds, the dream faded.

We had recorded brain waves from my left and right cerebral hemispheres so that the amounts of alpha activity during the two tasks could be calculated by a computer. Rhythmic alpha waves are generally interpreted as the indication of a resting or inactive brain. So, if during the performance of a given task one of the hemispheres is doing most of the work, the other hemisphere—the less active one—will show more alpha activity. Since the right hemisphere is involved during the singing and the left hemisphere during the counting, we expected to find more alpha in my left hemisphere during singing. And this is exactly what we found. Repetition of this experiment with two other subjects yielded consistent results: the brain seemed to show the same patterns of selective activation during singing and counting during REM sleep as it did during wakefulness.

Sexual Activity

Sexual activity seems to form a prominent part of the lucid dreams of many individuals, especially women. Patricia Garfield reported that two-thirds of her lucid dreams have sexual content and about half of these dreams culminate in orgasm. In *Pathway to Ecstasy*, Garfield describes her lucid dream orgasms as being of "profound" intensity. "With a totality of self that is only sometimes felt in the waking state," she found herself "bursting into soul- and body-shaking explosions."

These are incredibly impressive experiences, to say the least. However, the lucid dream reports of several of our female oneironauts contained similar accounts. I was intrigued by the possibility of an experiment to determine whether or not sexual activity in lucid dreams is accompanied by physiological changes similar to those that take place during waking sexual activities.[5]

Walter Greenleaf, a Stanford graduate student engaged in psychophysiological research on human sexual response, collaborated with me on several experiments. We decided to work with women at first, since they reported orgasm in lucid dreams much more frequently than men. I asked several of our female oneironauts if they would be willing to try, and "Miranda" was the first to succeed. She spent a night sleeping in our laboratory while we recorded sixteen channels of physiological data, including the usual EEG, EOG, and EMG, as well as respiration rate, heart rate, vaginal EMG, and vaginal pulse amplitude. These last two measures were obtained from a comfortable vaginal probe (inserted in privacy) that was worn while sleeping. The probe registered vaginal muscle activity by means of two electrodes on its surface. Pulse amplitude, a measure of blood flow to the vaginal walls, was obtained by means of an infrared light source and photocell detector embedded in the surface of the probe. Light emitted from the probe is reflected back to the photocell to an extent that varies with changes in the amount of blood flowing to the vaginal walls. Experiments in the waking state had clearly demonstrated that when women become sexually aroused, their vaginal pulse amplitude shows a significant increase. Thus we anticipated finding similar increases coupled with sexual activity during lucid dreams.

We asked Miranda to signal four times in her lucid dream, using standard eye-movement signals. The first signal was to be at the moment she realized that she was dreaming; the second when she began sexual activity in her dream; the third when she experienced orgasm; and the fourth only when she felt herself to have awakened.

At about five minutes into her fifth REM period of the night, Miranda had a three-minute lucid dream in which she successfully carried out the experimental task—exactly as agreed upon. In her report, she said that she seemed to be lying in bed still awake, with someone's hands rubbing her neck. Recognizing the improbability of someone being in her room, she suspected she was dreaming, and tested her state by trying to float into the air. As soon as she found herself floating, she was convinced she was dreaming and made the agreed-upon signal as she floated through her bedroom wall. Finding no one in the polygraph room, she proceeded through an unopened window outside. Continuing to fly, she found herself over a campus resembling both Oxford and Stanford. She flew through the cool evening air, free as a cloud, stopping now and then to admire the beautiful stone carvings on the walls. After a few minutes, however, she decided it was time to begin the experiment. Flying through an archway, she spotted a group of people—apparently visitors touring the campus. Swooping down to the group, she picked the first man within reach. She tapped him on the shoulder, and he came toward her as if knowing exactly what he was expected to do. At this she signaled again, marking the beginning of sexual activity. She says that she must have already been excited from the flying, because after only fifteen seconds she felt as if she were about to climax. She signaled a third time, marking her experience of orgasm as the final waves began to die down. Shortly after this she let herself wake up, and signaled, according to plan, as soon as she felt herself back in bed. She said the dream orgasm had been neither long nor intense, but was quite definitely a real orgasm.

The graph of vaginal blood flow during the several minutes of her lucid dream appears to correspond in every particular with Miranda's report of her lucid dream. During the portion of dreamed sexual activity, between her second and third signal, her respiration rate, vaginal muscle activity, and vaginal blood flow all reached their highest levels of the night. However, her heart showed only a moderate increase in rate. The increases in respiration rate and vaginal blood flow are fully comparable to those typically observed during waking orgasm—and the lucid dream orgasm was described as being "not very strong"! This experiment provided the first objective evidence for the validity of Miranda's reports (and, by extension, those of others) of vividly realistic sex in lucid dreams.

Before leaving Miranda's lucid dream, I would like to mention the fact that at least a part of it would have undoubtedly delighted Freud, had he lived another half-century to hear it. I am speaking of the flying, which seemed to have served as very effective foreplay, considering the remarkably short interval between the start of sex and orgasmic culmination. What is the meaning of flying dreams? Freud's unhesitating answer to this question was that flying in dreams symbolically expresses nothing other than the desire to engage in sexual activity! For once, this interpretation seems to fit the dream without forcing.

Having recorded an impressive female sexual response, we next wondered what males might show. Although males report orgasmic lucid dreams less frequently than females do, we decided to try the experiment anyway. "Randy," a first-rate oneironaut, volunteered for this perilous mission.

While Randy slept, we recorded the same physiological measures as we had done in Miranda's experiment, with the exception that we equipped him with a penile strain gauge (a loop of flexible tubing filled with mercury, about an inch in diameter)—the device generally used for measuring sexual response. Just before going to sleep, Randy put the strain gauge around the base of his penis. As the strain gauge expands during erection, its electrical resistance increases, allowing polygraphic monitoring of penile tumescence (enlargement). Although REM periods are normally associated with spontaneous erections of varying degrees, we hoped to observe a further increase during dreamed sexual activity.

Randy agreed to follow the same signaling procedure as Miranda had. After a few nights' practice, he succeeded perfectly. Awakening from his fourth REM period of the night, he made the following report:

A bizarre detail made me realize that I was dreaming. I made an eye-movement signal, then proceeded through the roof, flying Superman-style. Having landed in the backyard of a house, I wished for a girl. A cute little teenager walked out of the patio door, followed closely by her mother. For some reason, the mother seemed to know me, and with a wink sent her daughter out to play with me. We went in the backyard, and I signaled the beginning of foreplay. An instant later her blouse was on the ground and the nipples of her blossoming breasts stood out. She kneeled on the ground and began to kiss me in a most stimulating manner. I felt myself about to climax and closed my eyes in ecstasy as I had the orgasm, and again signaled. When I opened my eyes, I seemed to have awakened from a wet dream. I was very excited at the accomplishment of my experiment, then I realized it was only a false awakening, and at this I actually awoke. Although I found I had not actually ejaculated, I still felt the tingling in my spine and I marveled at the reality that the mind could create.

As in Miranda's case, Randy's polygraph record revealed a precise correspondence with his lucid dream report. During the thirty seconds of sexual activity marked by his second and third signals, his respiration rate reached its maximum for the REM periods, exactly as it had for Miranda. His penile strain gauge indicated that his erection, after having begun shortly before the onset of the REM period, only reached its maximal level between signals two and three. Remarkably, a slow detumescence began almost immediately following the dream orgasm.

Randy's heart, like Miranda's, showed only a moderate increase in rate during the lucid dream orgasm. In general terms, these orgasms seemed to trigger very similar physiological responses in their sleeping bodies. This was especially true of the dramatic increases in respiration rate shown by both. An important implication is that in some respects, lucid dream sex has as powerful an impact on the dreamer's body as the real thing.

The extent to which this is true may vary from dreamer to dreamer, and from one sex to the other. One significant gender-related difference may be that while Miranda experienced vaginal muscle contractions during lucid dream orgasm, Randy apparently did not experience corresponding pelvic muscle contractions. Randy's failure to actually ejaculate in his dream, in spite of having vividly experienced the sensations of ejaculation, is consistent with my own experience in this regard. Among the nearly nine hundred lucid dream reports in my personal record are about a dozen instances in which I dreamed that I reached orgasm. In all of these cases, the sensation of ejaculation was convincingly vivid, so much so that these lucid dream orgasms were usually followed by false awakenings in which I dreamed that I *had* in fact had a wet dream. Yet as soon as I awoke in actuality, I always discovered that I was mistaken.

Insofar as all this proves typical of lucid dream sex, it would seem that the wet dreams experienced by adolescents and other males lacking regular sexual outlet result from very different causes. As it happens, the reports of genuine wet dreams are sometimes completely devoid of any sexual or erotic elements whatsoever. Since, at the same time, every dream period is accompanied by spontaneous erections, wet dreams may result from genital stimulation and reflex ejaculation.

Although nonerotic wet dreams do occur, they are not the usual case. Why, then, do most wet dreams take on the guise of a sexual encounter? I would propose that these experiences result from the dream's incorporation of sensory information coming from the genitals, naturally elaborated into a "likely story" explaining the experienced sexual arousal. Following this line of reasoning, wet dreams would be the result of actual erotic sensations accurately interpreted by the dreaming brain. In other words, first comes the ejaculation, then comes the wet dream.

Apparently, the opposite normally holds for lucid dream orgasms. The erotic dream comes first, resulting in orgasm "in the brain." However, in this case, the resulting impulses descending from the brain to the genitals are evidently too inhibited to trigger the genital ejaculatory reflex. So, lucid dreams are only wet in the dream.

Because our data are derived from only one observation of two subjects, caution in interpreting these preliminary results is obviously necessary. However, I am willing to risk the conclusion that sexual activity and the experience of orgasm in lucid dreams appears to be associated with physiological changes that are very similar to those occurring during corresponding activities in the waking state.

An important exception to this conclusion is the fact that only very slight increases in heart rate accompanied the sexual activity in these lucid dreams. During waking sexual activity, heart rate may double or triple. This fact may have a practical benefit. For patients recovering from heart disease, sex can be a dangerous and sometimes fatal form of exercise. Dream sex, in contrast, appears to be completely safe for everyone, and for many paralyzed people, it may be the only form of sexual release available.

Significance

We have seen that dream sex is like "real" sex, dream singing and counting is like "real" singing and counting, and dream time is like "real" time. So what? You may be wondering what difference this all makes to *you*. These results have implications of considerable importance for every dreamer; let me explain how.

In the singing and counting experiment, we asked our subjects to do two things as controls. One was to actually do the tasks while awake, and the other was merely to imagine doing them. When we looked at imagined singing and counting we found that neither task produced any consistent shifts in brain activity. But singing and counting in the lucid dream produced large shifts equivalent to those that occurred during the actual performance of the tasks. This suggests that lucid dreaming (and by extension, dreaming in general) is more like actually doing than like merely imagining.

According to a theory widely accepted among psychologists and neuroscientists, when a person imagines an object, a pattern of brain activity occurs that is very similar to that which occurs when he or she actually perceives an object. If this is true, the difference between imagination (or memory) and perception may be merely a matter of degree—determined by the vividness or intensity of an experience. But an imagined or remembered apple is neither as palpable nor as tasty as a real apple.

In general, images and memories are pale reflections, much less vivid than the original perception. Otherwise, we would have difficulty in distinguishing inner from outer experiences, as sometimes happens to those prone to hallucinations. Our normal ability to distinguish memories of past perceptions from current perceptual experiences has obvious survival value. When our distant ancestors came face to face with a saber-toothed tiger, the hunters who were flooded with such vivid memory images of all the tigers they had ever seen, and did not know which tiger to run from, were probably eaten by the real tiger! As a result, they would have had no further descendants, and so none of us are likely to have inherited their dangerous imaginations! Thanks to evolution, most of us have inherited the ability to readily distinguish inner events from outer ones— except in dreams, of course. But this is because during the

REM state, the part of the brain that normally inhibits the vividness of imagery is itself inhibited, allowing memories and mental images to be released with undiminished vividness—as if they were waking perceptions. And this is exactly what we ordinarily take them to be, mistaking dreams for external reality—unless, that is, we happen to be lucid.

It is plausible to assume that the varying degrees of perceived vividness have their neurophysiological basis in corresponding variations in the intensity of patterns of neuronal discharge in the brain. This being so, the accounts of lucid dreamers, as well as the results of the experiments described earlier, suggest that the level of brain activity associated with lucid dreaming is at least comparable to, and frequently of even greater intensity than, the activity accompanying waking perceptions.

Perceptual vividness is probably the main criterion we use to judge how real something is. In a famous story, Samuel Johnson kicked a stone to demonstrate what he thought was "really" real. But if by some devilry he happened to be dreaming at the time, it would have been a dream stone he was kicking, and it could easily have seemed just as solid and "real." From the point of view of the brain, what seems real is as real as real can be.

Taken together, our work at Stanford has amassed strong laboratory evidence indicating that what happens in the inner world of dreams—and lucid dreams especially—can produce physical effects on the dreamer's brain no less real than those produced by corresponding events happening in the external world. The results of the experiments summarized in this chapter show that the impact of certain dream behaviors on brain and body can be fully equivalent to the impact produced by corresponding actual behaviors. This fits hand in glove with the fact that dreams are normally *experienced* by the dreamer as fully real, and indeed it is not unusual for dreams (especially when lucid) to seem more real than physical reality itself. This is far from the view prevalent in Western societies, seeing dreams as "airy nothings" devoid of meaning and reality. On the contrary, what we do in dreams (or leave undone) can at times affect us as profoundly as what we do (or do not do) in our waking lives.

I believe our findings have a number of exciting implications. The most exciting would seem to be in the areas of philosophy, psychophysiology, and neuroscience. All three of these disciplines have had a longstanding interest in the relationship between the mental and physical worlds. This, the "mind-body problem," is really many problems—or else a single problem that takes many forms. Among these forms is whether and how the subjective (mental) events of the dream and the objective (physical) events occurring in the dreamer's brain are connected. At this point, I can only give a partial answer: our research indicates that dream events are closely paralleled by brain events. The extent to which this model of psychophysiological parallelism will provide an accurate picture of reality remains a goal for future research. But in whatever details it may ultimately prove to be wrong, our model at this point seems empirically to rule out dualistic conceptions of dreaming, such as the traditional favorite of the soul (or "astral body") flying about the dream world completely free from brain and body.

Our results also should encourage psychologists, neuroscientists, and psychophysiologists attempting to discover correspondences between objectively measured physiology and behavior, and subjective experience. We are just at the beginning of mapping out the relationships between the human mind and brain, but our Stanford work may have brought us one small step closer to the day when we will discover the structure of our minds within the microcosm of the human brain.

5

~~~~~~~~~~

The Experience of
Lucid Dreaming

Let us begin *in medias res*—as is the way of dreams: I was
walking along a gradually ascending mountain path with a
friend. As far as the eye could see, the only thing moving
was the silent mist that veiled the majestic peaks in mystery. But suddenly we found ourselves before a narrow
bridge that precariously spanned a chasm. When I looked
down into the bottomless abyss beneath the bridge, I became dizzy with fear and could not bring myself to proceed. At this, my companion said, ''You know, Stephen,
you don't *have* to go this way. You can go back the way
we came,'' and pointed back down what seemed an immense distance. But then the thought crossed my mind that
if I were to become lucid, I would have no reason to fear
the height. A few seconds of reflection were enough for
me to realize that indeed I *was* dreaming. My confidence
was restored and I was able to cross the bridge and awaken.

In another dream world, an anonymous dreamer quoted
by Ann Faraday found herself facing an unpleasant di-

lemma; she had two choices: either she could have sex with "a fantastic dream lover" who would afterwards strangle her, or she could simply decide never to have sex again. She explained that "her growing desire for a life lived to the full rather than a living death led her to choose the former, and as she was being led into the arena she suddenly became lucid." Wishing to make the most of her lucid dream, "she decided to trick them all and go along with the game; and as she laughed to herself about how she would get up and walk away at the end, the environment expanded, the colors deepened, and she was high." But when the scene changed, "she found herself flying. . . ." Later in her lucid dream, she reflected that "although she had been looking forward to the sex, now her deprivation did not seem to matter because she was enjoying other even more exhilarating experiences."[1]

Oliver Fox described one of his lucid dream adventures as follows:

> . . . eventually we left the carnival and fire behind us and came to a yellow path, leading across a desolate moor. As we stood at the foot of this path it suddenly rose up before us and became a roadway of golden light stretching from earth to zenith. Now in this amber-tinted shining haze there appeared countless coloured forms of men and beasts, representing man's upward evolution through different stages of civilization. These forms faded away; the pathway lost its golden tint and became a mass of vibrating circles of globules (like frog's eggs), a purplish-blue in colour. These in their turn changed to 'peacock's eyes'; and then suddenly there came a culminating vision of a gigantic peacock, whose outspread tail filled the heavens. I exclaimed to my wife, 'The Vision of the Universal Peacock!' Moved by the splendor of the sight, I recited in a loud voice a mantra. Then the dream ended.[2]

The three very different accounts quoted above illustrate

something of the diversity of form and content shown by
lucid dreams. After reading a variety of the fascinating
stories people have reported of their lucid dreams, you
might naturally be inspired to have your own lucid dreams.
The lucid dreams described in this book will give you a
sufficiently detailed picture to appreciate the complexity of
the phenomenon. You will be well informed about what
lucid dreamers *say* they feel, but will you know what it is
really like to have a lucid dream? You cannot know fire
without being warmed by it (and a little burned as well!)—
any more than you can know the taste of a fruit you have
never eaten or the sound of a Beethoven string quartet you
have never listened to. In just the same way, you cannot
really know what lucid dreaming is like until you have
done it yourself. Having made my disclaimers, I will try
to give you a feeling of what lucid dreams are like, gen-
eralizing from some of the more familiar experiences of
your daytime and nighttime lives.

Take a few minutes, now, to observe your present state
of awareness. First of all, notice the richly varied and vivid
impressions harvested by your visual sense alone—shapes,
colors, movement, dimensionality. Next, register the various sounds taken in by your ears—a diverse range of in-
tensities, pitches, and tonal qualities, perhaps including the
commonplace miracle of speech or the wonder of music.
Observe the experiential dimensions uniquely afforded by
each of your other senses: taste, smell, and touch. Continued introspection in this manner reveals your self to be
contained within, and oddly enough, always at the center
of a multifarious universe of sensory experience. Also note
the subtle but essential difference the process of reflection
has contributed to your experience. Not only are you aware
of all the sensory impressions just surveyed, but you can
also, if you try, be aware that you are noticing these things.

Normally, awareness focuses on objects outside ourselves, but sometimes it turns in on itself. If you focus

your attention on *who* is focusing your attention, it is like standing in front of a mirror face to face with your own reflection. This inner state of self-reflection is called consciousness. I am warning innocent readers that I intend to use this word exclusively to mean reflective awareness, as just described. (Other writers have been known to use the word *consciousness* to refer to the mental abilities of hydrogen atoms! This is *not* what I have in mind, but enough said.)

All right, I trust you have been able to uncover your "inner eye" of conscious self-reflection. Well, now what? What is it good for? If you value freedom very highly, logic demands that you put a similar value on consciousness. Why? Because consciousness is what allows you to act most freely and flexibly. With habitual action, we can only do what we have already learned. But with consciously directed, intentional action, we are free to do things we have never done before. In any case, by means of consciousness you are able to deliberately attend to whatever interests you. You could put this book down now or turn the page. You could freely remember a vast number of facts about your life, and you could, if put to the test, think clearly.

This sketch of your current experience could serve as a description of lucid dreaming—with some important modifications. First of all, in that state you would know it was all a dream. Because of this, the world around you would tend to rearrange and transform itself (including the dream characters in it) much more than we are used to in daily life. "Impossible things" might well happen, and the dream scene itself, rather than fading into nothing, might increase in vividness and beauty until you found yourself rubbing your eyes in disbelief. Further, if you were willing and able to own the dream as *yours*, you would see it all as your own creation. This would imply that you were responsible for what was happening, and with this might come a wondrous feeling of freedom—for lucid dreamers nothing is impossible! Inspired by this realization, you might fly to heights as yet undared. You might choose to face someone or something that you have been fearfully avoiding; you might choose an erotic encounter with the most desirable partner you can imagine; you might visit a dead loved one to whom you have been wanting to speak; you might seek self-knowledge and wisdom in your dream. The possibilities are endless, which leaves plenty of room for prosaic lucid dreams, too. So it is important to have a goal—something you want to do the next time you have a lucid dream. Although the particulars of lucid dream content vary tremendously, there are certain characteristics of lucid dreams that apply to most and perhaps all of them.

Who Is the Dreamer?

A lucid dream implies a lucid dreamer. Obvious as that may seem, there are subtleties here. First of all, *who* exactly is the lucid dreamer? Is the lucid dreamer identical to the person we seem to be in the dream? Or to the person who is actually asleep and dreaming? The question of the identity of the dreamer is in a certain sense mysterious; to solve the mystery, we first need a list of suspects.

The most obvious suspect would seem to be the sleeper. It is, after all, the brain of the sleeping person that is actually doing the dreaming. But sleepers have a perfect alibi: they weren't there at the time of the dream, or any other time either—they were in bed asleep! Sleepers belong to the world of external rather than internal reality—because we can see and objectively test that they are asleep. But dreamers belong to the world of internal reality—we cannot see who, how, or what they are dreaming. So, we must turn our attention to the denizens of the dream world.

In a dream, there is usually a character present whom the sleeper takes to be himself. It is through the dream eyes of this dream body that we normally witness the events of the dream. The dream body is ordinarily who we think we are while dreaming, and this seems the obvious suspect. But actually we only *dream* we are that person. This dream character is merely a representation of ourselves. I call the character the "dream actor" or "dream ego." The point of view of the dream ego is that of a willing or unwilling participant—apparently contained within a multidimensional world (the dream), much as you probably experience your existence right now.

That the dream actor is not the dreamer is shown by the fact that there are some dreams in which we apparently play no part at all. In these dreams, we seem in varying degrees to witness, from the outside, the events of the dream. Sometimes we dream, for example, that we are watching a play. *We* seem to be in the audience while the action unfolds on stage. In this case we are at least represented as being present, though passively observing. A famous example of this type of dream is found in the Old Testament (Genesis 41:1–7):

> Pharaoh dreamed: and, behold, he stood by the river.
>
> And, behold, there came up out of the river seven well favoured kine and fat-fleshed; and they fed in a meadow.
>
> And, behold, seven other kine came up after them out of the river, ill favoured and lean-fleshed; and stood by the other kine upon the bank of the river.
>
> And the ill favoured and lean-fleshed kine did eat up the seven well favoured and fat kine. So Pharaoh awoke.

In other cases, the dreamer may not be present in the dream at all, as in the dream Pharaoh had when he went back to sleep:

And he slept and dreamed the second time: and behold, seven ears of corn came up on one stalk, rank and good.

And, behold, seven thin ears and blasted with the east wind sprung up after them.

And the seven thin ears devoured the seven rank and full ears. And Pharaoh awoke, and, behold, it was a dream.

I call this disembodied perspective the "dream observer." The dream observer is not contained in the dream proper but stands outside it.

Every dream contains at least one point of view with which we identify: the part we are playing in our dream theater. The nature of the role we play or choose to play in our dream allows us varying degrees of involvement, ranging from the complete participation of the dream actor to the uninvolved detachment of the dream observer. So the answer to "Who is the lucid dreamer?" seems to be that he or she is a composite figure—partly the dream ego or dream actor, and partly the dream observer.

There are usually other characters present in the dream besides the one we think we are. These are the animate and inanimate characters that make up the remainder of the *dramatis personae* of the dream. And, of course, if there is a single dream character with whom we fully identify at any given moment, this becomes the dream ego. We may dream, for example, that we are watching a play from the audience. Our identification at this point is with an outside observer. But if we sufficiently identify with one of the actors onstage, the results may be our suddenly *becoming* that character. Usually this happens in such a way that we forget that a moment earlier we were dreaming we were someone else. Our tendency to identify is so strong that we forget ourselves in the roles we play.

Which of these states of identification characterizes the

lucid dreamer—participant or observer? The answer is, a combination of both. Putting it all together, we could say that the dream ego is experientially in and part of the dream world, while the dream observer is neither. The combination of these two perspectives is characteristic of lucid dreaming and allows the lucid dreamer to be "in the dream, but not of it."

Lucid dreaming seems to require a balance between detachment and participation. A person who is too rigidly attached to a role while dreaming will be too involved to step back far enough to see the role *as* a role. On the contrary, a rigidly detached person will be too uninvolved and "out of it" to care.

In my own experience, participation seems a virtual requirement for lucid dreaming. Although I occasionally have dreams in which I am simply an observer, in none of these have I ever become lucid. In nearly all of the nearly nine hundred lucid dreams that I have recorded, I have been embodied in the dream in the accustomed guise of myself. In only three cases was I playing a role other than "Stephen LaBerge" when I realized I was dreaming. The exceptions are interesting: in one I dreamed I was simply a disembodied point of light; in another, a magic set of china; and in the third, I was Mozart—though only until I realized that I was dreaming. Then, I felt like "Stephen as Mozart"—an actor playing a role I knew was only a role. But somehow, behind the mask, *I* was not someone else, but *me*. There may be individual differences in this respect, but for me, being fully embodied (and the center of action, usually) seems a virtual prerequisite for attaining lucidity.

At the same time, a certain degree of detachment seems necessary in order to step back from the dream ego role and say, "This is all a dream." To say this is to *observe*— with a part of oneself, at least—the dream. So becoming lucid requires the observer's perspective, as well, and the lucid dreamer thus seems to possess at least two distinct levels of awareness.

In my own lucid dreams, I have sometimes found the emergence of this dual awareness perplexing. Recall the example from the beginning of this chapter: I first had the thought that if I were to become lucid, I would have no reason to fear. And then a moment later, I realized I *was* dreaming.

The fact that fully lucid dreamers realize their dream bodies are *not* who they really are has important implications, to be taken up in a later chapter. For now, it is sufficient to point out that such lucid dreamers realize their *egos* are only models of themselves, and cease to mistake them for the real thing.

Cognitive Functions

The form taken by lucid dreams is also determined by the lucid dreamer's mental state. Just as the quality of our memory, thinking, and will power varies in the waking state, so it varies in the dream state. At best, lucid dreamers can reason clearly, remember freely, and act as they wish to upon reflection; however, they do not always possess these mental abilities to a great extent. There are, in fact, degrees of lucidity, and probably only relatively experienced lucid dreamers function on a level comparable to their better moments while awake.

Minor flaws in thinking are not infrequent during lucid dreams. Some lucid dreamers, for instance, have problems keeping a clear distinction between their dream worlds and the physical world. Saint-Denys wrote that he experienced great difficulty remembering that the other characters in his lucid dreams were not actually real people sharing his experiences. He described a dream in which he was visiting a church tower with a friend and admiring the splendid panorama before them. He explained that he knew very well it was only a dream, but nonetheless asked his dream friend to remember the dream so they could talk about it the next day when they awoke.

Most lucid dreamers, however, have little difficulty realizing that the characters they find in their lucid dreams are imaginary. More commonly they are confused about the character they themselves play, and think *they* are real, but treat other dream characters as figments of "their" imagination. Nevertheless, fully lucid dreamers readily recognize that all the characters in their lucid dreams, including their dream egos, are nothing more than images.

A variation in how well we remember things also leads to differences in what occurs in dreams, lucid or otherwise. It may not be obvious, but levels of consciousness and memory are connected. The low level of consciousness of the usual dream state is accompanied by the dreamer's forgetting that he or she has recently gone to sleep. Questions concerning recent happenings are apt to be met with "confabulation"—a likely story mistaken for memory—rather than actual memory. For example, if someone were to ask you in a dream where you found all the money you had in your hand, you might answer, "I found it lying in a gutter," instead of remembering that you actually found it in a dream! In contrast, the full emergence of self-consciousness in the lucid dream brings with it continuous memory access; for example, the lucid dreamer can recall where he or she is sleeping at the moment—a useful fact when in the sleep laboratory.

There are individual differences in memory access during lucid dreaming, just as there are with thinking and volition. One relatively experienced lucid dreamer reported that "in none of my lucid dreams could I reason as clearly or remember as fully as when awake." Contrary to the scores of experiences of our lucid dream subjects at the Stanford Sleep

Laboratory, the same lucid dreamer claims that "in a series of experiments in which I tried to recall where I was sleeping, I never could remember very specifically."[3] We must keep in mind that there may be considerable individual differences in the mental abilities accessible to the lucid dreamer; nevertheless, they generally appear to approach those available to the individual while awake.

Motivation and Expectation

Motivations are what move us to act. They take many forms in the dream as well as in the waking state. We may distinguish four levels of motivation that can affect what happens in dreams, whether lucid or not. On the lowest level, there are *drives,* which, for example, motivate us to dream that we are visiting the bathroom when we need to. Then there are *desires,* which could lead us to find ourselves in bed with our favorite movie star. Next we find *expectations,* and finally, *ideals* or *goals.* While expectations are characteristic of the habitual level of our behavior, ideals are by their nature *deliberate.* We can only follow them if we are conscious; thus, it is only in our *lucid* dreams that we are able to act fully in accordance with our ideals. This ability will prove extremely useful to us later, when we discuss transpersonal dreams in Chapter 10. Since much more of our behavior is habitual than deliberate, expectations exert a more pervasive influence than ideals on our dreams as well as on the rest of our lives.

The general set of expectations guiding our ordinary waking experience also governs our ordinary dream state. We tacitly assume, in both cases, that we are awake, and so our perceptions during dreaming are distorted to fit this assumption. As an example of this, let us use psychology's most famous card trick. In a 1949 study, Bruner and Postman briefly flashed playing cards on a screen in front of subjects who were asked to identify what they saw. But the catch was that some of the cards were nonstandard— for instance, a *red* ace of spades. At first the subjects saw the anomalous card as an ace of hearts. Only after the cards were flashed for longer intervals did the subjects become aware that there was anything odd about the nonstandard cards. Still longer exposures were necessary for most subjects to correctly perceive the cards as unconventional. When given hints by the experimenters—along the lines of, "Although spades are *usually* black, they don't have to be"—some subjects were able to modify their perceptions and correctly perceive the unorthodox cards at very short exposures. But some subjects, when given the same hint, were unsure and required more exposure before they finally perceived the cards correctly.

The analogy to lucid dreaming is this: just as the subjects had the tacit expectation that spades are black and hearts are red, so we, as dreamers, normally assume that we are awake. When bizarre dream events occur, as they frequently do during REM sleep, we somehow assimilate them into what we consider possible. If we happen to notice or experience them as somehow unusual, we are usually able to rationalize them. The assumption is that "there must be a logical explanation," within the (delusional) conceptual scheme of the dreamer.

On several occasions, people have told me that on the very night they had a conversation with me about lucid dreaming, they had their first lucid dream. These people correspond to the psychology subjects who easily took the hints—they now knew that although apparent inconsistencies usually have "logical explanations" in the physical world, sometimes the explanation for anomalies is that we are dreaming.

Your expectations and assumptions, whether conscious or unconscious, about what dreams are like, determine to a remarkable extent the precise form your lucid dreams take. As I have said, this applies just as much to your waking life. As an example of the effect of assumed limitations on human performance, take the myth of the four-minute mile. For many years, it was believed impossible to run that fast . . . until someone did it and the impossible became possible. Almost immediately, many others were able to do the same. A *conceptual* barrier had been broken.

There is reason to believe that in the dream world, assumptions play an even more important role. After all, in the physical world there are actual limitations built into our bodies, not to mention the constraints of the laws of physics. Although the barrier of the four-minute mile was not insurmountable, there are absolute limits to human speed: with the bodies we have today, for example, a one-minute mile is probably impossible. In the dream world, however, the laws of physics are followed merely by convention, if at all: there is no gravity in dreams.

Nevertheless, there are equivalent laws of physiology that constrain a lucid dreamer's action, deriving from the functional limitations of the human brain. For example, lucid dreamers appear to find reading (more than a word or two) virtually impossible. As Moers-Messmer pointed out, letters in lucid dreams just won't hold still. When he tried to focus on words, the letters turned into hieroglyphics. (Note that I am not saying we can never read in dreams. I myself have had dreams in which I have done so, but these were not *lucid* dreams, in which the writing was being produced in response to voluntary intention.) Another example derives from Saint-Denys, who found that he was often unable to alter the level of illumination in his lucid dreams. I have experienced the same difficulty, which has been dubbed the "Light-Switch" phenomenon by Hearne. However, physiological constraints such as these seem to be far fewer than those imposed in waking life by physical laws, leaving more room in dreams for psychological influences, such as assumptions, to play a limiting role.

That expectations exert a powerful influence on the phenomena experienced by a particular dreamer is vividly illustrated by the following examples. The Russian philosopher Ouspensky believed, on theoretical grounds, that "man cannot in sleep think about himself *unless the thought is itself a dream.*" From this he concluded that "a man can never pronounce his own name in sleep." It should therefore come as no surprise that Ouspensky reported, "as expected," that "if I pronounced my name in sleep, I immediately woke up."[4] Rather than an experiment, Ouspensky's exercise should probably be seen as a clear instance of the influence that experience can have on the events of the dream state.

One of Celia Green's informants, referred to as "Subject C," heard of the philosopher's experiences and tested the effect of repeating her own name during a lucid dream. She reports that "I thought of Ouspensky's criterion of repeating one's own name. I achieved a sort of gap-in-consciousness of two words: but it seemed to have some effect; made me 'giddy,' perhaps; at any rate I stopped."[5]

Patricia Garfield described a lucid dream of her own that also bears on the issue: " . . . in 'Carving My Name,' I proceeded to do just that on the door where I was already carving. I read it and realized why Ouspensky believed it is impossible to say one's name in a lucid dream: the whole atmosphere vibrated and thundered and I woke."[6] Garfield, who was also familiar with Subject C's experience, concluded that it is "not impossible to say one's own name in a lucid dream, but it *is* disruptive."

When I read Ouspensky's account, I didn't accept his reasoning or his original premise, and I could see no reason why saying one's name while dreaming should present any difficulty at all. I decided to test *my* expectation, and in one of my early lucid dreams I spoke the magic word—

"Stephen, I am Stephen." Beyond hearing my own voice, nothing happened. The conclusion would seem to be that the experiences of Ouspensky, Subject C, and Garfield were all influenced by their prior expectations. An alternate explanation might be that we normally hear our names in sleep only when being woken up by someone, and may make that association in the dream.

Another illustration of the effect of assumptions on lucid dreams can be found in two contrary views of sexuality in lucid dreams. In the first case, a subject declared that "realization that one is dreaming brings a wonderful sense of freedom—freedom to try anything in the extended range of experience." She added, "The nature of lucid dream experience may range up to the mystical, whilst *there seems to be an inherent resistance to anything erotic* [my italics]."[7]

Patricia Garfield's experiences present a striking contrast. She reports that in "fully two-thirds" of her lucid dreams, she feels "the flow of sexual energy; this arousal culminates in an orgasmic burst on about half of these accounts." Garfield writes, *"Orgasm is a natural part of lucid dreaming* [her italics]: my own experience convinces me that conscious dreaming *is* orgasmic," and adds that "too many of my students have reported similar ecstatic experiences during lucid dreams to attribute the phenomena to my individual peculiarity."[8]

The point is not whether lucid dreaming is "naturally" erotic or the opposite, because the answer is probably that it is neither. Instead, it's most likely a matter of "as the dreamer, so the dream."

There are two related lessons to be taken from these examples. The first is that the assumptions a dreamer makes about what can happen during a lucid dream may wholly or in part determine what *does* happen. The second lesson follows as a corollary: namely, that individual differences may be very significant in the phenomenology of lucid dreaming.

Varieties of Action:
The Question of Control

The actions of lucid dreamers vary over the same range—from simple to complex—that they do when we are awake. Some of our actions are *reflexive,* as when we walk around in our lucid dreams without losing balance. Others are *instinctive,* as when we run because we are afraid. Still others are *habitual,* as when we continue to drive our cars to work even though we know we are dreaming. Finally, some of our actions are *deliberate*, as when we resist running away even though we are frightened by the events of the dream. (Not acting can itself be a form of deliberate action.) I have ordered these four forms of action from most unconscious and automatic to most conscious and voluntary. The higher the level on which we act, the more freedom we have. Freedom, however, means choice, and we do not always wish to have to choose—and in many cases, we always choose the same thing anyway. On the other hand, there are times when deliberate action is much more adaptive than habitual or instinctive action, as when we choose not to run away when afraid, but decide to face our fears voluntarily and master them. Most of our behavior consists of complex combinations of all four levels of action. The highest level of action available to us depends upon how conscious we are at the time.

Voluntary and conscious action is much more available to lucid dreamers than to non-lucid dreamers. The experienced lucid dreamer seems to be able to exercise at least as much free choice while dreaming as while waking. Just as you are free to read the next sentence or not, the lucid dreamer is able to choose what he will do next, as is illustrated by the following dream of Saint-Denys:

. . . I dreamt that I was out riding in fine weather. I

became aware of my true situation, and remembered the
question of whether or not I could exercise free will in
controlling my actions in a dream. 'Well now,' I said
to myself, This horse is only an illusion; this country-
side that I am passing through is merely stage scenery.
But even if I have not evoked these images by conscious
volition, I certainly seem to have some control over
them. I decide to gallop, I gallop; I decide to stop, I
stop. Now here are two roads in front of me. The one
on the right appears to plunge into a dense wood; the
one on the left leads to some kind of ruined manor; I
feel quite distinctly that I am free to turn either right or
left, and so decide for myself whether I wish to produce
images relating to the ruins or images relating to the
wood.[9]

In any case, the capacity for voluntary action seems to be
one of the most fascinating features of lucid dreams. Lucid
dreamers are often overjoyed to discover they can seemingly do anything they wish. They have, for instance, but
to declare the law of gravity repealed, and they float. They
can visit the Himalayas and climb to the highest peak without ropes or guides; they can even explore the solar system
without a space suit!

This brings up two questions regarding control of lucid
dreaming. The first is, how much is possible? This appears
to depend upon a number of factors: how experienced the
lucid dreamer is; what degree of psychological development he or she has reached in the waking state; what assumptions he or she has about lucid dreams and their
control.

Aside from these psychological factors, there appear to
be physiological determinants as well. The momentary state
of the lucid dreamer's brain limits the degree of deliberate
control available; this is especially true in regard to voluntary control of the dream environment as distinct from
the dream ego. Saint-Denys himself admitted that he had

never managed to master all the parts of a dream. On the other hand, the Tibetans claim that masters of the lucid dream yoga can do just about anything in their dreams, including visiting any realm of existence they desire.

The second question regarding dream control involves what kind is desirable. A distinction can be drawn between two kinds of dream control. One involves magical manipulation of dream characters other than the dream ego— controlling "them" or "it." This is just the type of control that does not always work (for any of us except the most advanced masters), yet this limitation may actually be a blessing: if we learned to solve our problems in our lucid dreams by magical alteration of dream content, we might mistakenly hope to do the same in our waking lives. Suppose, for instance, in my "ogre dream," I had chosen to turn my adversary into a toad, and I was in fact able to dispense with the unpleasantness that way. How would it help me if at another time I were to find myself in conflict with a boss or other authority figure whom I might well see as an ogre, in spite of my being awake? Turning him into a toad would hardly be practical; however, a change in attitude might resolve the situation.

The other kind of control open to lucid dreamers is *self-control,* exercised over our own dream egos. We are free to regulate our responses to dream content, and what we learn in so doing readily applies to our waking lives as well—thus we dream in order to learn how to live better both by day and by night. For example, in my "ogre dream," I gained a measure of self-control and confidence by confronting the monster that could serve me well in the waking world. For this reason, among others, I would advise the lucid dreamer who would be wise: "Control yourself, not your dreams."

Emotional Quality

What does it *feel* like to be in a lucid dream? This is a question many readers may be asking. As has already been said, feeling in lucid dreams, while generally positive or relatively neutral, can vary over the entire range of human emotions—from agony (mitigated by the realization that "it is only a dream") to the ecstasy of sexual or religious bliss.

The realization that one is dreaming is frequently accompanied by very positive emotions, as the following sample of quotations should make clear. For Rapport, the emergence of lucidity "instantly" transformed his dream into "an incommunicably beautiful vision."[10] For Faraday, "immediately the light became almost supernaturally intense . . . space seemed expanded and deeper, just as it does under psychedelic drugs."[11] Similarly, for Yram (1967), " . . . the transformation was instantaneous. As if under a magic spell I suddenly became as clear headed as in the best moments of my physical life."[12] Fox (1962) described the onset of his first experience of lucidity this way: "Instantly, the vividness of life increased a hundredfold . . . never had I felt so absolutely well, so clear brained, so divinely powerful, so inexpressibly *free*!"[13]

Of course, these are the most extraordinary cases. However, even the most prosaic lucid dreams tend to begin with an unmistakable sense of excitement and delight. This is still true for me even after hundreds of lucid dreams—although the novelty is gone, the thrill seems somehow to remain.

The emotional arousal characteristically accompanying the beginning of lucidity presents all lucid dreamers, and especially novices, with a certain problem. This is the tendency to awaken immediately, particularly if lucidity begins during a nightmare. The solution is simply expressed: "Don't panic! Remain calm." At first this is more easily said than done, but with practice the response becomes automatic and eventually effortless.

According to Celia Green, "Habitual lucid dreamers almost unanimously stress the importance of emotional detachment in prolonging the experience and retaining a high degree of lucidity."[14] There are two issues involved here. Guarding against loss of lucidity is one. One danger of emotional involvement is that the lucid dreamer's consciousness may be reabsorbed by the dream, and as the lucid dreamer becomes emotionally absorbed, he reidentifies with the dream role. This is a problem more often experienced by beginners than experienced lucid dreamers, and with practice, one can easily learn to maintain lucidity during intense emotional involvement with the dream.

The second issue, prolonging the lucid dream state, also requires a degree of emotional control. However, lucid dreamers are by no means unanimous about the extent to which this is necessary. At one extreme, Green's "Subject A" claimed that "emotional detachment is of paramount importance."[15] Oliver Fox seemed to feel the same:

> It was so difficult to maintain the role of an impersonal observer in this strange Dream World, to realize that if I allowed my emotions to get the better of my mental control the dream would come to an abrupt end. I would enter a restaurant and order a meal, only to wake after savoring the first few mouthfuls. . . .
>
> Similarly I would visit a theatre, but could never stay in the dream more than a few minutes after the curtain had risen, because my growing interest in the play broke down my mental control of the experience. I would encounter a fascinating lady and even talk to her for a little while, but the mere thought of a possible embrace was fatal.[16]

It is probably emotional *conflict* rather than emotions in general that most often threatens lucid dreamers with pre-

mature awakening. What, for Fox, "the mere thought of
. . . was fatal" to his lucid dream has been taken much
further by other, perhaps less inhibited, lucid dreamers.
Garfield, for example, writes that in her early experiences
with lucid dreaming she awoke immediately before, during, or just after orgasm. Later, with practice, and as she
became less sexually inhibited in her waking life, she "began experiencing dream orgasms of profound intensity with
a totality of self that is only sometimes felt in my waking
state. I found myself bursting into soul-and-body-shaking
experiences."[17]

Perceptual Quality

Just as in their cognitive and emotional aspects, lucid
dreams vary tremendously in terms of the perceptual quality of the experience. In some the scene is dimly lit or
vaguely delineated; others take the lucid dreamer's breath
away with their intense beauty and extravagant detail. Some
seem, indeed, "more real than real." In general, though,
the lucid dream seems to be more perceptually vivid than
the non-lucid dream. There are at least two sources of support for this contention. An indirect source is our psychophysiological research indicating that lucid dreams are
characterized by relatively intense brain activation, which
probably correlates with perceptual vividness.

Psychologist Jayne Gackenbach is one of the foremost
authorities on lucid dreaming. She and her team at the University of Northern Iowa have undertaken extensive studies
of personality factors influencing lucid dreaming ability, as
well as the content differences of lucid and non-lucid
dreams. Of relevance here, Gackenbach demonstrated that
lucid dreams were indeed more vivid than ordinary
dreams.[18]

We have completed our sketch of the dimensions of the world of lucid dreams. Having considered what it is like being in a lucid dream, now let us ask, How do dreamers get there?

Entry into the Lucid Dream State

Lucid dreaming can be conceptualized as the union of two separate elements, dreaming and consciousness. Lucid dreaming can therefore be initiated in two general ways: either from the dream state, while the person is dreaming and consciousness is added; or when the person is conscious and dreaming is added. In the second case, the initial state is waking consciousness, while in the first case, the initial state is ordinary, nonlucid dreaming.

The most common form of lucid dream initiation occurs when the dreamer realizes during a dream that he or she is dreaming. This realization can either be gradual or relatively sudden. When it is gradual, the realization sometimes shows two distinct phases. The lucid dream opening this chapter provides an illustration of this two-part process. In another example, I had been magically manipulating part of my dream environment when I had the thought that if I stepped through a door in front of me, *then* I would become lucid, and that is exactly what happened.

For the inexperienced dreamer, lucidity is perhaps most likely to arise from a nightmare or anxiety dream. We have already seen a number of examples of anxiety-initiated lucid dreams. Other intense emotions like embarrassment or delight are also commonly associated with the initiation of lucidity. But for most dreamers, the recognition of anomaly—inconsistency or bizarreness—is the factor most frequently leading to consciousness in dreams. In most cases, anomalous dream content is not fully recognized as such by the dreamer. Depending upon the degree to which reality is tested, the dreamer will attain a varying degree of lucidity. Oliver Fox believed critical thinking to be the key to lucid dreaming, and provided an unexcelled account of the progressive degrees of reality testing and increasing perception of anomaly:

> Let us suppose, for example, that in my dream I am in a cafe. At a table near mine is a lady who would be very attractive—only, she has four eyes. Here are some illustrations of those degrees of activity of the critical faculty.
>
> 1. In the dream it is practically dormant, but on waking I have the feeling that there was something peculiar about this lady. Suddenly I get it—"Why, of course, she had four eyes!"
> 2. In the dream I exhibit mild surprise and say, "How curious, that girl has four eyes! It spoils her." But only in the same way that I might remark, "What a pity she has broken her nose! I wonder how she did it."
> 3. The critical faculty is more awake and the four eyes are regarded as abnormal; but the phenomenon is not fully appreciated. I exclaim "Good Lord!" and then reassure myself by adding, "There must be a freak show or a circus in the town." Thus I hover on the brink of realization, but do not quite get there.
> 4. My critical faculty is now fully awake and fully refuses to be satisfied by this explanation. I continue my train of thought, "But there never was such a freak! An adult with four eyes—it's *impossible*. I am dreaming."[19]

Frequently a dreamer for whom the question of a situation's reality arises will decide that he or she is in fact awake and *not* dreaming. A dream in which the dreamer has at some point raised this question, without arriving at the correct conclusion, is commonly termed "pre-lucid." These pre-lucid dreams are generally the result of partial or inadequate reality testing, such as Fox's third stage. Dreamers who suspect they are dreaming may test their state in a variety of ways. However, few of these tests are reliably effective in distinguishing dreaming from waking. For example, pre-lucid dreamers too often conclude that they couldn't be dreaming because everything seems so solid and vividly real. Or they may pinch themselves, according to the classical test. This most often has the result not of awakening the dreamer, but merely producing the convincing sensation of a pinch!

A better test used by many lucid dreamers seems to be trying to fly. I find this method most effective in the form of attempting merely to prolong a hop into the air. However, the most reliable test, in my experience, is the following: I find some writing and read it (if I can!) once, look away, and reread it, checking to see if it stays the same; in all my lucid dreams, writing has yet to do so. Dreams are more readily distinguishable from waking perceptions on the basis of their instability rather than their vividness. But the last word on reality testing has been suggested by Charles McCreery, who points out that while awake we never doubt whether we are awake or not. Therefore, if you wonder whether or not you are dreaming, you probably are!

With experience, the perception of anomaly can lead directly to lucidity, without further explicit reality testing. In my case, when a bizarre event takes place, I no longer ask "Am I dreaming?" I simply directly realize that I am, as the following dream illustrates:

I was walking down a familiar street when I noticed what at first I took for a majestic new church. On closer examination, I realized this imposing structure was in fact a magnificent mosque. I reflected that as I had been on this very street only a week ago, there was only one way I could have missed such an impressive sight: I must be dreaming! As I approached this wonder with a mixture of curiosity and awe, its huge rose window blasted forth the theme from *Close Encounters of the Third Kind* in organ tones that shook the street beneath my feet. I was thrilled with the "realization" that I was in fact in the presence of a spaceship in disguise. Still fully lucid and with great excitement (though not entirely without trepidation), I mounted the steps and stepped into brilliant light pouring through the open door. What happened next I cannot say, for when I awoke, all my attempts to retrieve the memory of this vision failed completely.

Memory can sometimes play an important role in the initiation of lucidity. Lucid dreamers sometimes realize they are dreaming as a seeming result of *"déjà rêvé"*—an actual or apparent recollection that they have had a similar dream before. This is illustrated by another of my own experiences: I was walking with M. when I recognized we were in a place I had dreamed of before—"the museum of uninvented inventions"—and that this, therefore, was a dream. I thought how M. would like to have lucid dreams, but I knew that this "M." was a dream character, not my actual friend. Nevertheless, I suggested to him that even though he was only a dream character, perhaps he could realize that he was dreaming. Perhaps he did, for *I* woke up!

Closely related are lucid dreams in which the dreamer realizes he or she is dreaming by means of a particular *memory cue*. In a dozen lucid dreams, I realized I was dreaming by noticing that my contact lenses seemed to be multiplying. After a non-lucid dream in which this multiplication had occurred, I reflected that I should have realized thereby that I was dreaming. Shortly thereafter, the imagery recurred and I said to myself, "If this were a dream, it would be a dream!" After a double take, I realized the implication of this and became lucid. In subsequent similar dreams—during that moment before the full realization I was dreaming—I have reflected, variously:

"Too bad this isn't a dream, in which case it would be a dream"; "This proves this can happen in waking life as well as in dreaming"; and, quoting myself in jest, "If this were a dream, it would be a dream."

In most of my other lucid dreams, by the time I explicitly realize I am dreaming, I already seem to be implicitly aware of my state. But during the dreams in which lucidity is stimulated by a memory cue, I ordinarily haven't the slightest suspicion that I'm dreaming. So when I am compelled, by logic, to conclude that I *must* be dreaming, I am completely astonished. Readers can imagine my state by considering the shock and amazement they would feel if they were to discover, while reading this sentence, absolutely certain proof that they are dreaming *now!*

Self-reflection during dreams frequently leads to lucidity in experienced lucid dreamers. In my own case, I usually observe that I have been exhibiting wishful thinking, engaging in magic or "dream composition," and realize I must be dreaming. In one case I would have been dead had I not been dreaming as I drove my car too fast down a street that had a tanker truck blocking it. However, I was magically able to avoid the collision, and because I recalled other revisions of reality I had been doing, I realized that I must be dreaming.

The most common dream symbol involved in the initiation of lucidity seems to be light. Light is a very natural symbol for consciousness. Karl Scherner, one of the nineteenth century's three great pioneers of dream research, wrote in 1861: "Light in dreams is the expression of clear thinking and of sharpness of will." Scott Sparrow gives several examples of lucid dreams apparently initiated by the appearance of light. In one he reported that while he was sitting outdoors composing a speech, he looked up at the eastern sky and saw "a large orb of white light many times the size of the moon."[20] At this he realized he was dreaming.

The form of initiation of some lucid dreams is difficult to classify. The following, for example, combines elements of both anomaly and symbolic representation: "In my dream I was crossing a large room, in which several people were gathered, when I saw a pure white dove fly down obliquely and alight on my forehead. Immediately I found myself in a state of conscious projection [lucidity] and profited by the occasion to go and visit some friends." The dreamer was especially impressed by the sudden initiation of lucidity, adding that "as soon as the dove had touched me, the transformation was instantaneous. As if under a magic spell I suddenly became as clear-headed as in the best moments of my physical life."[21]

Five years ago I had an interesting experience that may clarify the notion of symbolic stimulation of lucidity. A friend and I were riding a train alongside "the Ocean." I was carelessly leaning out the window taking in the sights, when the beautiful dark intensity of the sea moved me to admire it aloud. Just then, some sort of falcon or hawk landed on a nearby branch, and without thinking I immediately extended my hand in its direction. To my delight and surprise, the bird alighted on my outstretched hand, and I immediately remembered a Sufi saying:

> When a bird will land in your outstretched hand,
> *Then* you will understand.

Remarkably enough, I *did* understand at once—that I was dreaming! As for my friend and the bird, they left the story, for the dream faded.

Since I have been using memory as a lucid-dream induction technique (see "MILD," Chapter 6), I have had increasingly frequent instances in which I became lucid without anything unusual in my dream content. In these I simply *remember* that I'm dreaming: "Oh yes! This is a dream!'' One morning, as a result of practicing MILD, I had lucid dreams of this kind in each of three successive REM periods. Here is the relevant section of the third: I was in bed looking at a picture book entitled something like *Russian Dance and Magic*. As in the preceding two dreams, I suddenly simply *remembered* that I was now doing what I wanted to remember to recognize: dreaming.

We have seen examples of three major ways that dreamers recognize they are dreaming: perception of inconsistencies, emotional arousal, and a sort of direct realization of the dream-like nature of the experience. These are the main triggers of consciousness during the dream state. But dream consciousness can also be initiated from the waking state.

It is possible to maintain continuous reflective consciousness while falling asleep, and hence to enter a lucid dream directly from the waking state. This form of initiation is relatively rare, for me, under ordinary conditions, accounting for about eight percent of my total sample of lucid dreams. But in circumstances of greatly increased motivation—characteristic of the nights I spent in the sleep lab—my proportion of lucid dreams initiated from the waking state increased five-fold, suggesting that this form of initiation is a skill that improves with motivation and practice. In fact, its cultivation has been described by Tibetan yogis, by the American psychiatrist Nathan Rapport, by the Russian philosopher Ouspensky, and—as the reader will discover in Chapter 6—by the author of this book.

In my typical induction of this sort, I am lying in bed in the early morning or afternoon after awakening from a dream; hypnogogic (sleep onset) imagery sometimes appears, and then suddenly I find myself fully in the dream scene, and lucid. Once I am in the dream state, this lucid dream continues exactly like the others. The following account is one of Ouspensky's lucid dreams initiated from the waking state:

I am falling asleep. Golden dots, sparks and tiny stars appear and disappear before my eyes. . . . From the first moment to the last I observed how pictures appeared and how they were transformed into a net with regular meshes. Then the golden net was transformed into the helmets of the Roman soldiers. The pulsation which I heard was transformed into the measured tread of the marching detachment. The sensation of this pulsation means the relaxation of many small muscles, which in its turn produces a sensation of slight giddiness. This sensation of slight giddiness was immediately manifested in my seeing the soldiers, while lying on the window-sill of a *high* house and looking down; and when this giddiness increased a little, I rose from the window and flew over the gulf. This at once brought with it by association the sensation of the sea, the wind and the sun, and if I had not awakened, probably at the next moment of the dream I should have seen myself in the open sea, on a ship, and so on.[22]

This method of initiating lucid dreams combines both self-reflection and memory. To observe successfully that dream images *are* images requires a balance between participation and detachment. Methods for cultivating this mode of lucid dream initiation are also described in Chapter 6. Now, having seen how lucid dreams are initiated, let us turn to how they typically end.

Termination of the Dream State

Since the lucid dream is a compound of lucidity and the dream state, and there are in principle two modes of initiating it, there are also two general possibilities for terminating it: either lucidity is lost while the dream continues, or the dream ends with an awakening.

The first mode is probably the more common one for

less-experienced lucid dreamers. Neophytes are more likely to lose their lucidity once they have gained it. Scott Sparrow remarks that "as lucid dreams begin to occur within the life of an individual, they are likely to be rare and short-lived." Accordingly, after having become at least momentarily lucid, the inexperienced dreamer will frequently become reabsorbed by the dream, forgetting that it is a dream and continuing to dream non-lucidly. Forgetfulness can be countered by repeating to oneself: "This is a dream." Later, however, such talk is unnecessary. In my own case, lucidity was lost in about twenty percent of the lucid dreams I recorded (and thus remembered) during the first year of my study; it was lost in one percent or less during the subsequent years.

For experienced lucid dreamers, termination of lucidity by awakening is more common than the loss of lucidity characteristic of beginners. Ordinarily there is a high degree of continuity of consciousness during this transition from dreaming to waking. In contrast, there is usually momentary confusion when we wake from a non-lucid dream, as we make the transition from the non-lucid dream ego to the waking ego. But when we wake from a lucid dream there is no such transition, since the lucid dreaming ego is identical to the waking ego.

There are two other possible ways in which lucid dreams can come to an end. One possibility is that the lucid dreamer might enter non-REM sleep and cease dreaming. Typically, if awakened at this point, the dreamer would recall nothing. In the other case in which lucidity is lost, the person *dreams* that he or she has awakened.

The latter dreams are usually called "false awakenings" and are very commonly reported adjuncts of lucid dreams. Sometimes false awakenings occur repeatedly, with the lucid dreamer seeming to awake again and again only to discover each time that he or she is still dreaming. In some cases, lucid dreamers have reported enduring literally doz-

ens of false awakenings before finally waking up "for
real." Here is an example of one of Delage's (see Chapter
2) multiple false awakenings:

> One night, I was woken by urgent knocking at the door
> of my room. I got up and asked: 'Who is there?' 'Mon-
> sieur,' came the answer in the voice of Marty (the lab-
> oratory caretaker), 'it is Madame H _____' (someone
> who was really living in the town at that time and was
> among my acquaintances), 'who is asking for you to
> come immediately to her house to see Mademoiselle P
> _____' (someone who was really part of Madame H's
> household and who was also known to me), 'who has
> suddenly fallen ill.'
>   'Just give me time to dress,' I said, 'and I will run.'
> I dressed hurriedly, but before going out I went into my
> dressing-room to wipe my face with a damp sponge.
> The sensation of cold water woke me and I realized that
> I had dreamt all the foregoing events and that no one
> had come to ask for me. So I went back to sleep. But a
> little later, the same knocking came again at my door.
> 'What, Monsieur, aren't you coming then?'
>   'Good heavens! So it is really true, I thought I had
> dreamt it.'
>   'Not at all. Hurry up. They are all waiting for you.'
>   'All right, I will run.' Again I dressed myself, again
> in my dressing-room I wiped my face with cold water,
> and again the sensation of cold water woke me and made
> me understand that I had been deceived by a repetition
> of my dream. I went back to bed and went to sleep
> again.
>   The same scene re-enacted itself almost identically
> twice more.

When Delage "really" awoke the next morning, he could
see the "whole series of actions, reasonings and thoughts
had been nothing but a dream repeated four times in

succession with no break in my sleep and without my having stirred from my bed."[23]

Although false awakenings are also reported following non-lucid dreams, they appear to be more often associated with lucid dreams, probably because only in these does the question of being awake or asleep normally arise. Moreover, false awakenings seem to occur more frequently in experienced lucid dreamers than in inexperienced ones. (I had them in about fifteen percent of my first year's record, and in about a third of my lucid dreams in the next five years.) The difference is probably accounted for by the fact that the more lucid dreams you have had, the more you associate waking up with the lucid dream fading, and thus more strongly expect to awaken when a dream fades.

Very occasionally, a dreamer may recognize a false awakening as a dream. However, this is often difficult because the dreamer *already* believes himself to be awake and never thinks to question the assumption. During my earlier lucid dream experiences, I had about forty false awakenings without recognizing them as dreams. Considering how bizarre some of these dreams were, I began to feel rather embarrassed about constantly fooling myself with them! Finally my self-esteem required me to attempt to master these false awakenings, and with surprisingly little effort I succeeded, discovering that it was my expectation of waking up that was deluding me. All I had to do was change my expectation of what was going to happen at the apparent end of a lucid dream. Simply by expecting a "false" rather than an actual awakening, I was able to maintain lucidity during most subsequent dreams.

The Spinning Technique

I have recently developed a technique for preventing awakening and producing new lucid dream scenes at will. I had been concerned with the problem that the discovery of lucidity often leads to immediate awakening, cutting short what otherwise might be a rewarding lucid dream. Since dream actions have corresponding physical effects, I reasoned that relaxing my dream body might inhibit awakening by lowering muscle tension in my physical body. The next time I was dreaming lucidly, I tested the idea. As the dream began to fade, I relaxed completely, dropping to the dream floor. However, contrary to my intention, I seemed to awaken. But as I discovered a few minutes later, it had actually been a false awakening. Further lucid dream experiments repeating the procedure confirmed this effect, and suggested that the essential element was apparently not the attempted relaxation but the sensation of movement. In subsequent lucid dreams, I tested a variety of dream movements and found both falling backward and spinning to be especially effective in producing lucid dreams of awakening.

The technique is very simple. As soon as my vision begins to fade in the lucid dream, I either fall backward or spin like a top (with my dream body, of course!). For the method to work, it is important to experience a vivid sense of movement. Usually this procedure generates a new dream scene, which often represents the bedroom I am sleeping in. By repeatedly reminding myself that I'm dreaming during this transition, I can continue dreaming lucidly in the new scene. Without this special effort of attention, I will usually mistake the new dream for an actual awakening—and this in spite of frequent manifest absurdities of dream content!

The method is quite effective. Out of the one hundred lucid dreams in the last six months of the three year record reported in my doctoral dissertation, I used this technique forty percent of the time, and new dreams were generated in eighty-five percent of these cases. Lucid consciousness was retained in ninety-seven percent of the new dreams. When spinning led to another dream, the new dream scene almost always closely resembled the bed I was sleeping in, or some other bedroom.

The experience of other lucid dreamers who have employed this method was very similar to mine, but suggests that the new lucid dream need not necessarily be a bedroom scene. One of these lucid dreamers, for instance, found herself arriving at a dream scene other than her bedroom in five out of the eleven times she used the spinning method.

These results suggest that spinning could be used to produce transitions to any dream scene the lucid dreamer *expects*. In my own case, it appears that my almost exclusive production of bedroom dreams may be an accident of the circumstances in which I discovered the technique. Upon occasion I have tried, with very little success, to produce transitions to other dream scenes with this method. But although I definitely *intended* to arrive elsewhere than my dream bedroom, I cannot say that I fully *expected* to. Although I believe I will someday be able to unlearn this accidental association (if that's what it is), I am meanwhile impressed by the power of expectation to determine what happens in my lucid dreams. Verily—in dreams, at least—faith can move mountains!

Why should the hallucinated movement of spinning have any effect upon dreaming? There may be a neurophysiological explanation. Information about head and body movement, as monitored by the vestibular apparatus of the inner ear (which helps you to keep your balance) is closely integrated by the brain with visual information in order to produce an optimally stable picture of the world—so that, for instance, you know the world has not moved when you tilt your head.

Since the sensations of movement during dream spinning are as completely vivid as those during actual movements, it is very likely that the same brain systems are being activated to a similar degree in the two cases. An intriguing possibility is that the spinning technique stimulates the vestibular system of the brain, and thereby facilitates the activity of the nearby components of the REM-sleep system. Since neuroscientists have obtained indirect evidence for the involvement of the vestibular system in the production of rapid-eye-movement bursts in REM sleep,[24] the proposed connection is not entirely without foundation.

On the other side of the psychophysiological coin, Barbara Lerner has emphasized the importance of movement during dreaming to maintain the integrity of the body image.[25] If movement is a psychological function of dreaming, as Lerner suggests, there ought to be a mechanism connecting such imagery with the physiology of REM sleep. Moreover, since imagery of one particular sense decreases sensitivity to external stimulation of the same sense, hallucinated movement ought to suppress actual body sensation, and hence help prevent awakening. If the brain is fully engaged in producing the vivid, internally generated sensory experience of spinning, it will be more difficult for it to construct a contradictory sensation based on external sensory input. This is an example of what is called "loading stabilization" of a system. Charles Tart described this with an analogy: "If you want someone to be a good citizen you keep him busy with the activities that constitute being a good citizen, so he has no time or energy for anything else."[26] In these terms, "being a good citizen" means continuing to dream, and the "activities" mean dream spinning.

Another technique—less effective than spinning—works on the same principle, by focusing attention on something in the dream. Moers-Messmer described, in 1938, the technique of looking at the ground to stabilize his lucid dreams, and several others have apparently discovered this technique independently since then, including Scott Sparrow and Carlos Castaneda. "Don Juan's" variation on the theme was, of course, the famous technique of looking at one's hand.

Another way to prevent awakening or loss of lucidity is to stabilize the state of consciousness through "positive feedback." In Tart's analogy, this is rewarding the citizen for carrying out whatever activities are considered desirable. Several methods proposed for stabilizing the lucid dream state appear to fall under this classification. For example, there is the suggestion of using an affirmation that constantly reminds you of the dream state (repeating "This is a dream, this is a dream," and so on). Another idea is to "go with the flow" of the dream, not attempting to alter the drift of dream events. My spinning technique also involves positive feedback, if the neurophysiological explanation I gave above is correct. If dream spinning results in brain-stem facilitation of REM sleep, then we have a case of dream activity—spinning—resulting in more dream activity.

A third way of stabilizing a state of consciousness—in this case, a lucid dream—is called "limiting stabilization," and is described by Tart as limiting the citizen's opportunities for engaging in undesirable activities. In the context of lucid dreaming, "undesirable activities" are awakening or losing lucidity. A number of methods that have been proposed for stabilizing lucid dreams probably have limiting stabilization as their basis. Some people have recommended exercising, to obtain deeper sleep, and eating well and avoiding indigestion. Others have suggested using earplugs, or sleeping alone. It is universally recommended that you avoid emotional conflict and do not get too excited in your lucid dreams. Finally, lucid dreamers have been advised not to "daydream" or think too much during the dream and not to lose themselves in the dream.

A Coherent Knowledge of Sleep Life?

We have so far considered some of the wide variety of forms taken by lucid dreaming. However, what we have seen so far may represent only the tip of the iceberg: lucid dreaming may be capable of a far greater degree of development than has yet been seen in Western psychology.

The claim is often made by yogis and other specialists in "inner states" that they are able to retain consciousness throughout the entire night, including during dreamless sleep. Wrote a twentieth-century Indian master, Sri Aurobindo Ghose, " . . . it is even possible to become wholly conscious in sleep and follow throughout from beginning to end or over large stretches the stages of our dream-experience; it is found that then we are aware of ourselves passing from state after state of consciousness to a brief period of luminous and peaceful dreamless rest, which is the true restorer of the energies of the waking nature, and then returning by the same way to the waking consciousness. It is normal, as we thus pass from state to state, to let the previous experiences slip away from us; in their turn only the more vivid or those nearest to the waking surface are remembered: but this can be remedied—a greater retention is possible or the power can be developed of going back in memory from dream to dream, from state to state, till the whole is once more before us. *A coherent knowledge of sleep-life*, though difficult to achieve or to keep established, *is possible* [my italics]."[27]

This is a very exciting possibility that would—if proven true—have profound implications for the scientific study of sleep, dreaming, and consciousness. As for the proof, it remains only for such a wakeful sleeper to spend a night in a sleep laboratory!

The problem with claims of continuous awareness during sleep is that we cannot be conscious of being unconscious.

The moments or hours we pass unconsciously are forever veiled in oblivion. Not only do we fail to remember them, but we also forget that we forgot them! The fact is, we are normally fully conscious of our selves and our actions only for brief moments, even while being what we call "awake." But in spite of the fact that we are only occasionally conscious of our selves, we experience ourselves as being continuously present. This is because our minds operate in such a fashion as to construct coherence and continuity out of our experiences. Thus we gloss over the blank spots in our consciousness. Since the first thing we remember when emerging from unconsciousness or sleep is the last thing we were conscious of, we may mistakenly assume that our consciousness was never lost.

In spite of these reservations, I see no reason in principle why a higher development of the human mind could not result in a continuity of consciousness throughout sleep, as described by Aurobindo. Such an advanced level of consciousness would only reveal itself after an extensive course of mental discipline. But we may well be able to learn to dream with degrees of lucidity and control as yet undreamt of.

6

~~~~~~~~~~~~~~~

Learning Lucid
Dreaming

*The vast majority of people have enormous potentiali-
ties of thinking, far beyond anything ordinarily suspected; but so seldom do the right circumstances by
chance surround them to require their actualization that
the vast majority die without realizing more than a fraction of their powers. Born millionaires, they live and
die in poverty for the lack of favourable circumstances
which would have compelled them to convert their credit
into cash.*

A. R. ORAGE

Learning to Dream

Just as we ordinarily take for granted that we know how
to think, we may also presume that we know how to dream.
But there are vast differences in the degree to which these

two faculties are developed in different people. What the above quote says about thinking applies, I believe, just as much to dreaming. We possess undeveloped, undreamed-of capacities. Like conscious thought, lucid dreaming is an ability that can be gained or improved by training. This chapter outlines the kind of training required, and in so doing provides you with the key to lucid dreaming.

In order to recognize that you are dreaming, you need first of all to have a concept of what dreaming is. What happens when you "realize you are dreaming" will depend upon what you understand "dreaming" to be. To illustrate this point, let us look at the typical developmental stages children pass through in acquiring a concept of dreaming.

According to the celebrated developmental psychologist Jean Piaget, children pass through three stages of understanding of dreams. In the first stage, attained between ages three and four, children do not distinguish dreams from waking life; thus a child believes that dreaming takes place in the same (external) world as the rest of his or her experiences. At this age, a child might awake in terror from a nightmare and believe that dream "monsters" are in the room. Parents' assurances that it was "just a dream" are not greatly effective at this stage. The child needs to be shown that, say, the closet is actually empty.

Between the ages of approximately four and six—and after sufficient experiences with awakening from dreams that are denied reality by parental figures—children modify their concept of dreaming. Now they know that what was happening was "just a dream." However, they don't know exactly what "just a dream" is. A child treats dreams, at this stage, as if they were partially external and partially internal. He or she might reply, for instance, if asked where dreams come from, "My head." But when asked where dreams take place, the same child might say, "In my bedroom."

Somewhere between the ages of five and eight, this transitional stage gives way to the third stage, in which the child recognizes the dream as entirely internal in nature. The child now considers dreams to take place *only* in his or her head. In other words, they are now conceived of as purely mental experiences.

These developmental stages refer, of course, to how the child views the dream *after* waking up. While asleep and dreaming, children and adults alike tend to remain at the first stage, implicitly assuming that dream events are external reality. This is the dominant assumption of ordinary, non-lucid dreams.

People not uncommonly have the experience, in dreams, of seeming to have temporarily separated from their physical bodies. These "out-of-body experiences" with their somewhat contradictory mixture of the mental and the material, may provide examples of the second developmental stage. In the typical experience, you apparently find yourself in a sort of *mental* body floating around in what seems to be the *physical* world. This is reminiscent of the mixed metaphysics regarding dreams displayed by children at Piaget's second stage.

In a fully lucid dream, the dreamer reaches the third stage, realizing that the experience is entirely mental and that the dream world is completely distinct from the physical world. To be lucid in this sense presupposes that the dreamer has reached Piaget's third level and knows that dreams are only mental experiences. Since this is attained by some children at age five, we should expect that lucid dreams might appear as early as that age; indeed, my first lucid dreams took place at just that age, and many lucid dreamers report their first experiences beginning between the ages of five and seven.

Potential for Lucid Dreaming

Can anyone learn to have lucid dreams? Does it take some special talent possessed by a gifted minority, or is this remarkable ability merely one of the everyday miracles of the human brain?

This question has the same answer as the question, "Who can learn to talk?" Everyone attains as much proficiency in his or her native tongue as is required for everyday speech; beyond that, the degree of fluency depends upon motivation, practice, and innate ability. The degree of language mastery exhibited by great writers and poets far surpasses the level with which the ordinary person is content, and what I have said regarding this skill applies analogously to the skill of lucid dreaming. The Shakespeares of lucid dreaming are bound to be few, but why shouldn't everyone be able to attain at least some proficiency in the field?

In my view there are two essential requirements for learning lucid dreaming: motivation and good dream recall. The necessity of motivation is obvious enough: lucid dreaming, after all, demands considerable control of attention, and hence we must be motivated to exert the necessary effort. As for dream recall, if A. M. Nesia recalls no dreams at all, and we assume one percent of the dreams he has forgotten are lucid, how many lucid dreams does he recall? The answer, obviously, is none—since unless we remember *some* dreams, how can we remember lucid ones?

Dream Recall

In order to have a lucid dream and know about it when you awaken, of course you have to remember your dream. For one thing, the more frequently you remember dreams, and the clearer and more detailed your pictures become, the more likely you are to remember lucid dreams. The more familiar you become with what your own dreams are like, the easier you will find it to recognize them *as dreams* while they happen. Thus, if you want to learn to dream lucidly, you need first of all to learn to reliably recall your dreams. (Incidentally, there is probably a good reason why dreams are so hard to remember: see Chapter 8.)

One of the most important determinants of dream recall is motivation. For the most part, those who want to remember their dreams can do so, and those who do not want to do not. For many people, simply having the intention to remember, reminding themselves of this intention just before bed, is enough. One effective way to strengthen this resolve is to keep a dream journal beside your bed and record whatever you can remember of your dreams every time you wake up. As you record more dreams, you will remember more dreams. Reading over your dream journal can provide an added benefit: the more familiar you become with what your dreams are like, the easier it will be for you to recognize one while it is still happening and therefore to awaken in your dream.

An infallible method for developing your ability to remember dreams is to get in the habit of asking yourself, every time you wake up, "What was I dreaming?" This must be your first thought upon awakening; otherwise, you will forget some or all of the dream due to interference from other thoughts. You must not give up too quickly if nothing is recalled at first, but persist patiently in the effort to remember, without moving or thinking of anything else, and in most cases, pieces and fragments of the dream will come to you. If you still cannot remember a dream, ask yourself what you were just thinking and how you are feeling. Examining your thoughts and feelings in this way can often provide the necessary cues for retrieving the entire dream.

In developing dream recall, as with any other skill, progress is sometimes slow. It is important not to be discouraged if you do not succeed at first. Each of us masters the ability to recall our dreams at our own rate. But virtually everyone who stays with it improves through practice. As the saying puts it, "If you want to be a calligrapher, then write, and write, and write." If you want to be a dream recaller, then try and try and try to remember.

Learning Lucid Dreaming

Let us suppose that you are capable of remembering your dreams often enough to appreciate how rarely you are lucid in them. Your occasional lucid dreams might be likened to finding money on the street—a rare, though nonetheless rewarding experience. Cultivating the skill of lucid dreaming corresponds, in this analogy, to developing a gainful means of employment with which to earn the money. If this sounds like work, it is; and it requires a certain amount of discipline at first, but it becomes easier—even effortless—with practice.

Try to remember what learning to speak was like: it was simply impossible at first to do more than babble. But with days after days and years after years of practice, you have now so mastered the skill that you are able to talk without thinking.

Maybe you haven't yet said your first word in lucid dreaming, or maybe you've just said your first sentence. Can you realistically expect someday to be an effortlessly fluent lucid dreamer? That, I say, depends on you.

You may wonder whether it is possible to learn to dream lucidly at will. My own experience has shown *me* that it is. That it took me two-and-a-half years is probably due to the fact that nobody taught me how. Since I did not have a very clear idea at first of what I was doing, I wasted much of my time and effort. With the induction method that I finally developed, I believe anyone who is motivated can be successful in learning how to dream lucidly, and in a fraction of the time it took me. But before I describe this method, I will first briefly summarize what has already been written on learning to dream lucidly.

Eastern religious and psychological writings contain a number of hints and suggested methods for lucid dreaming. As far as I know, the earliest recorded mention of lucid dreaming as a learnable skill is found in the eighth-century Tibetan manuscript *The Yoga of the Dream State,* which outlines several methods for inducing lucid dreams. However, unless you are an advanced yogi, capable of complex visualizations of Sanskrit letters in many-petaled colored lotuses, most of the methods will not be of much use! Besides, the book is really intended as a students' manual to supplement the oral teachings of a dream master.

Only the first and most elementary exercise described in the manuscript is likely to be intelligible to Westerners. The technique, called "comprehending it by the power of resolution,"[1] involves two practices. First of all, during the day the novice is instructed to think continuously, that "all things are of the substance of dreams." This practice makes use of the effect waking experiences have on the dreams of subsequent nights. Moreover, we tend to dream about our current concerns. The practice also helps to remove one of the most effective barriers to lucidity: namely, that if we never question the nature of our experience during the waking state, why should we do so during the dream state? Thinking of waking experience as dreaming will break the automatic habits with which we are used to seeing and thinking about life. The mental flexibility that results from waking practice facilitates lucidity in the dream state.

The second technique, the "firm resolution" to "comprehend the dream state," is just as straightforward. During the night, before going to sleep, the student must invoke the aid of the guru and "firmly resolve" to comprehend the dream state—that is, to understand that it is not real, but a dream. Lucid dreaming rarely occurs without our intending it, which means having the mental set to recognize when we are dreaming; thus, intention forms a part of any deliberate effort to induce lucid dreams. And if the would-be lucid dreamer is not initially successful in his or her efforts, the manuscript exhorts him or her to make no fewer than twenty-one efforts each morning to "comprehend the nature of the dream state."

One aspect of this Tibetan technique would—if essential—severely limit its application in the West. I refer to the "prayer to the guru." It may be that the Tibetan disciple's complete trust in his or her guru results in an expectation of success that becomes a self-fulfilling prophecy. The Westerner who lacks both guru and gods may thereby be deficient in the degree of confidence necessary for success.

For the most part, modern Eastern methods for lucid dreaming are no less complex. Bhagwan Shree Rajneesh, an unworldly guru with sixty-two Rolls-Royces, describes three techniques that vary from the incomprehensible to the almost impossible. The first is: "With intangible breath in center of forehead, as this reaches heart at the moment of sleep, have direction over dreams," and if that is not enough—"over death itself."[2]

The second method is to "remember 'I am'—whatsoever you are doing."[3] This is intelligible at least, and probably designed to strengthen self-consciousness and the observer's perspective. Remembering "I am" is a technique designed to produce a state of mind called

"self-remembering" in esoteric psychology. "Self-remembering," wrote biochemist and esoteric psychologist
Robert S. deRopp, "is a certain separation of awareness
from whatever a man happens to be doing, thinking, feeling. It is symbolized by a two-headed arrow suggesting
double awareness of self. There is actor and observer,
there is an objective awareness of self. There is a feeling
of being outside of, separated from, the confines of the
physical body; there is a sense of detachment, a state of
non-identification. For identification and self-remembering can no more exist together than a room can simultaneously be illuminated and dark. One excludes the
other."[4] This sounds so much like lucid dreaming that it
is likely that the practice of self-remembering in the waking state encourages the occurrence of lucidity in the
dream state.

Rajneesh's third method is simple enough if you happen
to be the obsessive type. He advises the would-be lucid
dreamer to "try to remember for three weeks continuously
that whatsoever you are doing is just a dream."[5] In my
view, anyone who could remember anything at all for three
weeks *continuously* ought to be able to do pratically anything! For such a talented person, lucid dreaming should
present little difficulty.

Paul Tholey, a German psychologist, has recently described various techniques for inducing lucid dreams, derived from over a decade of research involving more than
two hundred subjects.[6] According to Tholey, the most effective method for achieving lucidity is to develop "a crit-
ical-reflective attitude" toward your state of consciousness,
by asking yourself whether or not you are dreaming while
you are awake. He stresses the importance of asking the
critical question ("Am I dreaming or not?") as frequently
as possible, at least five to ten times a day, and in every
situation that seems dreamlike. Asking the question at bedtime and while falling asleep is also favorable. Following

this technique, most people will have their first lucid dream within a month, Tholey reports, and some will succeed on the very first night.

Oliver Fox regarded a critical frame of mind as the key to lucid dreaming (as described in Chapter 5), and it is easy to see why asking the question "Am I dreaming or not?" ought to favor the occurrence of lucid dreams. We most often dream about familiar activities from our waking life, and if we never ask whether we are dreaming or not while awake, why should we do so while dreaming? Or, to put it more positively, the more often we critically question our state of consciousness while awake, the more likely we are to do so while dreaming.

There are several modern methods aimed at the maintaining of consciousness during the transition from waking to sleep—such as the method used by Ouspensky and Rapport. Rapport described his technique as follows: While lying in bed and drifting into sleep, he interrupted his reveries every few minutes, making an effort to recall what had been passing through his mind a moment earlier. With sufficient practice, this habit of introspection continued into sleep, and he found himself in lucid dreams that frequently inspired "raptures of delight."

There are many variations on the technique of falling asleep while maintaining consciousness. For example, a student of Tibetan Buddhism reports having been instructed to visualize an eight-petaled rose with a white light in its center in his throat—a technique supposed to focus concentration with an intensity that allows consciousness to persist into the dream state. Tarthang Tulku, a Tibetan lama teaching in Berkeley, describes a similar procedure: After relaxing very deeply just before sleep, you are to "visualize a beautiful, soft lotus flower in your throat. The lotus has light-pink petals which curl slightly inwards, and in the center of this lotus is a luminous red-orange flame which is light at the edges shading to darker at the center. Looking very softly, concentrate on the top of the flame, and continue to visualize it as long as possible."[7]

The flame, Tulku explains, represents awareness; the lotus, I may add, denotes in Buddhist iconography the awakening consciousness of Self. While continuing the visualization, you are to watch how your thoughts arise, observe their interaction with the image of the lotus, and see how they are connected with the past, the present, and by projection, the future. You are to "just observe" whatever images come into your mind, but continue to concentrate on the lotus image. Thus, "as long as the thread of the visualization remains intact, it will carry over into the dream." Tarthang Tulku cautions the practioner against "trying to interpret or 'think about' your visualization." This, he warns, will break the thread and your awareness will be lost. "So, be careful not to force your visualization; just let it happen, but keep your awareness on the lotus." Finally, you are to "let the form reflect into your awareness until your awareness and the image become one." He explains that at first you will tend to pass into the dream state forgetting that you are dreaming, but with practice your consciousness "will naturally develop until you will be able to see that you are dreaming. When you watch very carefully, you will be able to see that whole creation and evolution of the dream."

Tholey[8] has described three similar techniques for retaining lucidity while falling asleep. The methods are based on the general procedure of falling asleep while maintaining inner attentiveness, with variations depending upon the object of attention. In the "image technique," you focus on your hypnagogic imagery, as Ouspensky, Rapport, and others suggest. Tholey recommends allowing yourself to be passively carried into the dream scenery rather than attempting to enter it intentionally, which tends to cause the dream to fade.

Tholey's second method, "body technique," is related to procedures aiming at producing an OBE or "astral projection" (see Chapter 9). While drifting into sleep, you simply imagine that your body is somewhere else, doing something other than lying in bed. If you find yourself vividly "elsewhere," you will be lucid if you do not forget that it is a dream. Tholey's third method of lucid dream induction, "the ego-point technique," involves concentrating, while you are falling asleep, on the idea that you will soon no longer perceive your body. As soon as you have fallen asleep, it is possible to float freely, as a point of awareness, in "a space which seems to be identical with the room in which one went to sleep."

Five years ago, I developed a simple technique for maintaining conscious awareness during the transition from waking to sleep. The method is to count to yourself ("one, I'm dreaming; two, I'm dreaming," and so on) while drifting off to sleep, maintaining a certain level of vigilance as you do so. The result is that at some point—say, "forty-eight, I'm dreaming"—you will find that you *are* dreaming! The "I'm dreaming" phrase helps to remind you of what you intend to do, but it is not strictly necessary. Simply focusing your attention on counting probably allows you to retain sufficient alertness to recognize dream images for what they are, when they appear. This and similar techniques apparently work best for people who tend to fall asleep rapidly, and frequently experience sleep-onset (hypnagogic) dreaming.

I gained the most information about this technique through tutoring one of our oneironauts in its practice. Laurie C. regularly experiences vivid dreaming at sleep onset. Some of her sleep-onset dreams are like the "snapshots" people typically think of as characteristic hypnagogic imagery. Others seem more like full-blown dream films, with her vividly felt presence and active participation in what are sometimes quite extensive sequences of scenes.

Knowing that Ouspensky had been able to maintain awareness in the hypnagogic state, I suggested to Laurie that she too ought to be able to be lucid during sleep-onset dreaming. I helped her practice by watching her fall asleep while she made the effort to retain consciousness. She would often fall asleep within fifteen to thirty seconds, as I could tell by her rolling or rapid eye movements and body twitches. At that point, I would wake her with the question, "What was just happening?" She almost always recalled a vivid dream scene, but rarely became lucid at the time. It seemed to me she needed a reminder. So I asked her to silently repeat the phrase "I'm dreaming" while counting to herself as she fell asleep. And it worked! She would be repeating "one, I'm dreaming; two, I'm dreaming; . . . forty-four, I'm dreaming," until suddenly realizing she *was* dreaming.

After about a week of practice, Laurie was able to dispense with the "I'm dreaming" phrase, and found that simple counting to herself worked as well. In a surprisingly short time, she was able to become lucid in her sleep-onset dreams almost at will.

At this point, we decided to observe her in the sleep lab for three consecutive nights. On these nights, Laurie made an effort to retain consciousness while entering sleep-onset dream states.

On each of these experimental sessions, she repeatedly rested quietly, but vigilantly, and counted to herself ("one, two, three . . .", until she began to dream. She usually awakened five to ten seconds later and tape-recorded a description of what she had just experienced. Laurie reported having been lucid in twenty-five of the forty-two resulting dreams. Visual inspection of the polygraph records showed that all of these "dreamlets" (I use the term because none lasted more than several seconds) occurred, whether they were lucid or not, during NREM Stage 1 sleep, with slow eye movements. The following is a sample: "I was in the grocery store, going down an aisle; only I was standing on a cart. It was whizzing real fast. As I went by the Coke and Pepsi bottles, I realized that I was dreaming. I remembered to look at my hands, but they wouldn't move up to eye level."

Laurie's inability to look at her dream hands may point to a significant difference between these sleep-onset lucid "dreamlets" and REM lucid dreams. During REM lucid dreams, the dreamer normally has complete volitional control of his or her dream body. I had wondered if the same would be true at sleep onset, so I asked Laurie to carry out a prearranged dream action of putting her hands before her face when she found herself conscious of dreaming. This seemingly simple task proved impossible, at least in this one case; obviously, more research is needed in order to settle the issue.

An important factor influencing the kind of results you are likely to obtain with the foregoing technique is *timing*. Rather than attempting to enter the lucid dream state at the beginning of your sleep cycle, you would do much better to try later in the night, toward morning, especially after already awakening from a dream. This is because the lucid dreams characteristic of sleep onset at the beginning of the night typically take place in NREM Stage 1 sleep, and hence rarely seem to last more than a few seconds. In contrast, when these techniques are practiced upon awakening from REM periods later in the night, it is often possible to return to REM sleep and experience extended, full-blown lucid dreams. However, the optimal time for entering REM lucid dreams directly from the waking state may be in the afternoon. I base this suggestion on the fact that in my personal record, the proportion of waking-initiated lucid dreams to dream-initiated ones is six times higher during my afternoon naps than in nocturnal sleep.

The various techniques described above for entering the dream state from the waking state work on the same fundamental principle: you lie in bed deeply relaxed but vigilant, and perform a repetitive or continuous mental activity upon which you focus your attention. Keeping this task going maintains your inner focus of attention, and with it your wakeful inner consciousness, while your drowsy external awareness diminishes and finally vanishes altogether as you fall asleep. In essence, the idea is to let your body fall asleep while you keep your mind awake.

There is another, and for most people far easier, way to become lucid in a dream: become very familiar with your dreams, get to know what is dreamlike about them, and simply *intend* to recognize that they are dreams while they are happening. Evidently, simply intending to recognize that one is dreaming is enough to increase the frequency of occurrence of lucid dreams.

In the West, the earliest account of learning lucid dreaming was provided by the Marquis d'Hervey de Saint-Denys, who taught himself through the following method. By the age of thirteen, he had become fascinated with his dreams and devoted a great deal of time to recording and sketching them. He explained that:

> as a result of thinking about my dreams during the day, and analyzing and describing them, these activities became part of the store of memories of waking life on which my mind drew during sleep. Thus one night I dreamt that I was writing up my dreams, some of which were particularly unusual. On waking, I thought what a great pity it was that I had not been aware of this exceptional situation while still asleep. What a golden opportunity lost—I thought. I would have been able to note so many interesting details. I was obsessed by this idea for several days, and the mere fact that I kept thinking about it during the day soon resulted in my having the same dream again. There was one modification, how-

ever: this time the original ideas summoned up by association the idea I was dreaming, and I became perfectly aware of this fact. I was able to concentrate particularly on the details of the dream that interested me, so as to fix them in my mind all the more clearly on waking.[9]

After another year of obsessive preoccupation with his dreams, the Marquis reported that he was having lucid dreams almost every night.

R. T. Browne, one of the contributors to Volume II of Narayana's *Dream Problem,* described essentially this same method. Asserting that "under certain conditions" it is "possible for the dreamer to remain cognizant of the fact that he is dreaming during the dream state . . . one of the means by which he may accomplish this is by placing in his so-called subconscious mind the suggestion, clear-cut and positive, that he will be conscious of the fact, under a given set of circumstances, that he is dreaming."

This method was tested in the early 1970s by Patricia Garfield. She merely told herself, before going to sleep: "Tonight, I *will* have a lucid dream." Garfield said that with this method she obtained a "classical learning curve, increasing the frequency of prolonged lucid dreams from a baseline of zero to a high of three per week."[10] She used the method for five or six years, during which time she had an average of four or five lucid dreams per month. These results indicate that merely telling oneself to have a lucid dream can provide a starting point, at least, for deliberately inducing lucid dreams.

Before beginning my own efforts to learn to dream lucidly, I had had occasional spontaneous lucid dreams over the years, especially as a young child. At about the age of five, I had a series of dreams that I would intentionally redream on successive nights. I vividly recall a scene from one of them, as described in Chapter 4, in which I experienced momentary anxiety about having been underwater for a long time—but then I remembered that in dreams I could breathe underwater. How long I continued these practices I do not know, but the next lucid dream that I can recall took place almost twenty years later. For several years I experienced occasional lucid dreams (about one per month) that were sufficiently intriguing to persuade me to undertake a careful study of the phenomenon.

During the first year and a half of my research, I used self-suggestion for lucid-dream induction, with results equivalent to Garfield's.

By the end of phase one, I had observed two factors that seemed to be associated with the occurrence of my lucid dreams. The first, and most obvious, was motivation. During this period, there were two months during which I reported, respectively, two and three times more lucid dreams than the average for the rest of this period. During the first month, September 1977, I was preparing a Ph.D. dissertation proposal in which I claimed that I ought to be able to learn to have lucid dreams at will. During the second month, January 1978, I was attempting (successfully) to have lucid dreams in the sleep laboratory. During both of these months I was highly motivated, since I felt challenged to demonstrate the practicality of a laboratory study of lucid dreaming. However, I found it impossible to maintain this high level of motivation, as is seen by the decline in lucid-dreaming frequency following these two months.

Gradually, more self-observation led to the realization that a second psychological factor was involved: the intention to *remember* to be lucid during the next dream. This clarification of intention was accompanied by an immediate increase in the monthly frequency of my lucid dreams. Once I discovered that memory was the key to lucid dreaming, further practice and methodological refinements allowed me to arrive, within a year, at my goal: a method by which I could reliably induce lucid dreams.

Mnemonic Induction of Lucid Dreams (MILD)

MILD is based on nothing more complex or esoteric than our ability to remember that there are actions we wish to perform in the future. Aside from writing ourselves memos (a device of little use here, for obvious reasons!) we do this by forming a mental connection between what we want to do and the future circumstances in which we intend to do it. Making this connection is greatly facilitated by the mnemonic device—the memory aid—of visualizing yourself doing what it is you intend to remember. It is also helpful to verbalize the intention: "When such-and-such happens, I want to remember to do so-and-so." For example: "When I pass the bank, I want to remember to draw out some cash."

The verbalization that I use to organize my intended effort is: "Next time I'm dreaming, I want to remember to recognize I'm dreaming." The "when" and "what" of the intended action must be clearly specified.

I generate this intention either immediately after awakening from an earlier REM period, or following a period of full wakefulness, as detailed below. An important point is that in order to produce the desired effect, it is necessary to do more than just mindlessly recite the phrase. You must really *intend* to have a lucid dream. Here is the recommended procedure spelled out step by step:

1. During the early morning, when you awaken spontaneously from a dream, go over the dream several times until you have memorized it.

2. Then, while lying in bed and returning to sleep, say to yourself, "Next time I'm dreaming, I want to remember to recognize I'm dreaming."

3. Visualize yourself as being back in the dream just rehearsed; only this time, see yourself realizing that you are, in fact, dreaming.

4. Repeat steps two and three until you feel your intention is clearly fixed or you fall asleep.

If all goes well, in a short time you will find yourself lucid in another dream (which need not closely resemble the one you have rehearsed).

The mental set involved in this procedure is much like the one you adopt when you decide to awaken at a certain hour, and go to sleep after setting your mental alarm clock. The ability to awaken *in* your dreams may be regarded as a sort of refinement of the ability to awaken *from* your dreams.

The reason for the "early morning" specified in step one is that lucid dreamers from van Eeden to Garfield have reported that such dreams occur almost exclusively during the morning hours. Our research at Stanford indicates that lucid dreaming occurs during REM periods, and since most REM sleep takes place in the later part of a night's sleep, this is likely to be the most favorable time for lucid dreaming. Although some dreamers have successfully induced lucid dreams using MILD during the first REM period of the night, the technique seems to be most effective when practiced during the early morning after awakening from a dream.

If you find yourself just too drowsy to follow the procedure as described above, you might try to wake yourself up by engaging in several minutes of any activity that demands full wakefulness, such as writing down your dream, reading, or simply getting out of bed. This is because certain activities have been observed to promote lucid dreaming upon a subsequent return to sleep. Garfield, for example, found that "sexual intercourse during the middle of the night was often followed by a lucid dream." Scott Sparrow, in contrast, reported that early-morning meditation favored lucid dreaming (but only if he did the meditation for itself and not to have lucid dreams). Other lucid dreamers indicate early-morning reading or writing to be favorable. The diversity of these activities suggests that it is not the particular activity, but the wakefulness that facilitates lucid dreaming during subsequent sleep.

However, wakefulness presents the would-be lucid dreamer with disadvantages as well as advantages. Often it is impossible to return to sleep after waking up fully. Another problem is that since proximity to REM sleep while doing MILD probably favors successful lucid-dream induction, the longer you wait before returning to sleep, the less likely it is for lucid dreams to occur. When you awaken from REM dreaming, your brain persists in a REM-like state for several minutes afterwards. Scientists have demonstrated this by awakening people from both REM and NREM sleep and having them devise stories. The stories told after awakening from REM were more dreamlike than the NREM stories. Thus, something of the REM state carries over for a few minutes after waking from a dream. If we reenter our dreams immediately after waking from REM, which is the point at which our dreaming and waking worlds are closest, it is the optimal time for carrying over our lucid-dream intentions from the waking mind into the dreaming mind.

People are likely to differ as to which of these two factors—wakefulness and REM carryover—are more effective for them, and I recommend experimenting with both when using MILD to induce lucid dreams. Once I myself learned how to use MILD, I experienced as many as four lucid dreams in a single night, and indeed seemed able to attain lucidity on any night that I tried it. I see no reason why the same shouldn't be true for others.

Since motivation is an important factor in inducing lucid dreams, how can we be sure increased motivation doesn't account for the improvements I have attributed to MILD? During all the nights I attempted to induce lucid dreams while being physiologically monitored, my motivation was very high. Using self-suggestion, I had only one lucid dream in seven nights of laboratory recordings, but when I began practicing MILD, I had fifteen lucid dreams in thirteen recording nights. It should be clear that it is the method, and not merely the motivation, that accounted for these results.

MILD also seems to work well for others, especially those who meet the requirements of high motivation and excellent dream recall. "High motivation" means having a strong desire to develop the skill of lucid dreaming, and by "excellent dream recall" I mean being able to awaken from (and remember) dreams two to three times per night or more. Students in my workshops and courses have almost always succeeded with MILD if they met these two conditions. Two of my students increased their lucid-dream frequency from less than one per month to about twenty per month during an eight-week course. Even the average student had three or four lucid dreams in the same two-month period. All this should make it clear that it *is* possible to learn to have lucid dreams. What one dreamer can do, others can do as well.

Undoubtedly, the future will see the development of much more effective techniques for lucid-dream induction that promise to make this world available to anyone who needs or desires it. Who knows—perhaps entry into lucid dreams will one day be no more difficult than falling asleep. (Although many will still say that *that* is no easy matter!)

Future Access to the
Lucid Dream State

At present, it is possible to point to several techniques that could be developed to induce lucid dreams. One is hypnosis. "Auto-suggestion," or implanting in oneself the command to do something, is a form of hypnosis, and it is involved in practicing MILD. Many people have found it at least moderately effective in inducing lucid dreams. For the fortunate minority who are easily hypnotizable, post-hypnotic suggestions to have lucid dreams may be more effective when given by a hypnotist, rather than when given by oneself. Although I am only moderately hypnotizable, I have been hypnotized three times and given post-hypnotic suggestions to have lucid dreams and on two of the three occasions they worked.

Along the same lines, Charles Tart has mentioned some preliminary work suggesting "that post-hypnotic suggestions may have some potential in inducing lucid dreaming."[11] I think one could change Tart's "may" to "do." In my view, this is an area greatly deserving of cultivation, since hypnosis could help provide access to lucid dreaming for those hypnotizable individuals who might find the state very useful, but who may not be able to get there on their own steam. Such a technique would probably greatly further the therapeutic applications of lucid dreaming (see Chapter 7).

A Ph.D. dissertation by Joe Dane, recently of the University of Virginia at Charlottesville, provides the strongest support yet for the possible usefulness of post-hypnotic suggestion as a lucid-dream induction method. Dane's fifteen female subjects—all scoring above the median level on a measure of hypnotic susceptibility, all recalling at least one dream per month, and all claiming *no* prior experience of lucidity—were given post-hypnotic suggestions to dream lucidly when they were recorded on a single night. Fourteen of the fifteen reported at least a minor episode of lucid dreaming. Contrary to most other studies, Dane's turned up more reports of lucid dreaming from *non*-REM sleep than from REM sleep. Some of the NREM lucid dreams resembled the "dreamlets" described earlier in this chapter, so it is difficult to evaluate just how significant these results actually are. Counting only the five unambiguous REM lucid dreams verified by eye-movement signals gives a considerably more modest success rate of thirty-three percent. However, even that seems most impressive when it is taken into account that the subjects were all previously nonlucid dreamers. I believe that Dane has significantly advanced the state of the art with respect to lucid dream induction by means of post-hypnotic suggestion.

The use of some particular element of dream content (for instance, my "multiplying contact lenses") as a lucidity cue was mentioned in Chapter 5. A closely related technique involves presenting, during REM sleep, an external stimulus as a lucidity cue, since it is well known that environmental stimuli are at times incorporated into dreams. Almost everyone has had the experience of hearing an annoying sound, such as a neighbor's buzz saw, only to awaken a moment later to find that what had really been making the noise was the equally annoying alarm clock. If we have a kinder system for awakening, music or the news may find its way into our dreams. Stimuli in the rest of the sensory modes (smell, touch, sight, temperature, and possibly other senses as well) are also occasionally incorporated in dreams, and any of these sensory pathways could carry a reminder to the dreamer that he or she is dreaming.

This all might seem contradictory to the reader accustomed to thinking of sleep as being "dead to the world." But the fact is that the sleeping brain maintains a degree of contact with the environment, analyzing for meaning the information about external events that is received through the senses. After all, we are able to awaken when our own name is called, but remain asleep when someone else's name is called or an airplane flies overhead. And consider the mother who sleeps through her husband's loud snoring, but awakens to her baby's faint cries coming from another room. If we are monitoring the environment for the occurrence of significant events such as these, why couldn't we sleep with the intention of noting some prearranged external sensory cue as a reminder that we are dreaming?

The idea occurred to me that the most direct approach would be to use as a cue a sentence stating what the dreamer wishes to become aware of: "This is a dream." I first tried this out in 1978 at the Stanford Sleep Laboratory, in collaboration with Dr. Lynn Nagel. Lynn got the short end of the deal, staying up all night monitoring my brain waves and REMs while I slept. When he observed me in REM sleep, he turned on a tape recording I had made earlier, playing it at a moderate level from a speaker next to my bed. The recorded message said, in my own voice, "Stephen, you're dreaming" and after a few seconds added the suggestion that I continue to sleep but realize that I was dreaming. At the time, I had not been sleeping too well, still being a newcomer to the sleep lab, and it seemed to me that I was lying in bed awake. Then from the next room, I heard the voice of a doctor commenting in Germanic accents, "Amazing! Ze subject has had *no* REM sleep all night!" Hearing this, I was not surprised. As far as *I* knew, I had had no sleep of any kind. But the next moment, I was astonished to hear my own voice coming over the P.A. system, announcing, "You're dreaming!" I became lucid immediately. It had worked! I was very excited. In a dream world suddenly beautiful and more vivid than waking life,

I was awake in my sleep! But a few seconds later, the recording continued with a voice now loud enough to wake the dead, to say nothing of the sleeping, "Continue to sleep"—and I awoke!

This first experiment showed us that lucid dreams could indeed be induced by direct verbal suggestion during REM sleep. The fact that in the dream I heard "You're dreaming" loud and clear, but did not hear my name at all, is interesting. Perhaps unconsciously hearing my name stimulated my attention, allowing me to hear the rest of the message consciously.

We used my own voice to record the message for two reasons. First, we hoped that being reminded by one's own voice would seem more like reminding oneself mentally, and second, because an earlier study found that when subjects heard tape recordings of their own voices during REM, the result was dreams in which the subjects were more active, assertive, and independent than when they heard recordings of other peoples' voices.[12] Since these qualities are associated with lucid dreaming, we hoped that hearing my own voice would reinforce these qualities and facilitate the realization I was dreaming.

This was the beginning of a series of explorations that are still continuing. We asked four people interested in lucid dreaming to spend one or two nights in the sleep lab. They each made a recording that repeated the phrase, "This is a dream" every four to eight seconds. This was played, at a gradually increasing volume, five to ten minutes after the beginning of each REM period. The subjects were instructed to signal by means of a pair of left and right eye movements whenever they heard the tape or recognized they were dreaming. The technician turned off the tape recorder immediately upon observing this eye-movement signal on the polygraph. If the subjects did not awaken by themselves within two minutes of the signal, the technician awakened them and asked for dream reports.

The tape stimulus was applied a total of fifteen times, producing lucidity in a third of the cases and, in general, one of four results:

1. *Awakening.* In the majority of cases (fifty-three percent), the subjects reported hearing the tape only after they had been awakened by it.

2. *Incorporation with lucidity.* In twenty percent of the cases, the subjects reported hearing the tape *in the dream* and signaling while still dreaming (now lucidly). This is the same sort of result we obtained in our first experiments with taped stimuli.

3. *Incorporation without lucidity.* The subjects twice reported dream content obviously related to the taped stimulus—without, however, becoming lucid before awakening. The most curious example of this was when a subject awoke after the tape had been played and wrote a report of his dream. I asked him at that point whether he had heard the tape, and he replied he was sure he had not. I was most surprised when I later read his written report. Near the end of his dream, he complained that someone was trying to tell him something, but he wouldn't listen to them. What were they saying? ''You're dreaming!'' Remarkably, this subject had not even recognized the phrase while writing a report of it after awakening!

4. *Lucidity without incorporation.* On two occasions, our subjects attained lucidity and signaled (while the tape was being played) without consciously hearing the stimulus in their dreams at all. This is exactly the opposite of the preceding situation. In one of these cases, having been awakened from my first REM period by the tape, I was frustrated at having had my sleep disturbed for nothing, and decided I would try

to induce a lucid dream on my own during my next REM period *before* the tape had a chance to wake me up. So I performed the MILD technique while returning to sleep. The next thing I knew I was in a violent struggle with my father. I recognized I was dreaming and thought, "So this is the first ten minutes of REM," since I hadn't heard any tape. This thought seemed to lead to a fading of the dream, and I soon woke up. Shortly after I wrote my dream report, the technician entered my room and asked if I had heard the tape. "What?" I said, confused. "When? What tape?" It turned out the tape had been turned on about twenty seconds before I had signaled—which was, by the way, after twenty, not ten, minutes of REM. Apparently, my unconscious awareness of the message helped me realize I was dreaming.

The results of this study also gave us a sense of the complexity and the multiplicity of variables involved. First there is the question of when is the best time to apply the stimulus, since not every moment of REM sleep seems equally suited to lucid dreaming. As for the message itself, what is its optimal form? First person—"I'm dreaming"? Second person—"You're dreaming"? Or objective—"This is a dream"? Our research at Stanford is aimed at finding our way out of this tangle of questions, to gain a reliable means of inducing lucid dreams in people who have had no prior experience with the phenomenon.

Another significant question is whether or not a verbal cue is best. In principle, any stimulus in any sensory mode could be used as a cue to remind a dreamer that he or she is dreaming. Perhaps a melody (say, Bach's *Sleepers Awake!*) might be more effective than speech. Or—since smell is the only sense that does not pass through the relay station in the brain called the thalamus, and thus may not be as inhibited as the other senses during sleep— it may be that scent would function as an especially effective cue.

A classic study by Dement and Wolpert[13] examined dream incorporation in several sensory modes. They found that tactile stimuli were more frequently incorporated into dreams than either light or sound. This suggests that tactile stimulation might provide an effective lucidity cue. In fact, in Great Britain a few years ago, Keith Hearne was promoting a "dream machine" operating on this principle. Hearne's device measured breathing rate with a nasal temperature sensor, and applied a series of electric shocks to the dreamer's wrist when an increase in breathing rate was detected. The problem was that if the dreamer was lucky, the shocks would occur during REM sleep, but they could just as easily come during NREM sleep or even waking. If the shocks did not awaken the sleeper, but were instead incorporated into the dream, and if the dreamer recognized the incorporated stimuli as lucidity cues, a lucid dream could have been produced. These are big "ifs" and the scant scientific research available on this machine suggests it to be only marginally effective at best. Though the idea seems a good one, the execution was apparently less than optimal for the intended purpose. I believe it is probably only a matter of time before someone perfects and markets an effective lucid-dream induction device; this is currently one of the top priorities of my own research.

Such a piece of technology might do the same thing for would-be lucid dreamers that biofeedback machines do for novice meditators. In both cases, the technological aid might make it easier for the beginner to get started, perhaps saving him or her years of frustrating, misdirected effort. But a time will likely come when reliance on external assistance will hinder the learner's further development. Crutches may help us walk when we are weak, but until we set them aside we will never dance.

7

~~~~~~~~~~~~~~~~

The Practical Dreamer: Applications of Lucid Dreaming

Concerning electricity, a "scientific curiosity" of the eighteenth century, a woman is said to have asked Benjamin Franklin, "But what use is it?" His reply is famous: "What use, madame, is a newborn baby?" If at this stage the same question were asked in regard to lucid dreaming, a "scientific curiosity" of the twentieth century, the same answer could be given. Though for the moment we can only speculate, our work at Stanford and the accounts of other lucid dreamers suggest that, like electricity, lucid dreaming could also be harnessed to aid us in performing a variety of tasks with far greater ease. As they appear to me today, applications of lucid dreaming generally fall into four broad areas: scientific exploration; health and inner growth; creative problem solving, rehearsal, and decision making; wish fulfillment and recreation. Since the use and advantages of lucid dreaming in scientific exploration of the dream state have already been presented, we will only concern ourselves with the latter three categories.

All of the applications of lucid dreaming we will be examining are examples of *creativity,* Since the most general advantages offered by lucid consciousness—to both dream and waking—is the capacity for flexible and creative action, it should come as no surprise that the various applications of lucid dreaming are all, in a sense, examples of creativity. As biofeedback researchers Elmer and Alyce Green have observed,

> It seems increasingly certain that healing and creativity are different pieces of a single picture. Both Swami Rama and Jack Schwarz, a Western Sufi whom we recently had a chance to work with, maintain that self-healing can be performed in a state of deep *reverie* . . . But this "manner" of manipulation of images is also the same as that in which we find ideas being handled creatively . . . for the solution of intellectual problems.
> What an interesting finding![1]

The Greens go on to describe what creativity means on each of three different levels: physiological, psychological, and social. In physiological terms, creativity means physical healing and regeneration; in emotional terms, it means creating attitude changes that favor the establishment of inner harmony; in the mental sphere, it involves the synthesis of new ideas.

The Greens continue:

> The entrance, or key, to all these inner processes, [is] a particular state of consciousness in which the gap between conscious and unconscious processes is voluntarily narrowed, and temporarily eliminated when useful. When that self-regulated reverie is established, the body can apparently be programmed at will, and the instruc-

tions given will be carried out, emotional states can be dispassionately examined, accepted or rejected, or totally supplanted by others deemed more useful, and problems insoluble in the normal state of consciousness can be elegantly resolved.[2]

The state of consciousness the Greens refer to is not lucid dreaming but the hypnagogic or reverie state. Nevertheless, their conclusions would seem to apply even more practically to the lucid dreaming state, in which the conscious mind confronts the unconscious face to face.

The Healing Dream

Testifying to the emotional healing power of dreams, Goethe wrote, "There have been times when I have fallen asleep in tears; but in my dreams the most charming forms have come to cheer me, and I have risen fresh and joyful."[3]

The use of dreams for healing was widespread in the ancient world. The sick would sleep in temples of healing, seeking dreams that would cure or at least diagnose their illness and suggest a remedy. I have mentioned this as a reminder that healing through lucid dreaming is a partly new and partly old idea. But before continuing, we need first to clarify exactly what the terms "health" and "healing" mean.

According to popular conception, a major function served by sleep and dreams is rest and recuperation. As it happens, there is scientific evidence supporting Macbeth's conception of sleep as "chief nourisher in life's feast." For example, there is a positive correlation, across many species, between the amount of sleep and the need for restoration as measured by metabolic rate. Accordingly, for

humans, physical exercise leads to more sleep, especially
delta sleep, which in turn releases more growth hormone.
On the other hand, mental exercise or emotional stress appears to result in increases in REM sleep and in consequence, dreaming. Sleep, as a time of relative isolation
from environmental challenges, allows the person to re-
cover optimal health or the ability to respond adaptively.
The healing processes of sleep are holistic, taking place on
all levels of the human system. On higher psychological
levels, these healing functions are probably normally accomplished during the dreams of REM sleep. I say "normally" because due to maladaptive mental attitudes and
habits, dreams do not always accomplish their functions,
as can be seen in the case of nightmares, which we will
discuss later in the chapter.

Human beings are extremely complex, multilevel living systems. It is useful, although an oversimplification, to
distinguish three main levels of organization that make up
what we are: biological, psychological, and social (as was
mentioned earlier in relation to the Greens' research). These
reflect our partial identities as bodies, minds, and members
of society. Each of these levels affects every other level,
to a greater or lesser extent. For example, your blood sugar
level (biology) affects how good that plate of cookies looks
to you (psychology), and perhaps even whether you are
hungry enough to steal (sociology). On the other hand, the
degree to which you have accepted society's rules and
norms affects how guilty you feel if you do steal. So how
the cookies appear (psychology) depends on how hungry
you are (biology) as well as on who else is around (sociology). Because of this triple-level organization, we can
view humans as "biopsychosocial systems." Now, since
environmental challenges (such as the one mentioned
above) occur on all levels of the individual's biopsychosocial organization, from cellular to social, and since we
are speaking of the *whole* individual's responses, the con-

cepts of health and of healing we have developed here are holistic.

Health has been defined as "a state of optimal functioning with freedom from disease and abnormality." The domain over which this functioning ranges is life in all its complexities. In the most general terms, health can be conceived as a condition of adaptive responsiveness to the challenges of life. For responses to be "adaptive" requires at minimum that they resolve a situation in a way that is favorable and that does not disrupt the integrity, or wholeness, of the individual. Adaptive responses in some way also improve the individual's relationship to his or her environment. There are degrees of adaptiveness; the optimum is what we have defined as health.

By this definition, being healthy involves more than simply maintaining the status quo. On the contrary, when our familiar behaviors are inadequate to cope with a situation, a healthy response will include learning new, more adaptive behaviors. And when we learn new behaviors, we grow; having done so, we find ourselves better equipped than before to deal with the challenges of life.

Lucid dreaming bears a family resemblance to daydreaming, hypnagogic reverie, psychedelic drug states, hypnotic hallucinations, and other types of mental imagery. Since many members of this family have found gainful employ in therapeutic circles, it would seem reasonable to expect that lucid dreaming might also prove effective here.

According to doctors Dennis Jaffe and David Bresler, "Mental imagery mobilizes the latent, inner powers of the person, which have immense potential to aid in the healing process and in the promotion of health."[4] However it works, imagery is used in a great variety of psychotherapeutic approaches, ranging from psychoanalysis to behavior modification.

The efficacy of imagery is to a certain extent dependent upon its believability as reality, so it seems likely that healing imagery occurring in the lucid dream state could be particularly effective. This is because lucid dreams are not merely experienced as being very realistic and very vivid; without exaggeration we can say that lucid dreaming is *the most vivid* form of imagery likely to be experienced by normal individuals. Thus what happens in lucid dreams has an understandably powerful impact on the dreamer, both experientially and physically.

Hypnosis is a therapeutic imagery technique that could possibly be relevant to lucid dreaming. People experiencing hypnotic dreams while in deep trance relate experiences that have much in common with lucid dreams. Hypnotic dreamers are almost always at least partly lucid in their dreams, and in the deeper states they, like lucid dreamers, experience imagery as real, or almost as real, as real can be. Deeply hypnotized subjects are able to exert remarkable control over many of their physiological functions: inhibiting allergic reactions, stopping bleeding, and inducing anesthesia at will. Unfortunately, these dramatic responses are limited to the five or ten percent of the population capable of entering hypnosis very deeply, and this capability does not seem to be trainable. Lucid dreaming *is,* on the other hand, a learnable skill, and lucid dreams could hold the same potential for self-regulation as deep-trance hypnosis, yet be applicable to a much greater proportion of the population.

One of the most intriguing therapeutic applications of mental imagery is Carl Simonton's work with cancer patients. Dr. Simonton and his colleagues report that patients with advanced cancer who supplemented standard radiation and chemotherapy treatment with healing imagery survived, on the average, twice as long as expected by national averages. While caution seems appropriate in interpreting these results, they still suggest some very exciting possibilities. Given the direct connection between mind and body that we have demonstrated in our lucid dream experiments, it seems justifiable to hope that healing imagery during lucid dreaming might be even more effective.

The fact that our laboratory studies have revealed a high correlation between dream behavior and physiological responses presents a rare opportunity for developing an unusual degree of self-control of physiology that might prove useful for self-healing. You could conceivably carry out actions in your lucid dreams specifically designed to have whatever precise physiological consequences you may wish.

A frequently described part of the techniques commonly used by so-called "paranormal healers" consists in imagining the patient to be in a state of perfect health. Since while dreaming we generate body images in the form of our dream bodies, why shouldn't we be able to initiate self-healing processes during lucid dreams by consciously envisioning our dream bodies as perfectly healthy? Further, if our dream bodies do not appear in a state of perfect health, we can heal them symbolically in the same manner. We know from our investigations at Stanford that such things can be done. Here is a question for future lucid dream research to answer: if we heal the dream body, to what extent will we also heal the physical body?

The possibility of voluntary self-control of physiology during lucid dreaming is attractive for another reason. In general, an individual can only learn to control a physiological parameter (heart rate, brain waves, blood pressure, and so on) within the normal range of variation for a given state of consciousness. For instance, while awake, you can only deliberately alter the frequency and intensity of your brain waves within the normal limits of waking brain activity. You can increase or decrease the amount of alpha waves you produce, since they are associated with waking, but you cannot get your brain to produce delta waves as it does when you are deeply asleep.

Now, of all the normal states of consciousness an individual passes through every day and night, the state with the widest range of physiological variability is REM sleep. Lucid dreaming, which occurs in REM sleep, thus affords those interested in voluntary self-control the widest possible parameters in which to operate. A person with high blood pressure could probably lower his or her blood pressure with greater ease, and to a greater extent, in lucid REM sleep than in the waking state. How practical this will prove to be, and what long-term effects it might have, are open questions. But it is possible that lowered blood pressure during lucid dreaming could result in lowered blood pressure during subsequent wakefulness.

The other side of the hypothesis that positive dream imagery can foster health is that negative dream imagery can contribute to illness. Harold Levitan of McGill University has studied the dreams of psychosomatic patients. Their dreams typically involved injury to the body, and Dr. Levitan suggested that "the repetitive experience of consummated trauma contributes to the malfunctioning of the physiological systems, and therefore, to the production of illness."[5] This seems plausible enough. If we are willing to accept the possibility that dreams can cure, it seems we must also accept the possibility that they may harm.

Since health means increased wholeness, psychological growth often requires the reintegration of neglected or rejected aspects of the personality, and this can be consciously and deliberately achieved through the symbolic encounters of lucid dreaming. The content of a healing dream often takes the form of an integration or union of images. The self-image (or ego) is often unified with elements of what Jung called the "shadow." For simplicity, let us divide our personalities into two categories. On one side, we put all the characteristics we find agreeable and "good." These qualities are the aggregate of our self-representation or "ego." On the other side, we put all those traits and qualities we consider "bad" or dislike in ourselves, and consciously or unconsciously wish to deny. We disown them by projecting them on the mental image of an "other"—the "shadow." Note that the self-representation is incomplete, not whole: it leaves out the shadow. According to Jung, when the ego intentionally accepts aspects of the shadow, it moves toward wholeness and healthy psychological functioning.

The ability to act voluntarily according to ideals, rather than habits, allows the lucid dreamer consciously to accept, and thereby integrate, previously repressed aspects of the personality. It is the stones rejected by the builder of the ego that form the foundation of the new Self.

The importance of taking responsibility for even the "shadow" elements in one's own dreams is illustrated by the difficulties that plagued Frederik van Eeden's dream life. "In a perfect instance of the lucid dream," wrote van Eeden, "I float through immensely wide landscapes, with a clear blue, sunny sky, and a feeling of deep bliss and gratitude, which I feel impelled to express by eloquent words of thankfulness and piety."[6] But for some reason, van Eeden found that these pious lucid dreams were very frequently followed by what he called "demon-dreams," in which he was typically mocked, harassed, and attacked by what he supposed to be "intelligent beings of a very low moral order."[7]

Jung would have probably considered van Eeden's demon-dreams as examples of compensation, striving to correct the mental imbalance produced by his ego's sense of self-righteousness and inflated piety. Nietzsche would probably have responded more aphoristically: "If a tree grows up to heaven, its roots reach down to hell." In any case, for van Eeden, the apparent existence of these demonic holdovers from the Middle Ages was a source of considerable embarrassment—was it not, after all, the twentieth century? Nevertheless, as a dedicated explorer of inner space, he felt compelled to account for their presence in his dreams. It was awkward, but demons they were, without question. However, van Eeden could not bring himself to believe *his* mind was responsible for "all the horrors and errors of dream-life." Since it was impossible for *no one* to be responsible, it must be someone else—and thus van Eeden was forced to embrace the demon hypothesis. Because of this belief, he was never able to free himself from his demon-dreams, and his efforts to rid himself of them met resistance throughout his life.

Van Eeden is not the only lucid dreamer to have had problems with dream demons. Saint-Denys also met his share of "abominable monsters" in his dream explorations; how he regarded them provides an instructive contrast to van Eeden's attitude. At one time, the Marquis found himself plagued by a "dreadful" recurrent nightmare:

> I was not aware that I was dreaming, and imagined I was being pursued by abominable monsters. I was fleeing through an endless series of rooms. I had difficulty in opening the doors that divided them, and no sooner had I closed each door behind me than I heard it opened again by the hideous procession of monsters. They were uttering horrible cries as they tried to catch me, I felt they were gaining on me. I awoke with a start, panting and bathed in sweat.

The same nightmare, "with all its attendant terrors," recurred four times in the course of six weeks. But, "on the fourth occurrence of the nightmare," Saint-Denys wrote,

> Just as the monsters were about to start pursuing me

again, I suddenly became aware of my true situation. My desire to rid myself of these illusory terrors gave me the strength to overcome my fear. I did not flee, but instead, making a great effort of will, I put my back up against the wall, and determined to look the phantom monsters full in the face. This time I would make a deliberate study of them, and not just glance at them, as I had on previous occasions.

In spite of his lucidity, he "experienced a fairly violent emotional shock at first," explaining that "the appearance in dreams of something one has been dreading to see can still have a considerable effect on one's mind, even when one is forewarned against it." Nevertheless, the intrepid lucid dreamer continued,

I stared at my principal assailant. He bore some resemblance to one of those bristling and grimacing demons which are sculptured on cathedral porches. Academic curiosity soon overcame all my other emotions. I saw the fantastic monster halt a few paces from me, hissing and leaping about. Once I had mastered my fear his actions appeared merely burlesque. I noticed the claws on one of his hands, or paws, I should say. There were seven in all, each very precisely delineated. The monster's features were all precise and realistic: hair and eyebrows, what looked like a wound on his shoulder, and many other details. In fact, I would class this as one of the clearest images I had had in dreams. Perhaps this image was based on a memory of some Gothic bas-relief. Whether this was so or not, my imagination was certainly responsible for the movement and colour in the image. The result of concentrating my attention on this figure was that all his acolytes vanished, as if by magic. Soon the leading monster also began to slow down, lose precision, and take on a downy appearance. He finally changed into a sort of floating hide, which resembled the faded costumes used as street-signs by fancy-dress

shops at carnival-time. Some unremarkable scenes followed, and finally I woke up.[8]

And that was the end of Saint-Denys' nightmares.

The nearest thing I have had to a "demon-dream" was
the "riot in the classroom" lucid dream (quoted in Chapter
1) in which I successfully accepted and integrated one of
my demons—the repulsive ogre. It seems clear on several
levels that this was a healing dream. In the first place, the
initial conflict—an unhealthy condition of stress—was resolved positively. Also, the dream ego was able to accept
the barbarian as a part of itself, and thus move toward
wholeness. Finally, there is more direct evidence—the feeling of increased wholeness and well-being that I experienced upon awakening.

There are alternatives to this technique of intentional acceptance and assimilation. Another of my dreams provides
an example of a healing lucid dream that made use of symbolic transformation. I had just returned from a journey and
was carrying a bundle of bedding and clothes down the
street, when a taxi pulled up, blocking my way. Two men
in the taxi and one outside it threatened me with robbery
and violence. Somehow I realized I was dreaming, and
immediately attacked the three muggers, heaping them into
a formless pile and setting fire to them. Out of their ashes
I arranged for flowers to grow, and I awoke feeling filled
with vibrant energy.

In contrast to the receptive strategy I followed in the
classroom riot dream, I took an active approach in this
dream, using the purifying symbol of fire to transform the
negative image of the muggers into the positive image of
the flowers. The main justification I have for considering
this a healing dream was how good I felt after I awoke.
And the muggers? I somehow felt they were happier being
flowers!

The two lucid dreams I have just discussed illustrate an

important psychotherapeutic principle: it may not be necessary to interpret the dream in order to resolve personality conflicts. In many cases, these conflicts can be resolved symbolically in the dream itself. While the barbarian and the muggers might well have symbolically represented some hidden attitude, quality, or aspect of myself that I had been attempting to reject and deny admission to my "ego" or self-image, I was able to resolve them without even having to know what they represented. So, my acceptance or transformation of the dream characters represented a symbolic acceptance or transformation of whatever unidentified emotion, behavior, or role they stood for. Interpretation may cast an interesting sidelight on the matter, but it would seem to me, in these cases, to be an entirely optional one.

The same two dreams provide illustrations of another important guiding principle in the psychotherapeutic use of lucid dreaming. In both cases, I attributed healing qualities to the lucid dreams on the basis of how I felt upon awakening. I have found from experience that the feelings I am left with after a lucid dream reliably indicate my intuitive evaluation of my behavior in that dream. Please do not misunderstand me. I am *not* saying that "if it feels good, it *is* good." What I *am* saying is that "if it feels good *afterward,* it *was* good." This is the compass by which I have charted my personal explorations through the lucid-dream world. If I do something in a lucid dream that I feel good about later, I do it in future lucid dreams. If I feel bad about what I have done, I avoid that action in later lucid dreams. Following this policy, of course, leads to increasingly good feelings in my lucid dreams. And rather than recommending to my students any more particular course of action in their lucid dreams, I advise them to follow the same general path: "It's your dream. Try it and see how you feel afterward. If you listen to your own conscience, you need no other rule."

Nightmares and Anxiety Reduction

Nightmares, according to Freud, are the result of masochistic wish-fulfillment. The basis of this curious notion was Freud's unshakable conviction that every dream represented the fulfillment of a wish. "I do not know why the dream should not be as varied as thought during the waking state," wrote Freud, tongue in cheek. " . . . In one case it would be a fulfilled wish, in another a realized fear, or again a reflection persisting into sleep, an intention, or a piece of creative thought."[9] For his own part, Freud wrote, "I should have nothing against it. . . . There is only a trifling obstacle in the way of this more convenient conception of the dream; it does not happen to reflect reality."[10] If, for Freud, every dream was nothing but the fulfillment of a wish, the same must be true for nightmares: the victims of nightmares must *secretly wish* to be humiliated, tortured, or persecuted.

Since the mirror in which I see reality reflected is different from Freud's, I do not necessarily see every dream as the expression of a wish; nor do I view nightmares as masochistic wish-fulfillment, but rather as the unhappy result of unhealthy reactions. The anxiety experienced in nightmares can be seen as an indication of the failure of the dream process to function effectively. Anxiety arises when we encounter a fear-provoking situation against which our habitual patterns of behavior are useless. If a person experiences a recurring anxiety dream, what he or she obviously needs is a new approach for coping with the situation represented by the dream. This may not be easy to find, since the dream undoubtedly results from unresolved conflicts that the dreamer does not want to face in waking life. It may be difficult to fix the nightmare without fixing the personality that gave rise to it. But this qualification applies mainly to chronically maladjusted personalities. If you are a relatively normal person who has nightmares only occasionally, the prognosis is much more favorable. That is, provided you meet a certain requirement—being willing to take responsibility for your experience and, in particular, for your dreams. If you fulfill this condition, then an exceedingly powerful tool for coping with anxiety dreams is available to you: lucid dreaming.

To find out how lucidity aids the dreamer in working through anxiety-provoking situations, consider the following analogy. Let us compare the non-lucid dreamer to a small child terrified of the dark. The child really believes there are monsters there. The lucid dreamer would perhaps be an older child, still afraid of the dark yet no longer believing that there are really monsters out there. This older child might be afraid, but would know there was nothing to be afraid of, and could master the fear. Thus it is with the lucid dreamer. Biologically speaking, anxiety serves a special function. It results from the simultaneous occurrence of two conditions: one is fear in regard to some situation we find threatening; the other is an assessment that an unfavorable outcome is unavoidable. In other words, we experience anxiety when we are afraid of something, and have nothing in our repertoire of learned or habitual behaviors that will help us overcome or evade what we fear. Anxiety functions to prompt us to scan our situations more carefully and reevaluate possible courses of action in search of an overlooked solution—in short, to become more conscious. This is likely to be adaptive just because the conclusion that no habitual behavior will help calls for nonhabitual, intentional, or novel behavior.

So when we experience anxiety in our dreams, the most adaptive response would be to become lucid and face the situation in a creative manner. In fact, anxiety does seem to result fairly frequently in spontaneous lucidity, even in children. It may even be the case that our anxiety dreams would *always* become lucid, if we were taught about this response.

Regarding the treatment of childhood dream anxiety, Mary Arnold-Forster mentioned having helped children overcome nightmares with a touch of lucidity, and I can relate a similar experience myself. Once, when I was making long-distance small talk with my niece, I brought out my favorite hobby-horse and inquired, "How are your dreams lately?" Madeleina, then seven years old, burst out with the description of a fearful nightmare. She had dreamed that she had gone swimming, as she often did, in the local reservoir. But this time, she had been threatened and terrified by a little-girl-eating shark! I sympathized with her fear and added, matter of factly, "But of course you know there aren't *really* any sharks in Colorado." She replied, "Of course not!" So I continued, "Well, since you know there aren't really any sharks where you swim, if you ever see one there again, it would be because you were *dreaming*. And, of course, a dream shark can't really do you any harm. It's only frightening if you don't know that it's a dream. But once you *do* know that you're dreaming, you can do whatever you like—you could even make friends with the dream shark, if you wanted to! Why not give it a try?" Madeleina seemed intrigued and soon proved that she had bitten the bait. A week later, she telephoned to announce proudly, "Do you know what I did? *I rode on the back of the shark!*" Whether this approach to children's nightmares always produces such impressive results I have no way of knowing, but it is certainly worth exploring.

Is there any evidence that lucid dreaming in this manner leads to any lasting benefits? I believe there is, and my own earlier experiences fit this pattern. Anxiety appeared to lead to lucidity in thirty-six percent of my first year's lucid dreams (sixty percent during the first six months.) In contrast, by the second year, anxiety was present when I recognized that I was dreaming in only about nineteen percent of my lucid dreams. During the third year, anxiety appeared in only five percent, and in one percent or less in the following four years. I attribute the decrease in the number and proportion of anxiety dreams to my practice of resolving conflicts during lucid dreams. This reduction seems especially impressive in light of the fact that my life has become *much* more stressful and demanding in the latter years. If something weren't resolving the stress of my daily life, I would be experiencing waking anxiety with concomitant increases in dream anxiety. It may therefore be the case that lasting benefit comes from "responsible" lucid dreaming of the sort I have been practicing—facing and dealing directly with dream conflict and anxiety in lucid dreams can result in more adaptive behaviors while asleep and perhaps while awake. In regard to my lucid dreams, I believe there is a convincing argument that this is so. First, suppose it were not. Suppose, on the contrary, that facing my fears and loving my dream enemies was an ineffective—or worse, unhealthy—activity. If this were the case, I should have found that I was continuing to have as many or even more anxiety dreams than before. Even if my methods of so-called "self-integration" were merely harmless palliatives—putting, as it were, a bandage on the dream—still there would be no reason to expect improvement. Yet the fact is that my lucid dreams became significantly more anxiety-free from one year to the next. Obviously, I was doing *something* right.

Yet someone could reasonably object that I have merely learned not to become lucid during anxiety dreams. This is by no means a far-fetched objection; however, it fails to account for all the relevant facts. First of all, the dreamer is always supposed to awaken from the classical anxiety dream. According to Freud, the function of anxiety in a dream is to wake the dreamer whenever the going gets too rough. Thus we would not expect a dreamer to sleep through the worst of his nightmares. But in my case, as I explained earlier, I have learned to utilize anxiety itself as an *infallible* lucidity cue. In the past six years, I have not been awakened once from a dream by anxiety, as should have happened if I were having non-lucid nightmares. During this period, sufficient anxiety has always led to my awakening *in* my dream rather than from it, thereby affording me the opportunity to face my fears and resolve my conflicts.

This is a very important potential of lucid dreaming, since when we "escape" from a nightmare by awakening, we have not dealt with the problem of our fear or our frightening dream, but merely relieved the fear temporarily and repressed the fearful dream. Thus we are left with an unresolved conflict as well as negative and unhealthy feelings. On the other hand, staying with the nightmare and accepting its challenge, as lucidity makes possible, allows us to resolve the dream problem in a fashion that leaves us more healthy than before. So if, as I have suggested, healing was the original intent of the dream that became a nightmare, lucidity can aid the redemption of the dream gone wrong.

The flexibility and self-confidence that lucidity brings in its wake greatly enhances the dreamer's ability to master situations presented by dreams. I believe the habit of flexibility to be well worth developing in lucid dreams. In addition to being highly effective in the dream world, it is also generally applicable in the waking world. Indeed, it may at times be the only course of action open to you. In most situations, it would be unrealistic to expect other people to change in the ways you may want them to. You cannot always, or even often, get others to do what you want; you may not not even be able to prevent them from doing exactly what you *don't* want. Nonetheless, at every moment, whether dreaming or waking, you have the power to reframe the way you see the circumstances you find yourself in. You define your own experience. Who and how you want to be, how much and which part of yourselves you choose to bring to the situation you are confronted with: the choice is yours. Finally, if in spite of what I have said, you still think that it is external events that determine your outlook on life, reflect on the following couplet:

> Two men looked out prison bars;
> One saw mud, the other stars.

It is often not so obvious which outlook or course of action is best. Life often presents us with difficult decisions, and as it happens, lucidity may help us to choose wisely.

Decision Making

Of course, decision making is only a problem when there is uncertainty about the information involved. Otherwise, the optimal choice is clear-cut. So how might lucid dreams help you to make effective ("correct") decisions under conditions of uncertainty?

In order to answer this question, we must make a short digression and discuss two distinct varieties of knowledge. To take the lesser first, there is knowledge you know that you know, and can spell out explicitly, such as how to add a pair of numbers or what your name is. This is called explicit knowledge. The second kind of knowledge, sometimes called "tacit" knowledge, refers both to what you know how to do but can't spell out (how to walk or talk), and to what you know, but don't know that you know (say, the color of your first-grade teacher's eyes). This latter form of knowing has been demonstrated by recognition tests in which the individual thinks he or she is only guessing, but in fact does better than chance would allow. Of the two kinds of knowledge, the "tacit" variety is incontestably the more extensive: we know much more than we realize we know. As an aside, an argument can be made that in nonlinguistic animals, such as a cat or dog, *all* knowledge is tacit. There was also a time when, as a newborn infant, you couldn't put anything you knew into words. It is easy to see that linguistic, "explicit" knowledge develops within a context of tacit knowledge and is ultimately dependent upon it.

A similar distinction may apply to "thinking" and "intuition." But the important point for us to realize in relation to problem solving is that under conditions of uncertainty, the intuitive process—drawing as it does on the broader information bases of tacit knowledge—is likely to have a certain advantage over directed, conscious thinking. Here is where the connection with dreams comes in. Everyone has had the experience of dreaming about a person they've met only once, yet in a dream produced an amazing likeness of that person, much better than anything they could have done while awake, with pencil and paper or with words. The explanation for this phenomenon is tacit knowledge. In our dreams we can draw upon the entire store of our knowledge; we are no longer limited to the tiny portion that we have conscious access to. What I am proposing is that we take advantage of our broadest data base in lucid dreams to assist us in making optimal decisions.

Creative Problem Solving

As we saw in Chapter 1, there have been many instances of creative dreams in art and science. We will examine here two examples in sufficient detail to illustrate the role played by dreams in the creative process.

First, let us consider the case of the Russian chemist Dmitri Mendeleev, who had been working for years to discover a way of classifying the elements according to their atomic weights. One night in 1869, he fell into bed exhausted after devoting many long hours to the problem. Later that night, Mendeleev "saw in a dream a table where all the elements fell into place as required." Upon awakening, he immediately wrote down the table just as he remembered it. Amazingly, Mendeleev reported that "only in one place did a correction later seem necessary."[11] Thus was the periodic table of the elements, a fundamental discovery of modern physics, first brought forth.

Let us take another example of creative dreaming. Elias Howe, the inventor of the sewing machine, had worked on his idea for years before attaining success.

> . . . Howe had been making the needles of his early failures with a hole in the middle of the shank. His brain was busy with the invention day and night and even when he slept. One night he dreamed, so the story goes, that he was captured by a tribe of savages who took him a prisoner before their king.
>
> "Elias Howe," roared the monarch, "I command you on pain of death to finish this machine at once."
>
> Cold sweat poured down his brow, his hands shook with fear, his knees quaked. Try as he would, the inventor could not get the missing figure in the problem over which he had worked so long. All this was so real to him that he cried aloud. In the vision he saw himself surrounded by dark-skinned and painted warriors, who formed a hollow square about him and led him to the place of execution. Suddenly he noticed that near the heads of the spears which his guards carried, there were eye-shaped holes! He had solved the secret! What he needed was a needle with an eye

near the point! He awoke from his dream, sprang out of bed, and at once made a whittled model of the eye-pointed needle, with which he brought his experiments to a successful close.[12]

The experiences of Mendeleev and Howe provide excellent and dramatic illustrations of how creative problem solving works. The process is commonly divided into four stages. The first is *preparation,* a phase of intense activity in which information is gathered, various unsuccessful approaches tried, and preliminary attempts made to solve the problem. Mendeleev and Howe had already been through this stage during the years they devoted to their respective problems. The next phase, *incubation*, begins when the person gives up actively trying to solve the problem. For Howe and Mendeleev, this phase was clearly in effect when they fell asleep and forgot their obsessions. If would-be problem solvers have "done their homework"—prepared themselves correctly—they may be rewarded by the *illumination* phase, in which the solution suddenly arrives unbidden. For Mendeleev and Howe, this literally meant their dreams had come true. Finally comes the *verification* phase, in which the viability of the solution is tested. For the Russian, this merely meant readjusting the position of a single element; for the American, the modification of the needle design on his machine. As we have seen in these examples, the dream seems most suited to play a role in the illumination phase of the creative process.

Illumination is also the part of the creative process over which we have the least amount of control. Preparation is a matter of working, and "incubation" of *not* working; verification is a fairly straightforward process. The difficult question seems to be how to get through the third stage. Lucid dreaming may provide an answer, and thus facilitate creative problem solving. Since we have access in our dreams to much more knowledge than we know that we know, perhaps we gain access to this knowledge when we become lucid. In the past, we had no way to ensure when, or even if, a creative dream might occur. It is possible that through lucid dreaming the extraordinary but heretofore unreliable creativity of the dream state could at last be brought under our conscious control. There is a little evidence available supporting this intriguing possibility. I myself have used lucid dreams for creative purposes in two areas: once I was able to effectively edit and alter the final form of my Ph.D. dissertation; and on other occasions, I successfully used lucid dreams to generate images for etchings and other graphic artwork.

It doesn't seem to matter what the specific nature of the problem at hand is. Sometimes it is even a physical one, involving the improvement of motor skills. Jack Nicklaus saw the solution to a problematic golf swing in a dream. After winning a number of championships, he had found himself in an embarrassing slump, but when he regained his championship form seemingly overnight, a reporter asked him how he had done it. Nicklaus replied:

> I've been trying everything to find out what has been wrong. It was getting to the place where I figured a 76 was a pretty good round. But last Wednesday night I had a dream and it was about my golf swing. I was hitting them pretty good in the dream and all at once I realized I wasn't holding the club the way I've actually been holding it lately. I've been having trouble collapsing my right arm taking the club head away from the ball, but I was doing it perfectly in my sleep. So when I came to the course yesterday morning, I tried it the way I did in my dream and it worked. I shot a 68 yesterday and a 65 today and believe me it's a lot more fun this way. I feel kind of foolish admitting it, but it really happened in a dream. All I had to do was change my grip just a little.[13]

Nicklaus's confession that he felt foolish admitting it really happened in a dream suggests that there may be others with similar experiences who have never mentioned the source of their inspiration. In fact, it is a little surprising to read about a case reported by Ann Faraday in which a gynecologist "discovered how to tie a surgical knot deep in the pelvis with his left hand—while dreaming!"[14]

Among the many letters I have received from lucid dreamers, there are similar anecdotes of motor skills perfected in dreams. One lucid dreamer claims to have improved her hockey skating in a lucid dream. Tanya writes that she was a fair skater, but something inside told her she was holding back—that there was much more to skating than the way she was doing it. And then one night, in a lucid dream, she experienced "complete skating."

> In the dream I was in a rink with a number of other people. We were playing hockey and I was skating in the manner I always had, competent yet hesitant. At that moment I realized I was dreaming so I told myself to allow my higher knowledge to take over my consciousness. I surrendered to the quality of complete skating. Instantly there was no more fear, no more holding back and I was skating like a pro, feeling as free as a bird.
>
> The next time I went skating I decided to experiment and try this surrender technique. I brought back the quality of that dream experience into my wakened state. I remembered how I was feeling during the dream and so in the manner of an actor in a role, I "became" the complete skater once again. So I hit the ice . . . and my feet followed my heart. I was free on the ice. That occurred about two and one-half years ago. I've skated with that freedom ever since and this phenomenon has manifested itself in my rollerskating and skiing as well.

Closely related to these mental "practice" dreams are those that serve a rehearsal function.

Rehearsal

Most readers have probably experienced instances of the rehearsal function of dreams. By dreaming about a significant event in advance, we can try out various approaches, attitudes, and behaviors, perhaps arriving at a more effective course of action than we otherwise would have. We may also be forewarned, by the dream, of certain aspects in a future situation that we might otherwise not be conscious of.

One of my own lucid dreams offers a clear illustration of the utility of previewing "coming attractions." A month before the 1981 meeting of the APSS, I dreamed I was at the dream symposium in Hyannisport. I was scheduled to give my lecture after the next speaker, who was just being announced. My heart skipped a beat when *I* was introduced as the next speaker, because even at this late stage I was unprepared. I was given a brief reprieve when the sequencing mistake was corrected, and I hastily looked for my notes. My anxiety increased when I couldn't find them. But in a real emergency, I knew I could always talk from my slides. As I looked through them to organize what I was going to say, I found I had brought the wrong slides. These were my art slides, not my science ones! I was panic-stricken—but only for a moment, because almost at once I realized I was dreaming. My anxiety vanished instantly, and I literally leapt for joy, spinning above the audience and announcing, "This is a lucid dream!" When I awoke, I was very glad I had a lot more than ten minutes to prepare my lecture! Up until then, I had been planning to wait a few weeks before working on it, but my lucid dream motivated me to begin at once, and it turned out that the month I spent was just enough.

In 1975 Dr. William Dement confessed that his "wildest speculation [was] that REM sleep and dreaming might have evolved to be utilized in the future." He prophesied that "the eventual function of dreaming will be to allow man to experience the many alternatives of the future in the quasi-reality of the dream, and so make a more 'informed' choice." One of Dement's own dreams provides a striking illustration of how effective this can be:

> Some years ago I was a heavy cigarette smoker—up to two packs a day. Then one night I had an exceptionally vivid and realistic dream in which I had inoperable cancer of the lung. I remember as though it were yesterday looking at the ominous shadow in my chest X-ray and realizing that the entire right lung was infiltrated. The subsequent physical examination in which a colleague detected widespread metastases in my axillary and inguinal lymph nodes was equally vivid. Finally, I experienced the incredible anguish of knowing my life was soon to end, that I would never see my children grow up, and that none of this would have happened if I had quit cigarettes when I first learned of their carcinogenic potential. I will never forget the surprise, joy, and exquisite relief of waking up. I felt I was reborn. Needless to say, the experience was sufficient to induce an immediate cessation of my cigarette habit. This dream had both anticipated the problem, and solved it in a way that may be a dream's unique privilege.
>
> Only the dream can allow us to experience a future alternative as if it were real, and thereby to provide a supremely enlightened motivation to act upon this knowledge.[15]

It would be the rare smoker who would continue smoking after such a dream! One wonders how many victims of lung cancer could have been saved by a dream preview of that likely outcome of their nicotine habit. Yet one also wonders how many smokers would choose to have such a dream if it became possible for them to do so. How many of us have the courage to face the possibilities of the future?

The recent movie *Dreamscape* presents a striking variation of Dement's life-changing dream. In the film, the president of the United States is plagued by gruesomely vivid nightmares on the theme of nuclear war. His dreams portray the postwar horrors so realistically that he is personally motivated to go to Geneva to negotiate a disarmament treaty with the Soviet Union.

Today, humanity seems poised between the ostrich and the eagle. Regardless of whether we choose to face the fact or not, the ecological and political situation of this planet will force enormous changes upon humanity within the next century. Among the future alternatives are such extremes as have been termed "utopia or oblivion." Certainly the planetary situation is one of unprecedented complexity. And just as certainly, what is needed is unprecedented vision: both to avoid the abysmal catastrophe of nuclear war, and to find the path to true humanity. With the future to gain, and nothing to lose, we shouldn't fear to take our heads out of the sand and into the dream, for dreams may have much to contribute here (for example, novel and creative solutions not thought of during waking life). But before this dream comes true, we will certainly need to increase our understanding of dream control greatly.

Since lucidity seems to provide the key to dream control, it seems reasonable to expect that attaining the goal of intentional dreaming will require considerable advances in the art and science of lucid dreaming. It may even seem unlikely that such an advanced degree of proficiency in dream control is possible. We know of no Western lucid dreamer more experienced than Saint-Denys, and he wrote that he had "never managed to follow and master all the phases of a dream," adding that he had "never even attempted it." However, some things "impossible" to the West are—like the rising of the sun—natural to the East. And indeed, when seeking the source of light, we should look eastward.

According to William Blake, "The philosophy of the east taught the first principles of human perception . . ." Regarding dream control, the existence of a 1200-year-old Tibetan "inner guidebook," *The Yoga of the Dream State*, testifies to the accuracy of Blake's assertion. One of the practices it describes is referred to as "transmuting the dream content." With this technique, the yogi is able to visit any realm of creation he desires to see. Not that the yogis attached particular significance to this activity, but it does serve as a test of proficiency through which the aspirant must pass before continuing to the next stage on the path toward enlightenment. I shall say more about this in Chapter 10, but the relevance here is simply to support the possibility of highly developed dream control. This would also make feasible the fulfillment of another potential of lucid dreaming, to which we now turn.

Wish Fulfillment

"Pleasant dreams!" Thus we bid each other goodnight. According to various surveys, however, most dreams are unpleasant. That is, of course, *non*-lucid dreams. As for lucid dreams, the opposite is probably true. Many lucid dreamers have remarked on the emotionally rewarding nature of the experience, since the lucid dreamer is free to act out impulses that might be impossible in the waking state. For example, we might fly, meet anyone we like from all of history, or indulge in any sexual adventures.

Patricia Garfield, as we have seen, has gone so far as to propose that lucid dreams are intrinsically orgasmic. She further speculated that during lucid dreaming, the reward or "ecstatic" centers of the brain are stimulated. This speculation may actually have some basis in fact, since neurophysiologists[16] have found evidence linking the neural circuits of REM sleep with the brain's "reward" system. It may be that in certain circumstances, lucid dreaming facilitates activity in this latter system. Whatever the neurophysiological case, lucid dreams are pleasurable experiences.

The lucid dream state might one day prove to be an ideal vacation site—a sort of poor man's Tahiti, a *real* "Fantasy Island." Lucid dreams could provide matchless recreation for those of us needing to get away from it all.

At the same time, lucid dreaming could provide the handicapped and other disadvantaged people with the nearest thing to fulfilling their impossible dreams. Paralytics could walk again in their dreams, to say nothing of dancing and flying, and even experience emotionally fulfilling erotic fantasies. Thus sings the contralto in Handel's *Messiah:*

> Then shall the eyes of the blind be opened,
> and the ears of the deaf unstopped.
> Then shall the lame man leap as an hart,
> and the tongue of the dumb shall sing!

It is the possibility of dream control more than any other potential application of lucid dreaming that seems to have captured the fancy and imagination of many people. By way of illustration, a recent article on dream control concluded with these terms of unrestrained enthusiasm:

> The keys to unimaginable power are within the reach of the entire terrestrial population. I am certain that the next leap for our species will not be launched from the

factories of physical technology, but from the night flights of creative dreamers. Think about the possibilities. An erotic encounter of unprecedented intensity with the most desirable woman you can imagine. A visit to an island paradise where intelligent natives sing solutions to your everyday problems. In one night, you could philosophize with Aristotle, joke with W. C. Fields, talk investments with J. P. Morgan and work out on the horizontal bar with Nadia Comaneci . . . Even if only remotely possible, the idea of controlling our dreams seems well worth pursuing. Sensual pleasure, inner wisdom, emotional tranquillity, extrasensory perception or even a hot tip for the seventh at Belmont—whatever the quest, the answer may be waiting for you just beyond the borders of sleep.[17]

8

Dreaming: Function and Meaning

Why do we have dreams, and what do they mean? For centuries these questions have been the subject of a debate that has recently become a heated controversy. In one camp we have a number of prominent scientists who argue that we dream for *physiological* reasons alone, and that dreams are essentially mental nonsense devoid of psychological meaning: "a tale told by an idiot, full of sound and fury, signifying nothing." The idea that dreams are nothing more than "meaningless biology" sounds absurd and rather blasphemous to the opposing camp, a coalition of Freudians and other dream workers committed to the view that we dream for *psychological* reasons, and that dreams always contain important information about the self that can be extracted by various methods of interpretation. This camp takes its credo from the Talmudic aphorism: "An uninterpreted dream is like an unopened letter." A third camp occupies the middle ground, believing that both sides' extreme positions on the function and meaning of dreams are partly right and partly wrong. Proponents of the middle way argue that dreams may have both physiological and psychological determinants, and therefore can be either meaningful or meaningless, varying greatly in terms of psychological significance.

This middle position is where I find myself most comfortable. I agree with Sir Richard Burton that

> Truth is the shattered mirror strown in myriad bits;
> while each believes his little bit the whole to own.

Perhaps, however, we may be able to put together enough of the pieces to reflect the reality of dreams reasonably well. Although people have argued for centuries over whether dreams represent the addled children of an idle brain, the heaven-sent embodiment of wisdom, or something in between, we will confine our discussion to "scientific" theories of dreaming at least as modern as the twentieth century. So, then, let us start with Dr. Sigmund Freud.

The Interpretation of Dreams Revisited

If we are to understand Freud's view of the dream, we need to consider his concept of the dreamer's brain. We know today that the nervous system contains two types of nerve cells: excitatory and inhibitory. Both types discharge and transmit electrochemical impulses to other neurons. Both do this spontaneously, without any kind of outside stimuli, as well as when they themselves receive excitatory impulses from other cells. However, one critical difference between these two types of neurons is that the excitatory type transmits impulses to other neurons that cause increased nervous activity, or "excitation," in them. The inhibitory type sends messages to other neurons that cause decreased activity, or "inhibition." The human brain is an unimaginably complex network of intricate interconnections between billions of each type of neuron. Generally, the inhibitory neurons play a more important role in the higher functions of the brain.

Before developing his theory of dreams, Freud had studied neurobiology intensively. But in his time, only the process of excitation had been discovered; the process of inhibition was not yet known. Based on the assumption of a completely excitatory nervous system, Freud reasoned that nervous, or in his terms, "psychic," energy could therefore only be discharged by means of motor action. This meant that once you got a notion in your head, it was doomed to run around in there forever until you finally decided to do something about it. Or, alternatively, until *it* found a way to trick you into unconsciously expressing it in some unintended action—like the famous "Freudian slip."

This older view of the nervous system has been caricatured as a "cat on a hot tin roof" model, "with the persistent internal drives generating blasts of energy that keep the ego and conscious system in frenzied movement."[1] We know today that a nervous system of this sort, if it could exist at all, would erupt into uncontrolled seizure activity. However, given the state of knowledge at his time, Freud's view of the unconscious mind as a cauldron seething with socially unacceptable impulses and desires appears perfectly reasonable, and likewise, his theory of dreaming can readily be seen to follow from it.

Let us imagine what might have happened if you were somehow able to ask the master himself why you had a particular dream. Freud, we may speculate, might have answered something like this: "In the first place, we may be sure that something happened to you a day or two before

the dream and that this 'day residue'—as we call it—stirred
up one of the many repressed wishes that you try to keep
closeted away in your unconscious. But when you drifted
off to sleep with no other wish in your conscious mind than
to sleep, you withdrew your attention from the external
world, setting the stage for your day residue and associated
unconscious wish to step forward, demanding satisfaction.
All this requires the cooperation of the chief executive of
your conscious mind, the ego. But because your pair of
supplicants were not, let us say, 'dressed in a socially acceptable manner,' they were at first denied admission to
your conscious mind. And that was as it should be! It is
the special function of the gatekeeper to prevent unruly and
unacceptable impulses, memories, and thoughts from disturbing your ego's conscious mind. The gatekeeper, which
we psychoanalysts call the 'censor,' is able to do his job
with the help of a big stick we call 'repression,' by means
of which these impulses, memories, and thoughts that conflict with personal and social standards of behavior are banished from the conscious mind, along with the painful
emotions and memories associated with the conflict. Since
the repressed contents cannot be banished entirely, they
settle to the bottom of your unconscious mind, where they
simmer and seethe like a witches' cauldron.

"But now and then, by the power of association, the
events of the preceding day dredge up these repressed
wishes. Naturally, they seek a way to achieve even partial
fulfillment. That is what your day residue and repressed
wish were doing, knocking on the door of the ego. However, after the censor threw them out, the vulgar pair,
knowing nothing of manners, continued to clamor for admission, raising such a ruckus as to threaten your precious
sleep and thereby frustrate your ego's only conscious wish.
Fortunately, you were able to continue to sleep, thanks to
your dream doing its job. As we say, 'Dreams are the
guardians of sleep.' Across the border, in your unconscious

mind, a special process that we call 'dreamwork' constructed a disguise for your repressed wish, made out of 'acceptable' imagery linked to it by association. Thus, transformed into a superficially presentable image, your wish was able to get by the censor and find expression in your dreams. And that is why," Dr. Freud might well have concluded, "you had that dream, and please note that your dream killed two birds with one stone: while preserving your sleep, it also allowed the discharge of one of your repressed instinctual impulses. That all this was a good thing seems undeniable. I need hardly add that we regard it as axiomatic that the nervous system obeys the 'nirvana' principle, forever seeking the reduction of tension and the ultimate cessation of action."

In some ways, of course, this aspect of psychoanalysis has strong parallels with Buddhism and other Eastern doctrines. But that brings us no closer to answering the original question, and you might well ask again: "But what did my dream *mean?* Or was it just nonsense?" In that case, Freud would probably have explained, "Every dream has some hidden meaning; the manifest content of the disguised dream (the dream itself) was the result of the dreamwork's transformations of the undisguised wish (the latent content of the dream). Therefore, in order to interpret your dream, it should simply be necessary to reverse the process. Since the dream disguised the latent content with images closely associated with the original wish, we can uncover the hidden message by reasoning backward from the image through a process of interpretation known as 'free association.' " If you had dreamed, let us say, that you were locking a door, Freud would have asked you, "What is the first thing that comes into your mind in connection with the word 'lock?' " If you said, "Key," Freud would continue, "Key?" And perhaps you would reply, "Tree." This, as you can see, might go on forever, except that Freud would probably have interrupted the process at this point and drawn on his knowledge of dream symbolism (key in lock . . .) explaining that your dream expressed a wish to engage in sex!

In other words, Freud believed that the function of dreaming was to allow the discharge of repressed impulses in such a way as to preserve sleep, and that the instigating force causing dreams to occur was always an instinctual, unconscious wish. Freud considered these unconscious wishes to be predominantly sexual in nature. In his "Introductory lectures on psychoanalysis," he wrote: "Though the number of symbols is large, the number of subjects symbolized is not large. In dreams those pertaining to sexual life are the overwhelming majority. . . . They represent the most primitive ideas and interests imaginable."[2] In any case, insofar as the instigating force behind every dream was an unconscious wish—whether sexual or otherwise—it follows from Freudian theory that every dream contained meaningful messages in disguised form: the original wish or "dream thought." The fact that all dreams contained unacceptable and unpleasant wishes explained why dreams are so regularly and so easily forgotten. This was because, reasoned Freud, they were (deliberately) repressed: blacklisted by the ego and sent by the censor to the bottom of the swamp of the unconscious.

We know today, thanks to thirty years of dream research, that dreams are not instigated by wishes or other psychological forces, but by a periodic or automatic biological process: REM sleep. If dreams are not triggered by unconscious wishes, we can no longer assume that these wishes play any role in dreams at all, and, even worse for the Freudian concept of meaning, we can no longer automatically assume that every—or even any—dream has meaning! This is not all the news that recent neuroscience has for Freud, but let us save the bad news for the next section. The good news for Freud is this: every period of dreaming sleep is accompanied by sexual arousal, as indicated in males by erections and in females by increased vaginal blood flow. Had Freud lived to hear of this phenomenon, he would almost certainly have regarded it as a complete vindication of his belief that at the bottom of every, or almost every, dream was sex.

The Activation-Synthesis
Model of Dreaming

In 1977, doctors Allan Hobson and Robert McCarley of Harvard University presented a neurophysiological model of the dream process that seriously challenged Freud's theory on virtually every point. In a paper they published in the *American Journal of Psychiatry*, "The Brain and a Dream State Generator: An Activation-Synthesis Hypothesis of the Dream Process,"[3] they suggested that the occurrence of dreaming sleep is physiologically determined by a "dream state generator" located in the brain stem. This brain-stem system periodically triggers the dream state, with such predictable regularity that Hobson and McCarley were able to model the process mathematically a high degree of accuracy. During the REM periods produced when the dream-state generator is switched on, sensory input and motor output are blocked, and the forebrain (the cerebral cortex, the most advanced structure in the human brain) is activated and bombarded with partially random impulses generating sensory information within the system. The activated forebrain then synthesizes the dream out of the internally generated information, trying its best to make sense out of the nonsense it is being presented with.

"The primary motivating force for dreaming," emphasize Hobson and McCarley, "is not psychological but physiological since the time of occurrence and duration of

dreaming sleep are quite constant, suggesting a pre-programmed, neurally determined genesis.'' They see the major drive toward dreaming as not only automatic and periodic, but apparently metabolically determined; of course, this conception of the energetics of dreaming flatly contradicts the classical Freudian notion of conflict as the driving force for dreams.

As for the *''specific stimuli for the dream imagery,''* they continue, these appear to arise from the brain stem and not from cognitive areas of the cerebral cortex. ''These stimuli, whose generation appears to depend upon a largely random or reflex process, may provide spatially specific information which can be used in constructing dream imagery.'' Hobson and McCarley argue that the bizarre distortions in dream content attributed by Freudians to the disguising of unacceptable content probably have a simpler neurophysiological explanation: such bizarre features of dreams as the condensation of two or more characters into one, discontinuous scene shifts, and symbol formation may merely reflect the state of the dreaming brain.

''In other words,'' the Harvard neurophysiologists argue, ''the forebrain may be making the best of a bad job in producing even partially coherent dream imagery from the relatively noisy signals sent up to it from the brain stem. The dream process is thus seen as having its origin in sensorimotor systems, with little or no primary ideational, volitional, or emotional content. This concept is markedly different from that of the 'dream thoughts' or wishes seen by Freud as the primary stimulus for the dream.''

Hobson and McCarley view, *''the elaboration of the brain stem stimulus* by the perceptual, conceptual, and emotional structure of the forebrain'' as primarily synthetic and constructive, ''rather than a distorting one as Freud presumed.'' According to the Activation-Synthesis model, ''best fits to the relatively inchoate and incomplete data provided by the primary stimuli are called up from memory. . . . The brain, in the dreaming sleep state, is thus likened to a computer searching its addresses for key words. Rather than indicating the need for disguise, this fitting of . . . experiential data to [genetically programmed] stimuli is seen as the major basis of the 'bizarre' formal qualities of dream mentation.'' Scoring one more point against Freud, they add that ''there is, therefore, no need to postulate either a censor or an information degrading process working at the censor's behest.''

Hobson and McCarley see our usual poor ability to recall dreams as ''a state-dependent amnesia, since a carefully affected state change, to waking, may produce abundant recall even of highly charged dream material.'' So if you are rapidly awakened out of REM sleep, you are likely to remember dreams that you otherwise would be just as likely to forget. Hammering a final nail into the coffin containing Freud's theory of dreams, they write: ''There is no need to invoke repression to account for the forgetting of dreams.''

As was only to be expected, Hobson and McCarley's paper stimulated counterattacks from the psychoanalytic establishment, which responded that Freud's neurological models were in no way crucial to his psychological theories. In the view of Morton Reiser, chairman of the department of psychiatry at Yale University and a past president of the American Psychoanalytic Association,

''McCarley and Hobson overextend the implications of their work when they say it shows that dreams have no meaning. I agree with them that their work refutes Freud's idea that a dream is instigated by a disguised wish. Knowing what we do now of brain physiology, we can no longer say that. The wish may not cause the dream, but that does not mean that dreams do not disguise wishes. The brain activity that causes dreams offers a means whereby a conflicted wish can give rise to a particular dream. In other words, wishes exploit—but do not cause—dreams.[4]

The degree of controversy stimulated by the Hobson and McCarley paper was truly remarkable. An editorial in the *American Journal of Psychiatry* a year later stated that the Harvard paper "provoked more letters to the Editor than the *Journal* had ever received before." Unexpectedly, what seemed to be stirring so many people up was not Hobson and McCarley's treatment of Freud, but their treatment of the dream. The view that "dreams were after all merely the senseless, random accompaniment of the autonomous electrical activity of the sleeping Central Nervous System" did not sit well with many researchers, to say nothing of therapists and other workers accustomed to putting dreams to a variety of practical uses.

Anybody who has ever awakened from a dream exclaiming with delight, "What a *wonderful* plot that was!" will know from experience that, sometimes at least, dreams are much more coherent than Hobson-McCarley's model of "the forebrain making the best of a bad job" would suggest. In my view, the fact that dreams can be such superbly coherent and *entertaining* stories is an indication of the need to concede to the forebrain at least an occasional or partial degree of control during dreaming. How could we construct such extended dream plots if the higher brain centers were limited to mere improvisation with whatever unrelated props, people, and scenes the "noisy signals" from the brain stem happened to kick upstairs? The dream Hobson and McCarley seem to envision would be like "And now for something completely different!" every minute or two. The fact that we *are* able, at times, to produce dreams so wisely and elegantly constructed that they can and do serve as teaching stories suggests that mental functioning of a higher order must in some way be able to influence the lower-order functioning of the dream state generator.

The phenomenon of lucid dreaming suggests even more strongly the influence of the cerebral cortex on the construction of dreams. For if your dreams were nothing more than the results of your forebrain producing "partially coherent dream imagery from the relatively noisy signals sent up to it," how would you be able to exercise volitional choice in a lucid dream? How would you be able to carry out a previously planned dream action? How would you be able to deliberately decide, let us say, to open a door to see what you might find there?

Lucid dream reports abound with examples showing that dreamers *can* have their own feelings, intentions, and ideas. When dreamers realize that they are dreaming, they often experience a feeling of exhilaration. This feeling is more like a response to a higher-order perception than one to a random brain-stem stimulus. As for intentions and ideas, when dreamers attain lucidity they typically remember what they wanted to do in their next lucid dream; they can also remember ideas and principles of behavior—such as "face your fears," "seek a positive outcome," and "remember your mission." Our oneironauts routinely make use of this last principle when sleeping in the laboratory.

Finally, if all the eye movements of REM sleep are randomly generated by a madman in the brain stem, how are lucid dreamers able to voluntarily execute eye-movement signals in accordance with pre-sleep agreements? Of course, the answer to all of these rhetorical questions is that the Hobson-McCarley hypothesis *cannot* be the whole story. I believe Hobson and McCarley are right about much of what they say about *physiological* determinants of the form of dreams; it is evident that dreams also have *psychological* determinants, and therefore any satisfactory theory of dream content ought to include both. It also ought to explain why and under what conditions dreams are sometimes coherent, brilliantly witty narratives, and under other conditions, incoherent ravings. And why in some dreams are we deluded and in others lucid? Why are some dreams profoundly meaningful and others pointless nonsense?

As for meaning and nonsense, the Activation-Synthesis model of dreaming seems to completely disregard the possibility that dreams could have any intrinsic or even interesting meaning whatsoever. Given this model of the forebrain struggling with random signals, the most we could reasonably expect would be what computer specialists term "GIGO," an acronym for "Garbage in, garbage out." Hobson, at least, seems to say as much in a recent interview: "Dreams are like a Rorschach inkblot. They are ambiguous stimuli which can be interpreted any way a therapist is predisposed to. But their meaning is in the eye of the beholder—not in the dream itself."[5] I can hear it now: A psychiatrist asks a patient, "What does this dream make you think of?" And the patient replies: "An inkblot!"

Among psychophysiologically minded dream researchers, a major criticism of the Activation-Synthesis model was that it was essentially a one-way street, allowing traffic to proceed only upward from brainstem to forebrain—from lower mental function to higher mental function. But the way the brain is actually put together would require a two-way street as a model, allowing forebrain control of brainstem activation, and therefore allowing higher cortical functions such as thinking and deliberate action to influence the dream. This is the same criticism I have just made regarding the inability of the Hobson and McCarley model to deal with lucid dreaming.

Some sleep and dream researchers argued that the Activation-Synthesis model missed the central question about dreaming altogether. According to Dr. Milton Kramer of the University of Cincinnati, Hobson and McCarley's approach was "not central to the functional problems of dreaming. When it comes to dreams, two things are important—meaning and function. Do dreams enlighten us about ourselves? Will they make us smarter, change our

personality, change our mood, solve our problems, have
an application to our daily lives?" Kramer concluded that
"I think the essence of dreams is psychological. It's all
very well to find in dreams that a person is walking. The
important questions are, 'Where is he walking? Why is he
walking there?' Those are the continuing mysteries of
dreams and that is what we want to know."[6]

So how does the Activation-Synthesis model measure up
if we use Kramer's two criteria, meaning and function? As
to the meaning of dreams, in Hobson and McCarley's
model there is none. Regarding function, Hobson has offered a possible function of the dream state:

> A crude analogy to computers helps to make a point
> even if it may violate the reality of brain function: Every
> information processing machine has both hardware and
> software components. To create a nervous system, the
> genetic code must program both a structural blueprint
> and a set of operating instructions. To maintain the neu-
> rons it would make sense to utilize a standard set of
> operating instructions to activate and test the system at
> regular intervals.
>
> From an intuitive point of view, it is appealing to
> consider REM sleep as the expression of a basic activity
> program for the developing CNS that would ensure the
> functional competence of neurons, circuits, and conn-
> plex activity patterns before the organism was called
> upon to use them. It would be particularly important for
> such a system to have a high degree of reliability in
> both time and in space. These features are to be found
> in the periodicity and duration constancy of REM and
> in the stereotyped nature of the activity.[7]

Elsewhere, he elaborates:

> I believe that dreaming is the (sometimes outward) sign
> of a genetically determined, functionally dynamic blue-
> print of the brain designed *to construct* and *to test* the

brain circuits that underlie our behavior—including cognition and meaning attribution. I also believe that this test program is essential to normal brain-mind functioning but that you don't have to remember its products to reap its benefits.[8]

Dreaming to Forget?

In a paper published in 1983 in the British journal *Nature*, Nobel laureate Francis Crick (one of the team that cracked the genetic code and unraveled the mystery of DNA) and his co-author Graeme Mitchison proposed that the function of dream sleep

> is to remove certain undesirable modes of interaction in networks of cells in the cerebral cortex. We postulate that this is done in REM sleep by a reverse learning mechanism, so that the trace in the brain of the unconscious dream is weakened, rather than strengthened by the dream.[9]

That, in a nutshell, is their "reverse-learning" theory of dreaming.

Crick and Mitchison's theory is derived from two basic hypotheses. The first is that the cerebral cortex, as a completely interconnected network of neurons, "is likely to be subject to unwanted or 'parasitic' modes of behavior, which arise as it is disturbed either by the growth of the brain or by the modifications produced by experience."

Their second hypothesis is even more tenuous than the first: *if* these 'parasitic' modes of neuronal activity do in fact exist, they might be "detected and suppressed by a special mechanism" hypothetically operating during REM sleep. This mechanism is described as having "the character of an active process which is, loosely speaking, the opposite of learning." Crick and Mitchison call this hypothetical process "reverse learning," or "unlearning," and explain that it "is not the same as normal forgetting," and "without it we believe that the mammalian cortex could not perform so well."

The mechanism Crick and Mitchison propose, drawing on the Hobson-McCarley conception of the neurophysiology of dreaming,

> is based on the more or less random stimulation of the forebrain by the brain stem that will tend to excite the inappropriate modes of brain activity . . . especially those which are too prone to be set by random noise rather than by highly structured specific signals. We further postulate a reverse learning mechanism which will modify the cortex . . . in such a way that this particular activity is less likely in the future. . . . Put more loosely, we suggest that in REM sleep we unlearn our unconscious dreams. 'We dream in order to forget.'

To reiterate: what they are suggesting is that everything that happens in any of your dreams is being actively unlearned by your brain. That is why you are dreaming about it—merely "in order to forget it."

What exactly does this mean? According to the reverse-learning theory, when we *remember* our dreams we are relearning exactly what we were trying to unlearn! This would seem to represent at least a partial failure of the mechanism, and "one might wonder what effects its failure might have." Crick and Mitchison suggest that complete failure (remembering *all* of one's dreams) might lead to "grave disturbances—a state of almost perpetual obsession or spurious, hallucinatory associations . . ." A partial failure (remembering several dreams a night) "should produce unwanted responses to random noise, perhaps as hallucinations, delusions, and obsessions, and produce a state not unlike some schizophrenias."

Crick and Mitchison seem to suggest that it would be

better for all of us to learn to forget our dreams. "In this model," they write, "attempting to remember one's dreams should perhaps not be encouraged, because such remembering may help to retain patterns of thought which are better forgotten. These are the very patterns the organism was attempting to damp down."

Certainly, if the reverse-learning model were followed to its logical conclusion, it would seem to call for the end of all psychological analysis of dreams, all attempts at remembering and interpreting them—in fact, the complete shutdown of the dreamwork industry. Fortunately, it appears there is absolutely no direct evidence for "unlearning" during REM. In fact, there doesn't even appear to be any evidence for "unlearning" of any kind in *any* state, in *any* living organism, anywhere. "Unlearning" as it now exists is only a hypothetical concept, perhaps of some relevance to computers, but there is no proof that it has any application to human beings. In fact, as Crick and Mitchison admit, "A direct test of our postulated reverse learning mechanism seems extremely difficult."[10]

There is, in short, no convincing argument for this theory. It just *might* be true or partially true, but until direct evidence supporting it is brought forward, it must be viewed as an unlikely possibility. Even if there were some substance to reverse-learning theory, Crick and Mitchison's conclusions about the desirability of dream recall are not necessarily correct. On the contrary, the strongest argument against the theory may be the catastrophic effects they predict from even a partial failure of the reverse-learning mechanism. Certainly, people who habitually remember their dreams do not seem any more prone to "hallucinations, delusions, and obsessions" than people who habitually forget their dreams. Similarly, if the unlearning theory were true, dream deprivation would interfere with the reverse-learning process, producing disastrous results. However, people have been deprived

of REM sleep for many nights—in some cases years—
without showing any signs of mental breakdown. So, for
any of you dreamers concerned about whether dream recall causes brain damage, I would suggest that there is
little reason to worry!

The Functions of Dreaming and the Advantages of Consciousness

Let us return to the question with which we began this
chapter: "Why do we dream?" Though we have considered only a few answers here, there are many more that
could be, and have been, proposed. But we can justifiably
rule out in advance any theory that does not make as much
sense when applied to the dreams of a tree shrew or a whale
as to the dreams of a hairless, speaking primate—meaning
us! Whatever the explanation for dreaming may be, we
must dream for the same reasons all mammals have
dreamed for more than a hundred million years. So, the
question is, why do all mammals dream? Because all mammals have REM sleep. Since humans are mammals, the
biologically correct answer to the question "Why do we
dream?" is: "For the same reason any mammal does—
because we have REM sleep." Yet while technically correct, this answer is not completely satisfactory, for it merely
leads to the question: Why do all mammals have REM
sleep?

This is a question for evolutionary biology. According
to the available evidence, it seems that active or REM sleep
evolved about 130 million years ago, when early mammals
gave up laying eggs and began to give birth viviparously
(offspring born live, not hatched). Non-REM or quiet sleep,
on the other hand, seems to have arisen some 50 million

years earlier, when warm-blooded mammals first evolved from their cold-blooded reptilian ancestors.

The evolution of sleep, and later of dreaming, was far too widespread and behaviorally significant to have occurred by accident, and thus presumably came about through the mechanism that Darwin made famous: natural selection. The idea is that only those genetic variations which provide the organism with some survival advantage are selected by evolution. Due to genetic variability, a wide range of characteristics is exhibited at any one time in the population of every species. Some of these characteristics, however, will be more favorable than others in a given environment. This increases the probability that individuals with a favorable variation will live long enough to reproduce, passing on their genes to progeny who in turn will be likely to survive long enough to replicate, and so on. If an inherited trait offers a great enough advantage, before long all members of a given species will possess it and carry the genes to pass it on. Since this must have been the case with sleep and dreaming, we can assume that they serve some adaptive (i.e., useful) function or functions.

All animals cycle once a day through a circadian (approximately twenty-four-hour-long) rhythm of rest and activity. Some animals, such as owls and mice, rest in daylight and are active at night; others, such as humans, usually act in the light and rest in the dark. Sleep tends to occur during the rest phase of the twenty-four-hour cycle. Thus, one of the primary adaptive advantages or functions of sleep is to enforce immobility on the animal during the rest phase of the circadian cycle, both to ensure its resting and to keep it safely in its nest, burrow, or home. Mother Nature's original idea of sleep (probably also familiar to your own mother) was to keep you off the streets after dark, and out of trouble.

If you recall that NREM sleep arose at the same time

mammals evolved from reptiles, you will have a hint about sleep's additional function. Reptiles were dependent upon external energy sources (primarily the sun) to maintain a high enough body temperature to allow them to undertake the business of living (principally feeding, fleeing, and breeding). Although reptiles enjoy a lifelong free-energy subsidy from the sun, it wasn't always at their disposal—for example, at night, when they might have an urgent need to escape from some hungry nocturnal predator. Warm-blooded mammals, on the other hand, were no longer completely at the mercy of the weather and the time of day—they maintained their own constant internal temperatures. The cost, however, was great: being warm-blooded took much more energy than being cold-blooded. Their inner fires were fueled with food, which had to be caught—at no small energy cost to the mammal. The need of warm-blooded mammals to economize energy therefore made energy conservation an adaptive survival trait.

To see how effectively sleep accomplishes this function, consider the case of two little mammals with high metabolic rates, the shrew and the bat. The shrew sleeps very little and has a life expectancy of no more than two years. The bat, in contrast, sleeps twenty hours a day and as a result can expect to live as long as eighteen years! If we convert these lifetimes into waking years, the bat is still ahead, with three years of active life compared to the shrew's two. There seems to be no doubt that sleep serves an energy-conservation function, keeping warm-blooded, fast-moving creatures from burning out too fast. This suggests there is more truth than fiction to the old aphorism about the importance of getting a good night's sleep!

All right, you might say, so that's why we have quiet sleep, but why did active sleep evolve, and with it, dreaming? Certainly there must have been very good reasons for it, since this state has many disadvantages. For one, your brain uses much more energy during dreaming than it does while awake or in quiet sleep. For another, the body is paralyzed during REM sleep, significantly increasing the sleeper's vulnerability. In fact, the amount of dreaming sleep for a given species is directly proportional to its degree of safety from predators; the more dangerous life is, the less a species can *afford* to dream.

Given these drawbacks, active sleep must have offered particularly useful advantages to the mammals of 130 million years ago. We can guess one advantage, if we remember that this was the point in evolutionary history when mammalian mothers gave up laying eggs in favor of bearing live young. What advantages might active sleep have offered our ancestral mothers? The answer can be seen, I think, if you recall that egg-hatched lizards and birds break out of their shells sufficiently developed to survive on their own if necessary. Viviparous offspring—of which the human baby provides an unexcelled example—are less developed at birth and often completely helpless. Viviparous infants have to go through a great deal of learning and development, especially of the brain, in the first few weeks, months, and years of life.

In contrast to the hour and a half an adult spends in REM sleep each night, a newborn baby, who sleeps sixteen to eighteen hours a day, is likely to spend fifty percent of this time dreaming—as much as nine hours a day. The amount and proportion of REM sleep decreases throughout life, suggesting to several dream researchers[11] that REM sleep may play an important role in the development of the infant brain, providing an internal source of intense stimulation that would facilitate the maturation of the nervous system as well as help prepare the child for the limitless world of stimulation it will soon have to face.

The foremost French sleep researcher, Michel Jouvet of the University of Lyon, has proposed a similar function for active sleep: dreaming permits the testing and practicing of genetically programmed (i.e., instinctual) behaviors without the consequences of overt motor responses—thanks to the paralysis of this sleep state. So the next time you see newborns smiling in their sleep, don't be surprised if they turn out to be practicing their perfect smiles to charm a heart they are yet to meet!

Well, then, we know why babies dream. But if that were all there is to it, why wouldn't REM sleep completely disappear by adulthood? It might, except that there *does* seem to be something more to it, providing adults with a good reason to continue to dream. The reason is this: active sleep has indeed been found to be intimately involved with learning and memory.

The evidence connecting the dream state with learning and memory is of two kinds. The most direct evidence is an extensive body of research indicating that learning tasks requiring significant concentration or the acquisition of unfamiliar skills is followed by increased REM sleep. The second type of evidence is less direct but still quite convincing: many studies have shown that memory for certain types of learning is impaired by subsequent REM deprivation. Psychologists distinguish two varieties of learning: *prepared* and *unprepared*. Prepared learning is easily and quickly acquired, while unprepared learning is difficult and only slowly mastered, with great effort. According to Boston psychiatrists Dr. Ramon Greenberg and Dr. Chester Pearlman, it is only unprepared learning that is REM-dependent. In one of their experiments, rats easily learned that cheese was located behind one of two doors—and an electric shock behind the other. This is called "simple position" learning, and most animals are well equipped for it. If, on the other hand, the positions of reward and punishment are reversed on successive trials, most animals find it difficult (or impossible) to learn where to expect what. In other words, for rats, "successive position reversal" is an instance of unprepared learning.

After Greenberg and Pearlman subjected the rats to these

two varieties of task, they deprived them of REM sleep and re-tested them for learning. The results were that while simple position learning was unimpaired by REM deprivation, successive position reversal was "markedly" impaired. "This finding is noteworthy," Greenberg and Pearlman remarked, "because successive position reversal is a task which clearly distinguishes the learning capacities of species with REM sleep (mammals) from those without it (fish)." The implication is that REM sleep makes more complex learning possible.

Greenberg and Pearlman conclude that dreaming sleep "appears in species that show increasing abilities to assimilate unusual information into the nervous system." They suggest that the evolutionary development of the dream state "has made possible the increasingly flexible use of information in the mammalian family. That this process occurs during sleep seems to fit with current thinking about programming and reprogramming of information processing systems. Thus, several authors have pointed out the advantage of a separate mechanism for reprogramming the brain in order to avoid interference with ongoing functions."[12]

One of these authors is the late Christopher Evans, whose computer-analogy theory of dreams is presented in his book *Landscapes of the Night: How and Why We Dream*. Dr. Evans, an English psychologist with an abiding interest in computers, proposed that dreaming is the brain-computer's "off-line" time—when the mind is assimilating the experiences of the day and at the same time updating its programs.

Not only is dreaming associated with learning and memory, but it also appears to play a somewhat broader role in the processing of information in the nervous system, including coping with traumatic experiences[13] and emotional adjustment. The dream state has been proposed as a restorative for mental functioning; according to Professor

Ernest Hartmann, REM sleep helps us adapt to our environments by improving our mood, memory, and other cognitive functions through restoring certain neurochemicals that are depleted in the course of waking mental activity.

Dreaming sleep has also been shown to play a general role in reducing brain excitability. It can have a favorable effect on our moods—making us, for example, less irritable. Janet Dallet, in a dissertation, has reviewed a number of theories of dream function, concluding that "contemporary theories tend to focus on the function of environmental mastery, viewed from one of three perspectives: (a) problem solving, (b) information processing, or (c) ego consolidation."[15]

Finally, psychologist Ernest Rossi has attributed a developmental function to dreams:

> In dreams we witness something more than mere wishes; we experience dramas reflecting our psychological state and the process of change taking place in it. Dreams are a laboratory for experimenting with changes in our psychic life. . . . This constructive or synthetic approach to dreams can be clearly stated: *Dreaming is an endogenous process of psychological growth, change and transformation.*[15]

It might be said that the diverse theories of dream function are all partly right and all partly wrong: right insofar as they say what *a* function of dreaming is, and wrong when they say what *the* function of dreaming is. The situation is analogous to the traditional tale of the blind men and the elephant. In this story, the blind men each seek to discover—by means of touch alone—the nature of an elephant. Each believes he knows, from the part he has grasped, the true nature of the whole. For the blind man who grasped it by the tail, the elephant was like a rope;

like a rug for the one who grasped its ear; like a pillar for the one who grasped its leg; and so on. In a similar manner, the proponents of various dream theories have each grasped not the whole, as they thought, but a part of the function of dreams. Freud, for example, in surveying the many opinions about dreams, judged almost all of the previous views to have missed the forest for the trees. He considered his own theory, which posited sex as the basis of all dream content, a "view from the heights." But—as it is perhaps apparent today—Freud himself mistook a wood for the world. Or, as the irreverent have put it, he seems to have grasped the elephant by the balls. Things could be worse, though, for others seem to have grasped the elephant by the feathers!

Putting aside, for the moment, the question of the special functions of dreaming, let us ask what is the most basic or general function that dreaming is likely to serve. Since dreaming is an activity of the brain, we must first ask what function brain activity serves. And since the most general biological purpose of living organisms is survival, this must also be the most general purpose of brain activity. The brain fosters survival by regulating the organism's transactions with the world and with itself. The latter transactions might perhaps be best achieved in the dream state, when sensory information from the external world is at its minimum.

As organisms proceed up the evolutionary ladder, new forms of cognition and corresponding actions emerge. The four major varieties of action are reflexive, instinctive, habitual, and intentional, in ascending order. Behaviors lower on the evolutionary scale are relatively fixed and automatic, while behaviors higher on the scale are more flexible. Automatic behaviors are best if the situation they are designed for is relatively invariable. For example, since we must breathe every minute of our lives, this is very efficiently accomplished by a reflexive mechanism. Likewise, instinctive action is effective as long as the environment we are in is not too different from the one our ancestors lived in. Habit, too, is useful if the environment doesn't change too much. But intentional or deliberate action has evolved in order to handle environmental changes that our habitual behavior is inadequate to cope with. The highest level of cognition, which allows for intentional action, is usually referred to as reflective consciousness. It is the same cognitive function that we call lucidity when speaking in the context of dreaming.

Reflective consciousness offers the advantage of flexible and creative action in the dream state as well as in the waking state. More specifically, consciousness allows dreamers to detach themselves from the situation they are in, and reflect on possible alternative modes of action. Lucid dreamers are thus able to act *reflectively,* instead of merely *reflexively.* The important thing for lucid dreamers is their freedom from the compulsion of habit; they are capable of deliberate action in accordance with their ideals, and are able to respond creatively to the dream content. Seen in this light, lucid dreaming does not at all appear as a mere abnormality or meaningless curiosity; rather, it represents a highly adaptive function, the most advanced product of millions of years of biological evolution.

The Meaning of Dreaming

Since the evidence indicates that dreaming serves important biological functions, dreaming cannot be "meaningless biology." On the contrary, dreams are, at very least, *meaningful* biology. But does this mean that dreams must be meaningful psychology? I think the answer is "Not necessarily." If you ask, "What do dreams mean?" the answer will depend upon just exactly what you mean by "meaning." But perhaps we can agree that "meaning" refers to placing anything—in this case, a dream—in some explanatory context or other. Please note, however, that explanatory contexts vary widely from person to person. For some, interpretation or translation will seem most appropriate, under the assumption that dreams are messages to ourselves. Others will seek mechanistic explanations in a physiological or psychological context; still others will be inclined to treat the dream on its own terms, as it relates to itself. Which approach is right? Or, rather, which is right for which dream?

Freud assumed that the events occurring in dreams (lucid or otherwise) were by their very nature symbolic of unconscious motives. This assumption, although undoubtedly correct in certain circumstances, is equally misleading in others. Many dream interpreters would like to believe that every element of every dream is equally subject to symbolic interpretation, or that "All dreams are equal." This is an understandable belief, for dream interpreters could not expect to stay in business for very long if they were to say of a dream presented for analysis: "This dream is meaningless," or even, "not very interesting." Dreamers meeting with such responses would be inclined to take their dreams elsewhere, until they found someone more willing to tell them what their dreams "really" meant. Also, it is a sensible working hypothesis, when presented with a dream for interpretation, to assume that it does have meaning, or at least that part of it does.

In the case of psychotherapists and their clients, the relevant kind of meaning assumed and sought is psychological. However, the assumption that every dream contains significant psychological information has yet to be subjected to rigorous testing. To me, asserting that every dream is equally informative—psychologically or otherwise—is like supposing that every sentence you say is equally interesting, coherent, or profound!

There is a contrary view of dreams, the "existential"

view, which treats dreams as *lived* experiences composed of imagined interactions and elements that could be symbolic, literal, or somewhere in between. Flying, for instance, could be the symbolic expression of any number of unconscious desires, such as the wish to transcend all limitation, or—as Freud would suggest—the wish to engage in sexual activity. In another case, flying might simply be the most convenient mode of travel available to the dreamer.

With these considerations in mind, we would probably be wiser to leave the degree of symbolic significance attributed to a dream event as an *empirical* rather than an *axiomatic* matter—as something to test rather than to assume. It seems safe to conclude that an interpretation is valid only if it impresses the dreamer as having sufficient explanatory power for his dream, or if it is otherwise supported by compelling evidence.

It is important to realize that just because a particular dream can *sometimes* be interpreted in symbolic terms doesn't mean it was intended as a communication in the first place. If dreams are important messages to ourselves—as suggested by the proverb "An uninterpreted dream is like an unopened letter"—then why do we throw most of them away? This is surely what we do when we forget our dreams, and we forget the great majority of them. The "letter-to-yourself" theory of dreams is in even worse trouble when we remember the mammalian origins of dreaming. Consider the family dog: of the tens of thousands of dreams Fido will dream in his lifetime, how many are likely to be interpreted? By Fido, none at all! By his owners, perhaps a few. But if humans are the only mammals equipped with the linguistic skills to use symbolic language, what purpose could dreaming serve for the thousands of species of non-human dreamers? And if dreaming served no purpose to our ancestors, how could it ever have evolved?

I think the answer is clear: dreaming must serve purposes other than talking-to-ourselves; moreover, these purposes must be achievable without requiring dreams to be remembered, to say nothing of interpreted. In fact, there is a good reason why remembering dreams might be maladaptive for all non-linguistic species, including our ancestors. To see why, consider how we are able to distinguish memories of dreamed events from those that actually occurred. It is something we have *learned* to do, thanks to language. Remember Piaget's account of the child's development of the concept *dream*. When, as children, we remembered our earliest dreams, we assumed that they had "actually" happened, just like everything else. After enough repetitions of our parents' telling us that some of our experiences were "only dreams," we learned to distinguish memories of inner dream events from memories of external physical events. But how would we ever have been able to untangle the two realities without the help of other people telling us which was which?

Animals have no way to tell each other how to distinguish dreams from reality. Imagine your pet cat living on the other side of a tall fence that protects it from a vicious dog. Suppose your cat were to dream that the wicked dog was dead, and replaced by a family of mice. What would happen if the cat were to remember this dream when it awoke? Not knowing it was a dream, it would probably hungrily jump over the fence, expecting to find a meal. But instead, it would find *itself* a meal—for the dog!

Thus, dream recall would seem to be a bad thing for cats, dogs, and all the rest of the mammalian dreamers except humans. This could explain why dreams are difficult to recall. They may be so, according to this view, because of natural selection. We and our ancestors might have been protected from dangerous confusion by the evolution of mechanisms that made forgetting dreams the normal course of affairs. But if the theory I have proposed for why dreams are difficult to recall is correct, then—contrary to Crick and Mitchison—remembering dreams should do humans no harm, precisely because we can tell the difference between dreaming and waking experiences.

In conclusion, I would suggest that the dream is not so much a communication as a creation. In essence, dreaming is more like world-making than like letter-writing. And if, as we have seen, an uninterpreted dream *isn't* like an unopened letter, then what *is* it like? Having demolished a popular proverb, let us replace it with another that seems to come closer to doing the dream justice: "An uninterpreted dream is like an uninterpreted poem."

If I am right, dreams have much more in common with poems than they do with letters. The word *poem* is derived from a Greek verb meaning *to create,* and I have already argued that the essence of dreaming is closer to creation than to communication. Are all poems equally worth interpreting? Are all poems equally coherent, effective, or beautiful? If you wrote a dozen poems a night every night of your life, what do you suppose you would find among your several hundred thousand poems? All masterpieces? Not likely. All trash? Not likely, either. What you would expect is that among great piles of doggerel, there would be a smaller pile of excellent poems, but no more than a handful of masterpieces. It is the same with your dreams, I believe. When you have to stage five or six shows every night, many of them are likely to lack inspiration. It is true that you can cultivate your dream life so that the time you spend there will grow more rewarding as the years pass. But why should you expect that every one of your dreams is worth taking the time to interpret? And yet, if a poem or a dream calls out to you to interpret it, by all means find out what it means to you.

It would be a very unusual poet who created poetry primarily for the amusement and instruction of critics or interpreters. Poets don't need a critic on hand in order to be affected, perhaps even transformed, by the poem's creation. When we read a poem, we don't need to interpret it to be deeply moved, edified, inspired, and perhaps even enlightened. Having said that neither poems nor dreams have any *need* of interpretation doesn't mean that it is never useful. On the contrary, intelligent criticism or interpretation can at times greatly increase the depth of our understanding of a poem, and in the best of circumstances, of ourselves as well. It is the same with the dream.

Dreaming, Illusion,
and Reality

"In the ages of the rude beginning of culture," wrote Nietzsche, *"man believed that he was discovering a second real world* in dreams, and here is the origin of all metaphysics. Without dreams, mankind would never have had occasion to invent such a division of the world. The parting of soul and body goes also with this way of interpreting dreams; likewise, the idea of a soul's apparitional body: whence all belief in ghosts, and apparently, too, in gods."[1]

I am inclined to agree with Nietzsche in placing the blame for belief in ghosts, gods, and life after death on the doorstep of the dream. Let us suppose that the idea of a soul-body derives from subjective experiences in the dream world. Whether or not the soul would be granted the status of objective reality would then depend on the reality status given to the dream.

If early humans believed they had discovered in the dream a second "real world," what might they have meant?

Did they merely mean that the dream world had a subjectively verifiable existence? That dreams were only real while they lasted? Or that dreams existed actually and objectively in some subtle plane of existence every bit as real as the physical world?

Is there any evidence suggesting that dreams can be objectively real? Several enigmatic phenomena seem to raise the possibility that, in some circumstances, the dream world may be at least partially objective. One of these enigmas is the uncanny experience in which a person feels he or she has somehow temporarily left his or her body. Survey data indicate that a surprising number of people have had such out-of-body experiences (OBEs) at least once in their lives.[2] Very frequently, those who have this experience become unshakably convinced that they, or at least some part of themselves, are capable of an existence independent of their bodies.

Another phenomenon whose existence is widely attested to is the mysterious mode of information transfer called extrasensory perception (ESP). A wealth of anecdotal evidence supports the idea that ESP occurs, working across both space and time. If it is indeed possible to perceive, in some fashion, events that are happening at a distance, or even those that have not yet happened, space and time must be other than what they seem, and the same thing goes for subjective and objective realities!

Accounts of "mutual dreaming" (dreams apparently shared by two or more people) raise the possibility that the dream world may be in some cases just as objectively real as the physical world. This is because the primary criterion for "objectivity" is that an experience is shared by more than one person—a fact supposedly true of mutual dreams. In that case, what would happen to the traditional dichotomy between dreams and reality?

These mysterious phenomena that threaten the simplicity of our commonsense view of life are all primarily "chil-

dren of the night.'' Surveys indicate that more spontaneous
psychic experiences are reported to occur during dreaming
than waking.[3] Most out-of-body experiences likewise tend
to occur while the person is dreaming or at least in bed.
Dean Shiels, an American anthropologist, studied OBEs in
sixty-seven different cultures around the world and found
that sleep was regarded as the most important source of
OBEs in about eighty percent of those cultures.[4]

How does all this relate to lucid dreams? I propose that
OBEs are actually variant interpretations of lucid dreams;
that dream telepathy will provide the basis for an explanation of the occasional accuracy of paranormal OBE vision; and laboratory experiments with mutual lucid dreams
will be suggested as a means of testing the objective reality
of shared dream worlds.

Although telepathic experiences also apparently occur
during the waking state, surveys do indicate that most instances occur in dreams. The following is a remarkable
example of such a dream:

Many years ago when my son, who is now a man with
a baby a year old, was a boy I had a dream early one
morning. I thought the children and I had gone camping
with some friends. We were camped in such a pretty
little glade on the shores of the sound between two hills.
It was wooded, and our tents were under the trees. I
looked around and thought what a lovely spot it was.

I thought I had some washing to do for the baby, so
I went to the creek where it broadened out a little. There
was a nice clean gravel spot, so I put the baby and the
clothes down. I noticed I had forgotten the soap so I
started back to the tent. The baby stood near the creek
throwing handfuls of pebbles into the water. I got my
soap and came back, and my baby was lying face down
in the water. I pulled him out but he was dead. I awakened then, sobbing and crying. What a wave of joy went
over me when I realized that I was safe in bed and that

he was alive. I thought about it and worried for a few days, but nothing happened and I forgot about it.

During that summer some friends asked the children and me to go camping with them. We cruised along the sound until we found a good place for a camp near fresh water. The lovely little glade between the hills had a small creek and big trees to pitch our tents under. While sitting on the beach with one of the other women, watching the children play, I happened to think I had some washing to do, so I took the baby and went to the tent for the clothes. When I got back to the creek I put down the baby and the clothes, and then I noticed that I had forgotten the soap. I started back for it, and as I did so, the baby picked up a handful of pebbles and threw them in the water. Instantly my dream flashed into my mind. It was like a moving picture. He stood just as he had in my dream—white dress, yellow curls, shining sun. For a moment I almost collapsed. Then I caught him up and went back to the beach and my friends. When I composed myself, I told them about it. They just laughed and said I imagined it. That is such a simple answer when one cannot give a good explanation.[5]

Anecdotes, though dramatic and numerous, do no more than convince one that precognitive dreams are a possibility. It takes scientific investigation to convert possibility to probability. Fortunately, there are perhaps half a dozen scientific demonstrations of dream telepathy.

The most famous of these were the experiments in dream telepathy carried out in the dream laboratory of the Maimonides Hospital in Brooklyn by Dr. Montague Ullman and Dr. Stanley Krippner in the late 1960s. These dream researchers monitored sleeping subjects. During the periods when a subject was in REM sleep, a person in another room focused on an art reproduction and attempted telepathically to transmit an image of the painting to the sleeper, who was awakened for dream reports at the end of each REM period. Afterward, judges were able to match which picture went with which dream report, with an accuracy significantly above chance.

One night, the target picture was *The Sacrament of the Last Supper* by Salvador Dali. The painting shows Christ at the center of a table, surrounded by the twelve disciples, with a glass of wine and a loaf of bread on the table, and a fishing boat on the sea visible in the distance. Dr. William Erwin was the subject that night. His first dream was about an ocean, which, he commented, had a "strange beauty about it. . . ." Remembering his second dream, he said, "Boats come to mind. Fishing boats. Small-size boats. . . . There was a picture in the Sea Fare Restaurant that came to mind. . . . It shows, oh, I'd say about a dozen or so men pulling a fishing boat ashore right after having returned from a catch." Erwin's third dream seemed to relate to the Christian theme: he was looking through a "Christmas catalogue." His following three dreams were about doctors (Christ the healer and spiritual physician?). His last two dreams of the night dealt with food. In the morning, Dr. Erwin's reflections on his dreams put the pieces together in a way that is very suggestive: "The fisherman dream makes me think of the Mediterranean area, perhaps even some sort of Biblical time. Right now my associations are of the fish and the loaf, or even the feeding of the multitudes. . . . Once again I think of Christmas. . . . Having to do with the oceanwater, something in this area. . . ."[6]

The findings of the Maimonides research offer scientific support for the possibility of telepathic influence on dream content.[7] Likewise, in 1962, L. E. Rhine concluded on the basis of a large body of anecdotal evidence that more spontaneous psychic experiences occurred during dreaming than during the waking state. That being so, we may accept dream telepathy as a working hypothesis.

But now let us return to the other enigma we were discussing—the out-of-body experience. The OBE takes on a confusingly wide variety of forms. A person having an OBE may, for example, find his sense of identity associated with a second, non-physical body: a "soul," "astral body," "spirit," or, to suggest a term having a certain charm, "out-of-body body" (OBB)! Equally, "out-of-body" one may dispense entirely with the inelegance of bodies of any sort, and experience oneself as a point of light or a freely mobile center of awareness. In some OBEs, one seems to see the sleeping physical body, while in other cases one finds an empty bed or someone else entirely.

Let us take the case of one "astral projector" who wrote that before he knew what his OBEs were, he "was much afraid each time" he had one. He explained that his projections always began with him lying in bed, feeling a weight holding him down. The next thing he knew he would be out of his body. During one OBE, he walked around his bedroom and looked down the stairs into the kitchen. He decided to look at himself in the mirror, but could not see anything when he did so. On another occasion, when returning from "astral adventures," he thought, "I'll look at myself on the bed." But when he looked, he saw his mother, who "had been passed over quite a long time." Yet, curiously, finding his dead mother in bed instead of his sleeping body didn't lead him to the conclusion that he was dreaming; he took this to mean that his mother's spirit would always be with him whenever he was "projected."[8]

Two features of this OBE report are particularly suggestive. One is that upon "leaving his body," the astral projector walked around "his bedroom" and looked into "the kitchen." This, added to the fact that he expected to find his own sleeping body in bed upon his return, indicates that he conceived of himself as being in a non-physical ("astral") body, but in an environment identical to the physical world. It is exactly this kind of contradictory and confused mixture of mental and material elements that is also characteristic of the pre-lucid or naive dreamer. Secondly, note the projector's failure to consider the possibility that if his physical body wasn't in the bed he was looking in, that might not be the real bed he was looking at, or the real bedroom, or the real kitchen, either.

These kinds of minor lapses of rationality, and the failure to question the anomalies that confront one, seem to me quite characteristic of non-lucid dreaming and OBEs. Here is an account by Keith Harary, a person who has impressed me in the waking state as quite rational and of superior intelligence, and who is, as well, unusually proficient at inducing OBEs:

> One night I awoke in an out-of-body state floating just above my physical body which lay below me on the bed. A candle had been left burning on the other end of the room during the evening. I dove for the candle headfirst from a sitting position and gently floated down toward it with the intention of blowing out the flame to conserve wax. I put my "face" up close to the candle and had some difficulty in putting out the flame. I had to blow on it several times before it finally seemed to extinguish. I turned around, saw my body lying on the bed and gently floated back and back into it. Once in the physical [body] I immediately turned over and went back to sleep. The next morning I awoke and found that the candle had completely burned down. It seemed as if my out-of-the-body efforts had affected only a non-physical candle.[9]

The fact that Harary considered the other objects as physical, and the candle alone as non-physical, is similar to the way in which normal dreamers account for anomalies occurring during a dream.

In addition to the anomalies that people tend to accept in OBEs, there is another similarity to dreaming. During the OBE, they are convinced that what they are experiencing is actuality. For example, the gentleman with the "astral mother'' testified that he had learned through his OBEs that ''the real Me is apart from, and working through, my physical body. I now know for sure that we have two bodies.''[10]

This feeling of knowing ''for sure'' is quite characteristic of the tenacity with which people cling to the conclusions drawn from their out-of-body experiences. Wherever else they may differ, persons who have had out-of-body experiences are quite unanimous in being certain that these were *not* dreams. Yet, during ordinary dreams, we are usually convinced of the actuality of what we later discover to have been delusions.

An example of one of my own experiences is, I believe, especially revealing in regard to the similarities between dreaming and OBEs. Previously, I had had several lucid dreams in which I dreamed I could see my ''sleeping body'' in bed. I refer to them as lucid dreams rather than OBEs because that is how I interpreted them at the time. In my opinion, lucid dreams and OBEs are necessarily distinguished by only one essential feature: how the person interprets the experience at the time. The primary qualification for an OBE is the sensation of being outside the body. Perhaps it would be less misleading to describe this experience as an ''out-of-body sensation'' (OBS) rather than an ''out-of-body experience.'' So, if you *believe*, in some sense, that you are ''out of your body,'' you are *having*, by definition, an ''out-of-body'' experience. This definition sidesteps the question of whether or not you have actually left your physical body. However, no experience guarantees the actual existence of the thing in question. In the dark forest, one may experience a tree as a tiger, but it is still in fact only a tree.

According to the traditional psychology of Tibetan Buddhism, all of our experiences are subjective and thus, by their very nature, no different in substance from what we call ''dreams.'' This is also the point of view of the cognitive psychology of the modern West. Granting this premise—and scientifically speaking, it is impossible to argue with it—it would be difficult to name any experience that was not a sort of dream.

Consequently, my assumption that OBEs are necessarily a certain species of dream made the following experience all the more startling. Aware that I was in a dream, but with the image of what I had been dreaming about fading, I tried to hold onto it. Throwing myself into the darkness, I found myself crawling down a dark tunnel on my hands and knees. At first I could see nothing, but when I touched my eyelids I was able to open them, and I suddenly found myself floating across the room toward Dawn, who was sleeping on the couch. I looked back to see my "body" asleep on the living room floor. Somehow, I was completely convinced that this was not a dream, but that I really was seeing my sleeping body. Dawn awoke and started to speak, and I felt myself magnetically drawn back into the body asleep on the floor. When I arrived, I got up in this body (which I took to be my physical body) and excitedly said to her, "Do you know what just happened to me? An out-of-body experience of the genuine kind!" After this I was looking through a stamp book, when I found myself flying (like Superman) in the air over Germany.

I was shocked to awaken a few minutes later in my bed and realize that I had been sleeping all along. By now my brain was working well enough to note the general implausibility of my previous interpretation of the recent events. I could see, for instance, the inconsistencies implied by my belief that the body I had seen asleep on the floor, and entered from my supposed "other body," was actually my physical body. Were it not for the physical impossibility of traveling to Germany once I had opened a stamp book, and the waking testimony of Dawn, I might still be convinced that what had happened was not a dream. And this in spite of all "reason" to the contrary. What we know "for certain," reason is powerless to doubt. When you see your hand in front of you, can you really doubt it is your hand? Actually, what we know for certain only means what we assume or believe we know. My "out-of-body experience of the genuine kind" serves as a reminder that we can be totally mistaken about what seems indubitable.

The lucid dream is sometimes considered an inferior form of the OBE. But I believe the opposite may be the case, as may have already occurred to readers who remember the progression of stages through which children develop an understanding of "dreaming." To review briefly: at the earliest stage, children believe that dreams take place in the same (external) world as the rest of their experiences. Having learned, mainly through their parents, that dreams are somehow different from waking experiences, they next treat dreams as if they were partially external and partially internal. This transitional stage gives way to a third stage in which children recognize that a dream is entirely internal in nature—a purely mental experience.

These developmental stages refer, of course, to the conceptual terms in which children think of the dream after awakening. While dreaming, children and adults alike tend to remain at the first stage, implicitly assuming that dream events are external reality. Likewise, "astral projectors," who explicitly believe that what they are experiencing is external reality, are at this same stage. However, most typical OBEs, with their somewhat contradictory mixture of the mental and the material, would seem to provide examples of the second stage. Only with the fully lucid dream does the dreamer arrive at the third stage of conceptual clarity: realizing that the experience is entirely mental and clearly distinguishing the dream from the physical world.

In support of the notion that OBEs are generally the result of misinterpreted dream experiences, let me offer a personal observation. In about one percent of the lucid dreams in my record, I felt I was in some sense out of my body. In every case, when examining the experience after awakening, I noted some deficiency in either my memory or my critical thinking during the experience. In one such situation, I tried to memorize the serial number of a dollar bill to verify later whether I really had been out of my body or not. When I awoke, I couldn't recall the number, but it hardly mattered. I remembered that I hadn't lived in the house I thought I was asleep in for several years. In another instance, I was floating near the ceiling of my living room, looking at some photos that I knew I hadn't seen before—on top of a cabinet—given my habitual confinement to walking on the floor rather than on the ceiling! My hopes of verifying this paranormally gained information evaporated in a flash when I remembered upon awakening that I hadn't lived in *this* house for more than twenty years!

In contrast, during most of my lucid dreams I can remember where I am sleeping (if it matters) and usually have as accurate a notion of the date as I normally have while awake. Frequently, I know what time it is to within a few minutes.

From this I suggest that imperfect brain function during REM sleep may at times give rise to incomplete lucidity during dreaming. This state is characterized by partial amnesia, inadequate reality testing, and interpreting the experience as being out-of-body rather than dreaming.

All in all, the quality of reasoning during OBEs seems to resemble Nietzsche's description of the reasoning typical of primitive humanity, and also of dreamers today: "The first *causa* which occurred to the mind to explain anything that required an explanation was sufficient and stood for truth."[9] This uncritical state of mind is like the one in which many pre-lucid dreamers accept implausible proof that they are *not* dreaming. I believe a similar state of mind characterizes the reasoning whereby people convince themselves that they really are out-of-body.

In fairness, it should be pointed out that the manner in which OBEs are typically initiated makes the out-of-body interpretation seem almost beyond questioning: the person finds oneself awake in bed, and then, with no more notice than a feeling of vibration or melting, one finds oneself "peeling," "stepping," or "floating" out of the body. Most people accept uncritically that what *seems* to be the natural explanation is the true explanation of the experience.

In accordance with Nietzsche's contention above, "leaving one's body" is the first *causa* to occur to the dreaming mind, and it is accepted on face value as *the* explanation. One of the reasons people might be likely to label such an experience as out-of-body rather than dreaming is that it seems to happen while they are awake. Obviously, if they are awake, they can't be dreaming, and if they aren't dreaming, they must be doing what it seems they are doing—traveling "out-of-body."

This all seems straightforward enough, except for one awkward fact: in a variety of circumstances, it may be extremely difficult to determine whether you are asleep or awake, only dreaming or really seeing. These states of confusion are especially likely to occur during the sleep paralysis, a condition that sometime results when a person partially awakens from REM sleep and finds himself unable to move. This occurs because the part of the brain that prevents him from acting out his dreams has for some reason temporarily continued to function even though the person is otherwise "awake." Although the physiological basis for sleep paralysis has only recently been uncovered, the state and the hallucinatory experiences associated with it have been known for many years. For example, Eleanor Rowland described some of her experiences during this confusing blend of dream and reality in a 1908 paper entitled "A Case of Visual Sensations During Sleep":

> It often happens that dream persons issue from behind
> a real door, a dream hand moves along a real wall, and
> a dream figure sits upon the real bed. Since my vision

is so accurate, I cannot reassure myself by being certain that I am asleep. Nor am I in a slumber deep enough to accept any dream that comes without comment. My reasoning powers are active at such times, and I commune thus with myself: "No one can have opened the door, for you know you locked it." "But I see a figure distinctly standing at my elbow, and it has knocked on the door twice." "You are probably asleep." "How can I be? I see and hear as distinctly as I ever do." "Why, then, don't you push the figure away?" "I will. Here I am doing it." "No—you are not doing it at all, for you can see that you have not moved an inch." "Then I am asleep after all—the figure is not there, and I need not be afraid of it."[12]

The lesson to be learned from all this is that it is not always easy to determine which world you are living in at any given time: telling dreams from reality is no easy matter. Neither biological nor cultural evolution has prepared you to any significant extent for this particular task. Distinguishing one state of consciousness from another is a cognitive skill learned in exactly the same way you learned, as a child, to comprehend the gibberish of sounds that became your native language— by practice. The more practice you gain in lucid dreaming, the easier you will find it not to be fooled into thinking you are awake when you are dreaming. The more experience you have had with recognizing false awakenings, sleep paralysis, and other phenomena associated with REM sleep, the more likely it is that when you "leave your body" you will recognize it as a lucid dream.

This, in fact, is what we have observed with most of our experienced oneironauts. They quite frequently describe lucid dreams initiated from brief awakenings within REM periods as "leaving their bodies," even though we all agree that while this terminology effectively captures the way the experience actually feels, it does not presumably describe what really happens.

As an example of the peculiar form taken by these experiences, consider one of Roy Smith's laboratory lucid dreams. While lying on his right side, he began turning to the left and felt as though he had "left his body." He saw a scene of a field, and signaled lucidity about seven times. Next appeared a glowing reddish light, so he turned to the right toward it, and flew down an alley. At this point, he resumed signaling although he was later unsure of exactly how many times he had moved his eyes—it might have been nine. In any case, he continued to fly down the alley until he saw the moon—full and strikingly luminous. Upon seeing the stars above, he decided to try to unite them with the moon. But it was too late. Already he felt his body paralyzed in bed. He wanted to wake up and signal someone, and after what seemed like a very strenuous effort, he succeeded in awakening and pressed the call button.

Before I offer an explanation for what I believe may actually be happening in experiences of this kind, I would like to describe one of my own wake-within-REM-initiated lucid dreams. It was the middle of the night, and I had evidently just awakened from a REM period since I effortlessly recalled a dream. I was lying face down in bed, drowsily reviewing the story of my dream, when suddenly I experienced a very curious sensation of tingling and heaviness in my arms. They became so heavy, in fact, that one of them seemed to melt over the side of the bed! I recognized this distortion of my body image as a sign that I was reentering REM sleep. As I relaxed more deeply, I felt my entire body become paralyzed, although I could still seem to feel its position in bed. I reasoned that this feeling was most likely a memory image and that actual sensory input was cut off just as much as motor output was. I was, in short, asleep. At this point, I *imagined* raising my arm and experienced this imagined movement as if I had separated an equally real arm from the physical one I knew to be paralyzed. Then, with a similar imagined movement, I "rolled" out of my physical body entirely. I was now, according to my understanding, wholly in a dream body in a dream of my bedroom. The body I had seemed to leave, and which I now dreamed I saw lying on the bed, I quite lucidly realized to be a dream representation of my physical body; indeed, it evaporated as soon as I put my attention elsewhere. From here, I flew off into the dawn. . . .

I would say that having awakened from REM sleep, I was (as always) experiencing my *body image* in a position calculated by my brain. Since this calculation was based on accurate information about the physical world obtained through my awake, and therefore functional, senses, the body position I experienced corresponded to my actual position of lying in bed. Since during sleep (particularly REM), sensory input from the external world is actively suppressed, my sensory systems at the point when I returned to REM sleep no longer provided my brain with information regarding the physical world. Thus, my brain's representation of my body image was no longer constrained by sensory information concerning my body's actual orientation in physical space and I was free to move it in mental space to any new position that I chose. With no sensory input to contradict me, I could freely "travel" anywhere in mental space.

Let us consider, for comparison, an alternate theory: OBEs as astral projection. The idea of the astral world was brought to the West and popularized by Madame Blavatsky in the last century. According to her doctrine of Theosophy, the world is composed of seven planes of existence, and each plane is made up of atoms of varying degrees of refinement. The physical world is the coarsest of all. On the next level, the "etheric" plane, we find a second body—but this is not yet the "astral body," only the "etheric body" normally attached to the physical body and serving to keep all seven bodies in communication. The next plane is the "astral one," where we find the body we have been looking for. The astral world is made of astral

matter, which is superimposed on physical matter, and
everything in the physical world has its counterpart in the
astral world. However, there are more things found on the
astral plane than on the physical, including a menagerie of
spirits, elementals, and discarnate entities of all sorts. What
is more to the point here is that the astral body is supposed
to be able to travel on the astral plane, free of the physical
body, and since the astral world is supposed to contain a
copy of everything in the physical world, it would seem an
easy matter to gain information from distant places by
speedy travel there. (There are many difficulties with the
astral-projection theory of dreaming and OBEs. Just to
name one, I can recall lucid dreams in which I viewed a
dream representation of my bedroom that was missing a
good deal of "astral" matter: a whole wall and window,
in fact!) But my intention here is not to expound the theory
of astral projection, rather to translate their terms into mine.

What occultists have termed "astral travel," I am calling
"mental travel"; instead of "astral world," I say "mental
world." As for the mysterious entity elsewhere referred to
as the "astral body," "second body," "double," or
"phantom," I regard it as an experiential reality that I have
identified with the body image, but the most straightforward term for it may simply be "the dream body."

This dream body is our mental representation of our actual physical body. But it is the only body that we ever
directly experience. We know, by direct acquaintance, only
the contents of our minds. All of our knowledge concerning the physical world, including even the assumed existence of our "first" or physical bodies, is by inference.

Just because our knowledge of external reality is indirect, it should not lead us to conclude that mind alone
exists or that the physical world is merely an illusion. Due
to its representational nature, it is our mental world that is
the illusion. Our mental experiences can be compared to
watching television. The televised events are merely proj-

ected pictures having only the semblance of reality. Whether or not the events we see on TV have any correspondence with actual events is another matter. When, for instance, we watch a news program, we trust we are witnessing the depiction of events that actually occurred. If we see a man killed we expect him to be, in fact, dead. In contrast, when we see an actor "killed" on a TV melodrama, we consequently expect *him* rather than his widow to collect his paycheck!

In both of these cases, what we experienced were illusions, in the sense that the events that apparently took place on our TV set were only the images of events that may or may not have actually occurred in external reality. This is the necessary condition of *all* of our experiences: as mental representations, they are the images of the things they represent—not the things themselves. It is informative to specify the relation between the image and the thing it represents. Our two examples represent opposite degrees of possible correspondence. In the case of the actor, there was no relationship between the theatrical "death" and actuality. In contrast, the news program showed us the image of an event that precisely corresponded to the occurrence of an actual event. Thus we accept the news as accurately expressing reality. One can easily imagine TV productions possessing degrees of truth anywhere between the two extremes we have considered, such as a dramatic enactment of a true story, or a news program mistakenly reporting that a man has been killed when he has in fact only been wounded.

Now imagine a person confined to a room; his entire experience of the outside world is limited to what he or she sees on television. Such a person might well regard TV as the primary reality, and "the outside world" as a derivative and unnecessary hypothesis.

I am suggesting by this metaphor that we are all in a very similar situation: the room we are confined in corresponds to our minds, and the TV programs to the news and fantasies of the external world brought to us by our senses. All of the foregoing references to television images equally apply to the mental images out of which we construct our worlds.

In the terms I have proposed here, being in the body means constructing a *mental* body image. Because it is based on sensory information, it accurately represents the body's position in physical space. While dreaming, we are out of touch with our bodies and consequently liberated from the physical constraints imposed by waking perception. Thus, no awkward sensory facts are present to limit our movement in mental space, and we are free to move out of the spatial orientation defined by "being in the (physical) body."

The part of us that "leaves the body" travels in mental, not physical space. Consequently, it would seem reasonable to suppose that we never "leave our bodies" because we are never in them. Where "we" are when we experience anything at all—OBEs included—is in *mental* space. Milton's famous phrase, "The Mind is its own place," goes not quite far enough. The mind is not merely its own place, the mind is its *only* place.

We are now ready to address an empirical aspect of the OBE phenomenon. Persons undergoing OBEs frequently believe they are paranormally perceiving happenings taking place in the physical world. Unfortunately, in most cases, this belief takes the form of an untested assumption. Like the events we see on TV, what we see during OBEs could have *any* degree of correspondence with physical reality.

The generally unquestioned assumption underlying OBEs is that the person is actually situated, in an unexplained way, somewhere in the physical world other than his or her physical body. An implication of this is that what the persons sees while "out-of-body" ought to be an accurate reflection of physical reality, entirely analogous to ordinary perception. Rarely are either of these assumptions subjected to a rigorous test or, for that matter, to any test at all. These are empirical questions that can and should be settled by scientific experiment.

Are there any scientific data that might allow us to arrive at a verdict on the claim that OBE vision is valid? In fact, a good deal of relevant evidence is available, along with a number of studies of OBE vision that meet the standards of rigorous control required by exact science.

There are two ways of broadly viewing the results of these studies. First of all, we have the summary of Karlis Osis, Director of Research at the American Society for Psychical Research. This society, in an effort to produce evidence for survival after death, undertook an extensive investigation of OBE perception.[13] In the course of the study, approximately a hundred subjects, all of whom believed they were proficient in inducing OBEs and possessed paranormal perceptual abilities during OBEs, were tested under controlled conditions. While confined to one room, the subjects induced OBEs and "visited" a distant target room, attempting afterward to describe in detail what they had "seen" while there. A comparison of their reports with the actual contents of the target room revealed, in all but a few cases, absolutely no indication of any correspondence whatsoever. In other words, in the great majority of these cases, there was no evidence supporting accurate OBE perception or the validity of the subjects' convictions that they had actually left their bodies. Moreover, these subjects were described by Osis as being "the crème of the claimants" of OBEs. I believe the results of this study strongly support my "OBE as misinterpreted lucid dream" theory.

As for OBE vision, in the words of Dr. Osis, "the bulk of the cases seem to be a mirage." At best, OBE vision seems a highly variable and unreliable mode of perception "ranging from fairly good (i.e., clearly distinguishing some objects) to complete failure (i.e., producing very foggy or totally incorrect images).'' Moreover, Osis added, ''of those individuals in our studies who have shown some signs of OBE perceptual power, we did not find a single one who could see things clearly every time he felt he was out of body.''

The great majority of alleged cases of OBE vision apparently show no greater degree of perceptual ability in regard to the external world than we would expect from ordinary dreams. This might, by itself, suggest that the nature of OBEs would require no additional explanation than that already offered.

But the existence of even occasional accurate OBE perceptions is a fact that still needs to be explained. The traditional explanation holds that OBE vision is a form of direct perception by means of the senses of a non-physical body. But there is an alternate explanation that is philosophically sound, economical, and (most importantly) in agreement with observation. It does not, in the first place, assume a condition of unvarying accuracy during OBE or lucid dream vision. Instead, it suggests that like all other mental imagery, this form of perception may be relatively more accurate at some time than others. Mental experiences can be ordered on a spectrum ranging from little or no relation to external reality (e.g., ''hallucinations'') at one end, to near perfect correspondence with actuality (e.g., ''perception'') on the other end. Moreover, there can be any degree of relationship in between, and it is somewhere in this middle ground that dreams and OBEs generally fall.

What I am proposing is that the select minority of accurate OBE reports are simply cases of dream telepathy. To some people, this may seem like explaining the mysterious in terms of the more mysterious. Dream telepathy is a fact only barely established and in no way satisfactorily understood or explained. A question for future research is whether lucid dreamers and OBE-ers are more liable to experience telepathy than ordinary dreamers.

Taken together, the out-of-body experiences with which we have become familiar do not seem to have lived up to the claim that they would "challenge our most basic assumptions concerning the nature of reality." I have saved for last what may be the most mysterious of the reality-shaking phenomena of the world of dreams: I am referring to what are variously called "mutual," "reciprocal," or "shared" dreams.

These are the perplexing experiences in which two or more people report having had similar if not identical dreams. In some of these cases, the reports are so remarkably alike that one is almost compelled to conclude that the dream sharers have been present together in the same dream environment. If this does occur, it would imply that at least in certain cases, the dream world—and likewise the dream bodies within it—can possess some sort of objective existence. On the other hand, we may only share dream plots in mutual dreams, not the dreams themselves. Let us examine a classical account of ostensible reciprocal dreaming.

In Elmira, New York, on Tuesday, January 26, 1892, between 2 and 3 A.M., Dr. Adele Gleason dreamed that she stood in a lonesome place in the dark woods and that great fear came over her, at which point she dreamed that John Joslyn, her attorney and friend, came to her and shook a tree by her, causing its leaves to burst into flame. When the two friends met four days later, Adele mentioned having had a "strange dream" last Tuesday night. John stopped her at once, replying, "Don't tell it to me. Let me describe it, for I *know* that I dreamt the same thing." At approximately the same time on Tuesday night, he had awakened from a no less strange dream of his own and written down the following remarkably similar account: He had found Adele in a lonely wood after dark, "apparently paralyzed with fear of something I did not see, rooted to the spot by the feeling of imminent danger. I came up to her and shook the bush, upon which the leaves that fell from it burst into flame''[14]

Although these two dream reports are remarkably similar, they are not quite identical. For example, Adele made a tree of what for John was only a bush; the leaves burned on her tree, while his turned to flame while falling. The original reports show other discrepancies as well. I would interpret this as an instance of shared dreaming as caused by Adele's telepathic transmission of an sos, along with highly charged dream imagery to her friend. John, for his part, responded to his friend's call for help by telepathically initiating and sharing a visionary experience strikingly reminiscent of Moses' burning bush. This is a truly amazing tale of two dreams, yet it does seem to me more strongly supportive of the hypothesis of shared dream plots rather than shared dream worlds.

A somewhat more convincing anecdote is provided by Oliver Fox. "I had been spending the evening with two friends, Slade and Elkington," wrote Fox, "and our conversation had turned to the subject of dreams. Before parting, we agreed to meet, if possible, on Southampton Common in our dreams that night." Later that night, Fox claimed that he dreamed he met Elkington on the common "as arranged." So far, so good, "but Slade was not present." According to Fox, both he and Elkington knew they were dreaming, and commented on Slade's absence, "after which the dream ended, being of very short duration." Fox tells us that that when he saw Elkington the next day he asked him whether he had dreamed. "Yes," Elkington replied, "I met you on the Common all right and knew I was dreaming, but old Slade didn't turn up. We had just time to greet each other and comment on his absence, then the dream ended." This, to Oliver Fox's mind, "perhaps accounted for" Slade's "inability to keep the appointment." What happened to Slade? Fox was able to settle the mystery to his own satisfaction. When the two friends finally found Slade and asked him what had happened, he replied that he "had not dreamed at all."[15]

Intriguing as this particular case appears, it is marred by Fox's failure to report the exact time of occurrence of the two lucid dreams. Although the dreams are described as occurring on the same night, if they happened at different times (that is, if Fox and Elkington were not in REM sleep at the same time), it would favor the hypothesis of shared dream plots rather than a shared dream. In any case, Fox was unable to repeat "this small success" in mutual lucid dreaming and expressed the belief that "it is an extremely rare occurrence for two people to share approximately the same dream experience."

The examples we have so far considered were both once-in-a-lifetime experiences for the dream sharers. In contrast, there are suggestions that mutual dreaming abilities have been cultivated to a high level by a number of Sufi mystics. Aside from various stories of Sufi masters being able to appear in the dreams of anyone they choose, there is the report of a group of dervishes who explored the world of dreams on the island of Rhodes in the sixteenth century. The dervishes were presided over by a sheikh, "a certain Hudai effendi" who not only "practiced all the virtues, cultivated all the sciences and read books in the majority of Classical languages" but "devoted himself to the cultivation of collective dreams." In an isolated monastery atop a small hill on the island, "master and disciples purified themselves bodily, mentally and spiritually together; they got into an enormous bed together, a bed which contained the whole congregation. They recited the same secret formula together and had the same dream."

A remarkable story is told of an encounter between this dream master of Rhodes and Suleiman the Magnificent, the sultan of Turkey. One day, during a military campaign in Corinthia, Suleiman found himself in a seemingly impossible dilemma, and none of his advisors could devise any plan of action whatsoever. Fortunately, the sultan remembered that Hudai effendi's emissary was still in his camp. Since the dreammaster had helped him in the past out of no less difficult circumstances, Suleiman summoned the dervish and, providing him with travel expenses and safe conduct passes, asked him how many weeks he would need to journey to Rhodes and return to the imperial camp with the sheikh.

"The dervish gave an involuntary smile. 'Sire,' he replied, 'I thank you for the travel expenses and the safe-conduct. I have no need of them. True, the vulgar the island of Rhodes is far from here, but the venerated Sheikh Hudai is no distance from Your August Highness's camp. I undertake to summon him tonight, even before morning prayers.' "

Misunderstanding the nature of the Sufi's words, the sultan was "astonished at the holy man's presence in the neighborhood of his camp," and gave the dervish purses full of gold and silver, but he refused them. In return, the dervish offered Suleiman a "soporific apple," which the Sultan peeled and ate.

"Then the mysterious man went to sleep," as did the sultan himself. Previously, he had ordered his men to awaken him at the arrival of Hudai effendi. But when the master failed to appear, they laughed at the dervish and mocked their sovereign's "credulity and senility." When at dawn the muezzin of the army began the morning call to prayer, the Great Eunuch gently woke the sultan, and after wishing him good morning as well as a brilliant victory over the enemy, whispered ironically: "Sire, no news of Sheikh Hudai effendi. It looks as if his disciple is a fraud."

"Silence, you utter imbecile," roared the sultan, "silence! The illustrious Master has deigned to visit me. I have had a long conversation with him and I tell you that my faithful armies have won the most brilliant of victories, less than an hour ago. Await the messenger's arrival." The enemy commander had passed out just as the battle was about to begin, and his subordinates were unable to carry on without him, with the result as described by the sultan via Sheikh Hudai.

Evidently, "at a dream signal from the humble disciple," Hudai effendi had visited and advised Suleiman—in a dream. Moreover, there is the suspicion that the dream master may have somehow been involved in the enemy commander's mysterious loss of consciousness, which resulted in what would seem "the most accidental" in spite of being called "the most brilliant" of victories for the armies of Suleiman the Magnificent.[16]

Fascinating as this and other anecdotes of mutual dreaming may be, they bring us no nearer to deciding between the competing interpretations of the phenomenon. One might wonder whether there is any way the question could definitely be settled. I propose that there is an empirical test: Two oneironauts could have simultaneous lucid dreams while being monitored in a sleep laboratory. They would agree to meet in their lucid dreams and signal simultaneously. If the experience were truly a mutual dream—that is, if the lucid dreamers actually sharing a dream world—simultaneous eye-movement signals would show up in their polygraph recordings. If, on the other hand, they reported carrying out this task in a mutual lucid dream but did not show simultaneous signals, we would have to conclude that they were at most sharing dream plots.

Let us be sure to appreciate the significance of such an experiment. If the mutual lucid dreamers failed to show simultaneous signals, it would be neither surprising nor especially significant. However, if they did produce simultaneous eye-movement signals, we have incontrovertible proof for the objective existence of the dream world. We would then know that, in certain circumstances at least, dreams can be as objectively real as the world of physics. This would finally raise the question of whether physical reality is itself some kind of mutual dream. Perhaps what

really happens is the balanced result of a myriad of interactions contributed by all of us dreaming the dream of con-
sensual reality. But if not, then there's always Bob Dylan's
offer: ''I'll let you be in my dream, if I can be in yours.''

10

〰〰〰〰〰〰〰

Dreaming, Death, and Transcendence

While ascending a mountain path I began to find it more and more difficult to climb. My legs took on the familiar leaden feeling they sometimes have in dreams, and a dull heaviness spread through my rapidly weakening body. My feelings of weariness deepened relentlessly until I could only continue by crawling—but finally even this was too much for me and I was overcome with the feeling of certainty that I was about to die of exhaustion. This realization of imminent death focused my attention with remarkable clarity upon what I wanted to express with the one act of my life I had left: perfect acceptance. Thus, gladly embracing death, I let go completely of my last breath, when to my amazement and delight a rainbow flowed out of my heart and I awoke from the dream.

Years after this experience, the profound impact of this dream of death and transcendence continues to influence my beliefs concerning what may happen to us when we die. Because of this dream, I am inclined to share Walt

Whitman's view that to die is "different from what anyone supposed and luckier." Yet I know that it was just a dream, and I wonder whether I, or others who have had similar experiences, have sufficient grounds for trusting the belief that they have seen the truth.

Whatever relation this dream of death may bear to reality, it illustrates an important truth about dreams. There is a common fear that if you die in a dream, you will not awaken at all. Consequently, people dreaming of death tend to fear and resist the experience. But my dream illustrates what could happen when the dreamer fully accepts a dream encounter with death. In cultures that consider death as transformation rather than annihilation, such dreams are easier to accept.

According to Greek mythology, sleep is the brother of death, an indication that the two concepts have long been closely associated in the human mind. The reason is easy to see: both states are characterized by an inactivity sharply contrasting with the animate movement of waking life. And since the soul was regarded as leaving the body temporarily during sleep and permanently at death, sleep seemed a short death and death a long sleep. The straightforward association of death and dreaming naturally follows from dreaming's connection with sleep. And the associations of sleep, dreaming, and death with the darkness of the underworld are all quite obvious.

Less obvious is that these symbolic associations have another side: dreams, the children of sleep, also represent the creative impulse to life, as expressed by the seed germinating in the dark womb of the earth. Moreover, sleep itself resembles the state of incipient life *in utero*. As Freud observed, "Somatically, sleep is an act which reproduces intrauterine existence fulfilling the conditions of repose, warmth and the absence of stimulus; indeed in sleep many people resume fetal position."[1] This brings us to the paradox that death, for the dreamer, most often signifies rebirth. As Ann Faraday suggests, "the most interesting dream death is our own, for this indicates the death of some obsolete self-image, from which comes rebirth into a higher state of consciousness and authentic self-being."[2]

The association between death and transformation has long been recognized in literature. In Thomas Mann's great alchemical novel, *The Magic Mountain*, Hans Castorp's initiation into the mysteries of life takes the form of a dream, and a lucid one at that, which answers and resolves all of his questions about the seeming contradictions of life and death. Mann describes his hero as "searching for the Grail—that is to say, the Highest: knowledge, wisdom, consecration, the philosopher's stone . . . the elixir of life."[3] Lost in the perilous mountains, battered and blinded by a blizzard that very nearly costs him his life, Hans loses consciousness of his surroundings and falls into the snow. During the same storm, he has seen in the "too perfect symmetry" of the flakes of falling snow the coldness of "the very marrow of death." But as he lies thoroughly immersed in the frozen ocean of death, he dreams himself another, wholly different world—this one as delightful a vision of sunshine, comfort, and harmony as the other one was a blinding vision of violence, elemental chaos, and harshness. Hans walks through this idyllic scene, joyously viewing the friendly and courteous behavior displayed everywhere by the happy, yet serious and in every way noble, people of his dream. But then he discovers, to his horror, a temple of human sacrifice in which he witnesses two hideously ugly hags tearing apart a child over a witches' cauldron. The shock brings him to his senses.

Upon half awakening to find himself lying nearly frozen in the snow, Hans Castorp says to himself, "I felt it was a dream, all along . . . lovely and horrible dream. I knew all the time that I was making it up myself. . . ."[4] Without moving, he continues to reflect for some time on his "dream poem of humanity," which he discovers possesses "both rhyme and reason. . . . It is love, not reason, that is stronger than death." His lucid dream, he declares, has brought him to this profound insight: "My dream has given it to me, in utter clearness, that I may know it forever."[5] Of this, Hans Castorp's creator wrote that "if he does not find the grail, yet he divines it, in his deathly dream."[6] Having done so, Hans awakens himself fully from his reverie, struggles to his feet, shakes off his frozen coat of snow, and returns to live another several hundred pages.

The reader may object that the experiences of fictional characters are, well, *fictional,* and therefore unrelated to actuality. But the fact is that—in life as well as in literature—people who have survived actual or imagined encounters with death frequently report them to have been accompanied by powerfully significant experiences. These life-changing visions currently are referred to most commonly as "near-death experiences" (NDEs). The particular contents of NDEs vary widely, as much as the contents of OBEs, visions, lucid and non-lucid dreams. A useful picture of a thing can be sometimes constructed by combining, features from a variety of different examples. Raymond Moody has provided the public with such a picture of the NDE in his best-seller, *Life After Life:*

> A man is dying and, as he reaches the point of greatest physical distress, he hears himself pronounced dead by the doctor. He begins to hear an uncomfortable noise, a loud ringing or buzzing, and at the same time feels himself moving very rapidly outside his own physical body, but still in the same immediate physical environment, and sees his own body from a distance as though he is a spectator. He watches the resuscitation attempt from this vantage point and is in a state of emotional upheaval.
>
> After a while, he collects himself and becomes more accustomed to his odd condition. He notices that he still has a "body," but one of a very different nature and

with very different powers from the physical body he has left behind. Some other things begin to happen. Others come to meet him and help him. He glimpses the spirits of relatives and friends who have already died, and a loving warm spirit of a kind he has never encountered before—a being of light—appears before him. This being asks him a question, non-verbally, to make him evaluate his life and helps him along by showing him a panoramic, instantaneous playback of the major events in his life. At some point, he finds himself approaching some sort of barrier or border, apparently representing the limit between earthly life and the next life. Yet, he finds that he must go back to earth, that the time for his death has not yet come. At this point, he resists, for by now he is taken up with his experiences in the afterlife and does not want to return. He is overwhelmed by intense feelings of joy, love, and peace. Despite his attitude, though, he is somehow united with his physical body and lives.[7]

It is important to remember that this account is a composite put together by Dr. Moody from a variety of diverse anecdotal accounts, no one of which possesses all of its features. It is really therefore closer to fiction than description, and may only provide us with an idealized picture of the NDE.

NDEs seem to exhibit varying degrees of completeness. Kenneth Ring, a psychologist specializing in the study of NDEs, describes the experience as unfolding in a five-stage continuum. "The first stage involves a feeling of extraordinary peace and contentment; the second stage is characterized by a sense of detachment from one's physical body, i.e., an OBE; the third stage is described as entering a transitional world of darkness; the hallmark of the fourth stage is a brilliant light of exceptional beauty; and the last stage is one in which the subject experiences himself as 'entering the light.' "[8] Dr. Ring found that each of the five stages was reported by decreasing numbers of NDE subjects.

The resemblance of the NDE to certain aspects of dreams is quite obvious. For example, there are the *images* of relatives and friends who have already died and would therefore be significantly associated with the person's idea of death, which itself has been brought up by his fear or expectation of his own impending death. There is also the obvious element of wish-fulfillment involved in seeming to be in a different body than one's own.

The popular press has treated the NDE in a credulous and sensationalistic manner, interpreting it as providing positive "proof" for life after death. Considering the fact that no one who ever had an NDE was *really* dead, the experience provides no more evidence for survival after death than OBEs provide for the existence of any kind of "astral" body independent of the physical body. A neurophysiologist would be quick to point out that when the NDE occurs, the person's brain is still sufficiently intact to produce the experience. In this regard, it is of interest to note that a deceased person's brain shows considerable activity thirty minutes or more after clinical "death"—that is, heart failure.

Like waking life, OBEs, and dreams, the near-death experience is still an *experience*. The question is, does it occur during death or during a more reversable sleep? Since our current sources of information concerning what is supposed to happen at and after death are limited to what we gain in seances and "phone calls from the dead," we are not in a very favorable position to determine the validity of NDE reports! I am not at all certain this is the most important question to answer, anyway. A dream need not be literally true to be significant and meaningful—for example, my rainbow dream, which began this chapter—and the same applies to NDEs, which often possess the profoundest significance for people who have had them.

People who have undergone near-death experiences frequently show fundamental and remarkably positive transformations in their approaches to life. Noyes summarized the changes as follows:

> A pattern of favorable attitude change resulting from near-death experiences was described that included the following: (1) a reduced fear of death; (2) a sense of relative invulnerability; (3) a feeling of special importance or destiny; (4) a belief in having received the special favor of God or fate; (5) a strengthened belief in continued existence. In addition to these elements that seemed directly related to the experience itself, several more appeared to be associated with a heightened awareness of death that resulted from it. These included: (1) a sense of the preciousness of life; (2) a feeling of urgency and reevaluation of priorities; (3) a less cautious approach to life; (4) a more passive attitude toward uncontrollable events. This pattern of change seemed to contribute to the emotional health and well-being of persons reporting it.[9]

Dr. Noyes added that "an opposite pattern was described by a few and appeared to be associated with psychopathology. . . ." However, for most people, the NDE has a profound and vivifying effect that those of us who haven't experienced it might well envy.

But is it possible to have an NDE or its equivalent without nearly dying? Kenneth Ring has suggested that the NDE experience can take many forms; he quotes a line from Plutarch that says, "At the moment of death the soul experiences the same impressions as those who are initiated into the great Mysteries." Ring notes that "the modern world is witnessing the emergence of a new mystery school where resuscitation techniques administered by physicians have replaced hypnotic procedures practiced by high priests. The initiates of course are those who have suffered clinical death and the intiation itself is the NDE.''

Ring regards the greatest benefit to be gained from the NDE (at least in its highest form) as the possibility of realizing "who and what we truly are," a self far more expansive and all-encompassing than the one we show in our daily lives.

According to Dr. Ring, a person who has found this out, whether by fasting and prayer, drugs, accident, or as it were, "by itself," is no longer concerned about personal survival after death, because he or she has experienced "eternal" existence. They could say, with Richard M. Bucke, the author of *Cosmic Consciousness*, " . . . I became conscious in myself of eternal life. It was not a conviction that I would have eternal life, but a consciousness that I possessed eternal life then . . ."[10] In my view, and I believe Kenneth Ring would probably agree, the NDE is one path to a mystical experience. It is an experience open to others so inclined, including perhaps lucid dreamers, as we shall see at the end of this chapter. It may not be clear why I am calling some NDEs mystical experiences. In that case, the following account from a woman who nearly died during the delivery of her baby may clarify this point:

> The next thing I knew, I was in—I was standing in a mist and I knew *immediately* that I had died and I was *so* happy that I had died but I was still alive. And I cannot tell you how I *felt*. I was thinking, "oh, God I'm dead, but I'm here. I'm me!" And I started pouring out these enormous feelings of gratitude because I still existed and yet I knew perfectly well that I had died. . . .
>
> While I was pouring out these feelings . . . the mist started being infiltrated with enormous light and the light just got brighter and brighter and, as everybody says, it was so bright but it doesn't hurt your eyes, but it's brighter than anything you've ever experienced in your whole life. At that point, I had no consciousness any

more of having a body. It was just pure consciousness.
And this enormously bright light seemed almost to cra-
dle me. I just seemed to exist in it and be part of it and
be nurtured by it and the feeling just became more
and more and more ecstatic and glorious and perfect. And
everything about it was—it just didn't bear any relationship to anything! The feeling—if you took the one thousand best things that ever happened to you in your life
and multiplied by a million, maybe you could get close
to this feeling, I don't know. But you're just engulfed
by it and you begin to know a lot of things. I remember
I knew that everything, everywhere in the universe was
OK, that the plan was perfect. . . . And the whole time
I was in this state, it seemed infinite. It was timeless. I
was just an infinite being in perfection.[11]

One element of the NDE, as described in Western accounts, finds independent support in the traditional teachings of the visionary culture of Tibet: "the Clear Light of
Reality," according to the Tibetan Buddhists, is briefly experienced by everyone at the moment of death. Moreover,
"unless the dying person possesses, as a result of having
successfully practised *yoga* while incarnate, the *yogic*
power to hold fast to the after-death condition in which the
Clear Light dawns, he mentally sinks downward, stage by
stage, and the Clear Light of Reality fades from his consciousness."[12]

Adepts who recognize the Light of the after-death state
as being of the same nature as dreams are supposed to
transcend the dream of life and death. The means by which
one attains this transcendence is the yoga of the dream
state. Through the practice of lucid dreaming during his
lifetime, the yogi is able to experience the "dream of
death" lucidly as well.

Dream yoga is not merely intended as a rehearsal for the
final sleep of death. The serious follower of dream yoga is
attempting to awaken before death: "The whole purpose

of the Doctrine of Dreams is to stimulate the *yogin* to arise from the Sleep of Delusion, from the Nightmare of Existence, to break the shackles in which *maya* [illusion] thus has held him prisoner throughout the aeons, and so attain spiritual peace and joy of Freedom, even as did the Fully Awakened One, Gautama the Buddha.''[13]

The first steps toward the dream yogi's goal of awakening involve becoming proficient in "comprehending the nature of the dream state." Once the yogi has become an accomplished lucid dreamer, he proceeds to the next stage, "transmuting the dream-content," in which the initial exercise is the following: "If, for example the dream be about fire, think, 'what fear can there be of fire which occurreth in a dream!' Holding to this thought, trample upon the fire. In like manner, tread underfoot whatever be dreamt." After gaining sufficient skill in controlling his reactions to the contents of his lucid dreams, the yogi goes on to more advanced exercises, and by means of these he masters the ability to visit—in his lucid dreams—any realm of existence desired.

The next stage of practice is called "realizing the dream-state, or dream-content to be *maya* [illusion]." According to Buddhist doctrine, the entire universe of forms, or separate existence, is an illusory appearance or "dream." This should be a familiar idea to readers of the previous chapter, where it was argued that all experiences are necessarily mental representations and, as the subjective products of our brains, are thus of the same nature as dreams.

At the third stage, the dream yogi is advised to practice the transformation of dream content into its opposite. For example, the lucid dreamer should transform the dream, if it be of fire, into water; if it be of small things, into large; if it be of one thing, into many, and so on. Thus, the text explains, the lucid dreamer comprehends the nature of dimensions and of plurality and unity.

After becoming "thoroughly proficient" in the art of

transforming dream content, the yogi turns his attention to his own dream body: this, he now sees, is just as illusory as any other element of his lucid dream. The fact that the fully lucid dreamer knows he is not his dream body plays a crucial role in self-transformation, as we shall see below.

The fourth and final stage of dream yoga is enigmatically termed "meditating upon the thatness of the dream-state." The text tells us that by means of this meditation, "the dream propensities whence arise whatever is seen in dreams as appearances of deities, are purified." It is, ironically, by means of these "appearances" that the ultimate goal is reached. The yogi is, of course, aware that these "deities" are his own mental images. Bearing this in mind, he is instructed to concentrate in the lucid dream state, focusing on the forms of these deities, and to keep his mind free of thoughts. In the undisturbed quiet of this mental state, the divine forms are said to be "attuned to the non-thought condition of mind; and thereby dawneth the Clear Light, of which the essence is of the voidness."

Thus, one realizes that the appearance of form "is entirely subject to one's will when the mental powers have been efficiently developed" through the practice of the yoga of lucid dreaming. Having learned " . . . that the character of any dream can be changed or transformed by willing that it shall be," the lucid dreamer takes "a step further . . . he learns that form, in the dream state, and all the multitudinous content of dreams, are merely playthings of mind, and, therefore, as unstable as a mirage." A process of generalization "leads him to the knowledge that the essential nature of form and of all things perceived by the senses in the waking state are equally as unreal as their reflexes in the dream state," since both waking and dreaming are states of mind. A final step brings the yogi to "the Great Realization" that nothing within the experience of his mind "can be other than unreal like dreams." In this light, "the Universal Creation . . . and every phenomenal thing therein" are seen to be "but the content of the Supreme Dream." And for the one upon whom "this Divine Wisdom" has dawned, "the microcosmic aspect of the Macrocosm becomes fully awakened; the dew-drop slips back into the Shining Sea, in *Nirvanic* Blissfulness and At-one-ment, possessed of All Possessions, Knower of the All-Knowledge, Creator of All Creations—the One Mind, Reality Itself.''[14]

Having described the realization reached by the successful seeker, let us consider some of the possible pitfalls on the path of inner growth through lucid dreaming. Primary among them is the tendency for the less than fully lucid dream ego to misunderstand and misuse the new access to power and control over dreams that lucidity brings. The semi-lucid dream ego is inclined to use "magical powers" to seek its own ends, which may be at odds with the person's real goals. Moreover, the semi-lucid dream ego's sense of greatly expanded power leads to a grandiose expansion of self-esteem, the condition Jung referred to as "inflation."

Although the inflated dream ego, like a power-intoxicated Roman emperor, bestows divinity upon itself, it proves to be filled with nothing but hot air. The hottest of the airs it puts on is the delusion that it *is* the self. The truth is that the dream ego is only a self-representation that tends to forget its nature.

The ego's tendency (whether awake or dreaming) to mistake itself for the true self is natural. The ego is a model of the self, designed to serve adaptive action; it is based upon disparate sources of information, ranging from how the self has actually behaved in the past to parental and social notions of how the self should behave in the future. From this collection of expectations, predictions of the self's future behavior can be made.

Since pretending to have a socially desirable feature is more frequently rewarded than truthfully admitting *not* to have it, much of our mental map of the self becomes pretense. The pattern of social pretense, of playing a role intended to deceive others, is later applied to oneself after society's standards have become internalized. If we are to pretend successfully to ourselves, we must also pretend that we are not pretending. Thus the person behind the mask forgets he has another face. The actor becomes his role, mistaking the part he plays for the whole he is; appearance usurps reality; the original plan is forgotten; and clothes mock the man.

All this has been said regarding the undeveloped or semi-lucid dream ego. Lucid dreams are experienced and interpreted, by such an ego, as *"my* dream." But the dream ego is not the dreamer; rather than dreaming, it is being dreamed. The unenlightened but semi-lucid dream ego falsely believes itself to be the only reality, of which all other dream figures are the mere projections.

The case of Ram Narayana vividly illustrates how far delusions of grandeur can be taken by the semi-lucid dreamer. Narayana, an Indian physician and editor, had been perplexed by the problem of how to convince "the creatures of his dream, during the dream state, that it really is a dream." He finally gave up trying, having decided that even if he succeeded, convincing them could serve no useful purpose. Therefore, Narayana resolved to enjoy himself instead and to pass his time while dreaming "as comfortably as possible." Consequently, next time he went to sleep, he addressed "the assembly of his dream characters" as follows: "Friends, why don't you try to attain the state of ecstatic and immortal bliss, entirely free from pain of every description? This state of bliss can be obtained only by entering into the celestial region, the abode of the Supreme Creator. To this region I go daily and enjoy its pleasures for twelve hours out of every twenty-four. I am the only incarnation and representative of the Supreme One."

Narayana indicated that "the majority of dream creatures believed in the above speech." A minority were skeptical of his claim of being the "only manifestation of the Supreme Deity." What about Krishna, Christ, Buddha, or Mohammed? demanded the doubters. They received the reply that "all those great men had come from lower regions and were only theoretical in their teachings and nobody ever attained salvation through them, that the dreamer alone came from the highest spiritual plane, and that he would teach them the only sure and practical method of reaching that region."

Having been made the usual promises, they were charged the usual price, being then told the chief condition of initiation was "to have implicit faith in their preceptor, the dreamer." Narayana went on to explain, in terms well known by the leaders of cults everywhere, that "the most effective means to hypnotize them all in a body was then employed, which consisted of looking intently into the eyes of the *guru,* the dreamer, while sacred hymns and songs of love and devotion were being recited in a chorus. They were further impressed with the idea that ultimately every one of them would reach the highest region, after one, two or more re-births, but one having complete faith in the dreamer would reach there the soonest."

Narayana claimed that "the method proved so satisfactory that the dreamer was actually worshipped by every one of the dream creatures and was pronounced to be the only true spiritual guide. He now considered himself in no way less fortunate than so many leaders of the various faiths, in the waking world, who enjoy the pleasure of being devotedly worshipped by their disciples."

This comical parody of spiritual cults would have its tragic aspect as well, were it not for the fact that Narayana was eventually able to progress beyond this state of inflation. He dreamed that he fell in among a group of yogis who managed to enlighten him in the following dream:

. . . another elderly figure from amongst the dream creatures rose from his seat and overawed the assembly with his long grey beard and his *yogi's* staff. He began his oration in a curious and amusing manner, though with an authoritative tone, his voice quivering with anger and his gaunt index finger pointing towards the dreamer: "What reason have you to call us your dream creatures and yourself the creator of us all? If you are our creator we say equally emphatically that so are we the creator of yourself. We are all in the same boat, and you can claim no sort of higher existence than ours. If, however, you want to be convinced of my statement, I can show you the Creator of us all, i.e., of yourself as well as ours." With these words, he struck the dreamer on the head with his heavy staff, who, in consequence, woke up and found himself lying in his bed with his mind extremely puzzled.[15]

The yogi's point is that the dream ego (mistaken for "the dreamer" by Narayana) is just another dream figure. The actual creator of the dream is not a part of the dream at all—being, in fact, the sleeping self.

This is an insight fully lucid dreamers realize through direct experience. They know that the persons they appear to be in the dream are not who they really are. No longer identifying with their egos, they are free to change them, correcting their delusions. As an immediate consequence of this, the self-representation of the ego becomes a more accurate map of the true territory of the self. The ego now encompasses the fact that "the map is not the territory," which makes it more difficult to mistake one's self-image for one's true self.

The fully lucid dreamer does not need to struggle to overcome his or her ego. He or she has become objective enough to no longer identify with it. In consequence, the ego now stands in proper relation to the self as its representative and servant. The lucid dreamer's ego now realizes its limitations: it knows it is only the limited part of the self that the person believes him or herself to be. Or perhaps even less—only what we can *explicitly* spell out about ourselves. This knowledge puts the ego's importance in modest proportion to the true, and perhaps as yet undiscovered, Self.

The fully lucid dreams we have been discussing are instances of transcendental experiences, experiences in which you go beyond your current level of consciousness. Lucid dreamers (at least during the dream) have gone beyond their former views of themselves and have entered a higher state of consciousness. They have left behind their former way of being in dreams, no longer identifying with the dream characters they play or thinking that the dream world is reality. In this way, fully lucid dreams are transcendental experiences.

Transcendental experiences are advantageous, in my view, in that they help us detach from fixed ideas about ourselves. The less we identify with who we think we are (the ego), the more likely it is that we may one day discover who we really are. In this regard, the Sufi master Tariqavi has written,

> The study of the Way requires self-encounter along the way. You have not met yourself yet. The only advantage of meeting others in the meantime is that one of them may present you to yourself.
>
> Before you do that, you will possibly imagine that you have met yourself many times. But the truth is that when you do meet yourself, you come into a permanent endowment and bequest of knowledge that is like no other experience on earth.[16]

Before they meet themselves, lucid dreamers are at first inclined to seek the dream fulfillment of what they believe they have always wanted. This is natural enough. Yet after too many "wish-fulfilling" dreams, where the action is motivated by the ego-associated drives, passions, desires, expectations, and goals with which we are so familiar, a point of satiation may be reached. Lucid dreamers may then tire of seeking their habitual satisfactions, which may have become less satisfying due to effortless gratification. They grow weary of dreaming the same dreams, and equally of being the same self, night after night. It is at this point that the need for self-transcendence may arise. Such lucid dreamers no longer know what they want, only that it is not what they used to want. So they give up deciding what to do, and resign from deliberate dream control.

Having recognized the limitations of goals determined by the ego, the lucid dreamer has surrendered control to something beyond what he or she knows him or herself to be. The form taken by this "something beyond" will vary in accordance with the individual's way of thinking. For those comfortable with traditional religions, the surrender might naturally be phrased in such terms as "submission to the will of God." On the other hand, those who find themselves uncomfortable with theistic terminology will probably prefer to express themselves differently.

If you follow the reasoning argued above for the self-representational nature of the ego, a very natural way to frame this surrender is available: giving control to your true self. Whatever you assume about the nature of your true self, surrendering control from who you *think* you are, to who you truly are, is likely to be an improvement. Including, as it does, everything that you know, your true or total self ought to be capable of making wiser decisions than your ego. Moreover, it knows what your ego may not—your highest goals.

Another formulation is surrender to "The Highest," whatever this may ultimately prove to mean. Such questions as whether this is a part of yourself or something beyond yourself need not be resolved at this point. It is with this term that I personally find myself most comfortable. Besides, it is, by definition, with "The Highest" that the ultimate decisions rightfully rest.

Though lucid dreamers give up control of the course of their dreams, they still require lucidity. But now they need it to respond creatively to whatever the dream presents and to follow intuitively the intentions of the higher will. The following lucid dream illustrates the process of self-transcendence we have been discussing. Although it is one of my own lucid dreams in the sense that *I* awoke from it, it felt more like *it* had me:

Late one summer morning several years ago, I was lying quietly in bed, reviewing the dream I had just awakened from. A vivid image of a road appeared, and by focusing my attention on it, I was able to enter the scene. At this point, I was no longer able to feel my body, from which I concluded I was, in fact, asleep. I found myself driving in my sportscar down the dream road, perfectly aware that I was dreaming. I was delighted by the vibrantly beautiful scenery my lucid dream was presenting. After driving a short distance farther, I was confronted with a very attractive, I might say a *dream* of a hitchhiker beside me on the road just ahead. I need hardly say that I felt strongly inclined to stop and pick her up. But I said to myself, "I've had *that* dream before. How about something new?" So I passed her by, resolving to seek "The Highest" instead. As soon as I opened myself to guidance, my car took off into the air, flying rapidly upward, until it fell behind me like the first stage of a rocket. I continued to fly higher into the clouds, where I passed a cross on a steeple, a star of David, and other religious symbols. As I rose still higher, beyond the clouds, I entered a space that seemed a vast mystical realm: a vast emptiness that was yet full of love; an unbounded space that somehow felt like home. My mood had lifted to corresponding heights, and I began to sing with ecstatic inspiration. The quality of my voice was truly amazing—it spanned the entire range from deepest bass to highest soprano—and I felt as if I were embracing the entire cosmos in the resonance of my voice. As I improvised a melody that seemed more sublime than any I had heard before, the meaning of my song revealed itself and I sang the words, "I praise Thee, O Lord!"

Upon awakening from this remarkable lucid dream, I reflected that it had been one of the most satisfying experiences of my life. It *felt* as if it were of profound significance. However, I was unable to say in exactly what way it was profound, nor was I able to evaluate its significance. When I tried to understand the words that had somehow contained the full significance of the experience—"I praise Thee, O Lord!"—I realized that, in contrast to my understanding while in the dream, I only now understood the phrase in the sense it would have in our realm. It seemed the esoteric sense that I comprehended while I dreamed was beyond my cloudy understanding while awake. About what the praise did not mean, I can say this: in that transcendent state of unity, there was no "I" and "Thee." It was a place that had no room for "I" and "Thee," but for one only. So which of us, then, was there? My personal "I," my dream-ego sense of individuality, was absent. Thus, what was present was "Thee." But in that realm, "I" *was* "Thee." So I might just as well have sung "I praise Me . . ." except that there was really no "me" either! In any case, it should be clear why I have called this lucid dream a transpersonal experience.

This brings us back to the question of whether it is possible to have the equivalent of a near-death experience without nearly dying. That the answer is "yes" should now be evident. I say this because the experience provided by transpersonal dreams (whether lucid or not) is symbolically synonymous with the process of dying to our old ways and being reborn to new lives. Whether this new attitude carries over into waking life is another matter, but from the point of view of dreaming, death and transcendence are the same thing.

Let us bring this chapter full circle by giving a reply to the question, "What will we be after death?" As far as we are individuals, death appears to be the end of us. Were we to leave it at that, this would be nothing more than the "modern" view of death as annihilation. Yet the preceding pages suggest that our individuality is not our truest being, but only a representation of it. What you take to be your individuality is a mental image of yourself. "Who you think you are" is only a thought, a transient process occurring in time and space, and doomed to pass like everything else that exists in time.

However, according to the point of view we have been considering, your essential being transcends space and time: your transpersonal identity transcends your personal identity. This, your transpersonal individuality, may in the end prove identical with the nature of ultimate reality—"the Shining Sea" referred to above: "Possessed of all possessions, Knower of the All-Knowledge, Creator of All Creations—the One Mind, Reality Itself." At death, "the dewdrop slips back into the Shining Sea." Thus it may be that when death comes, although you are annihilated as an individual and the dewdrop is lost in the sea, you at the same time return to the realization of what you have always essentially been: the drop recognizes itself to be not merely the drop it thought it was, but the *Sea*. So to the question "What will we be after death?", the answer may be given, "Everything and nothing."

Epilogue:

Alive in Your Life

At the beginning of this book I made the assertion that in our usual dream state, we are neither really awake nor fully alive. From this point of departure, I argued that until we become aware while dreaming that we *are* dreaming, we remain asleep within our sleep, and thus the third of our life that lies in the domain of sleep and dreams is all but lost to us. But fortunately, as every reader must know by now, this is not an unalterable condition, because we can develop the capacity to be awake in our dreams.

It is likely that what has already been said regarding the sleeping third of your life may apply, in equal measure, to the other two-thirds—the state you call "awake." Let us begin with some of the applications and implications the experience of lucid dreaming suggests for everyday life.

To what extent are the concepts of lucid dreaming relevant to waking life? The answer is that the attitudes characterizing lucid dreaming have certain parallels with an approach to life that might be called "lucid living." To gain a clearer concept of what this intriguing term entails, we can proceed by analogy, examining some of the contrasting attitudes and assumptions associated with lucid versus non-lucid dreaming.[1]

The most basic way in which the attitudes of lucid and non-lucid dreamers differ is derived from the very definition of lucidity.

During non-lucid dreaming, you tacitly assume that you are awake; during lucid dreaming, you know you are asleep and dreaming. I believe the corresponding pair of attitudes in the waking state to be as follows. On one hand, you might be making the non-lucid assumption that you are objectively experiencing reality. According to this point of view, perception seems a straightforward matter of looking through the windows of your eyes and simply seeing what is out there. Unfortunately, this traditional, "commonsense" view seems clearly inconsistent with the findings of modern psychology and neurophysiology. What you see is not "what is out there"; in fact, it isn't even "out there." What you see is only a mental model inside your head of what you perceive or believe is "out there." The lucid understanding of the nature of perception is derived from current knowledge about how the brain works. If you would like to follow this approach, I recommend the working hypothesis that your experiences are necessarily *subjective*: they are the results of your own construction based upon your current motivational state as well as what you see and believe of reality. In terms of visual perception, this point of view accounts for the optical illusions that can occur as a result of our expectations about the world, as well as how emotions can distort perception—causing, for instance, the camper to see "every bush as if a bear," and the lover to see "the beloved in every tree." To summarize, the more correct analysis of perception is that we do not experience reality directly, but rather through our models of the world. Thus, before we can see what is "out there," the visual information from our eyes must pass through a host of subjective factors such as expectations, feelings, concepts, values, attitudes, and goals. It is unavoidable that our models of the world limit what we experience of reality; the more distorted our maps, the more distorted the territory will seem.

A related pair of attitudes would be the tendency, while non-lucid, to assume passively that the events of a dream are "just happening to you," versus your realization, while lucid, that *you* are actively creating, or at least significantly contributing to, what happens in your dream. The corresponding waking state attitudes are exactly parallel. What was just said of your dream state applies equally to your waking state, if you substitute "experience" for "dream."

As a consequence of this passive attitude while non-lucid, you might hold the belief that the rules of your dream game are entirely determined by an external reality principle. As a non-lucid dreamer, you would thus remain earthbound due to your belief that gravity is a universal law of physics—even in your own dream. But if you are lucid enough to know that dream gravity is a mere convention, you are free to take it or leave it, flying at will. Lucid dreamers regard other "laws" of the dream world in a similar fashion—as self-made rules that could well be changed if there were a reason to do so. Here, the corresponding attitudes in the waking state do not translate as directly as those we have so far considered. In this case, I believe the non-lucid attitude is that the situation you are experiencing is defined and determined by external factors generally beyond your power to alter to any significant extent; if you hold this view, other people and the accidents of fate determine what happens to you. In contrast, the lucid attitude is that *you* define how you experience the situations of your life. So whether you view a given dream as a nightmare or an opportunity for self-integration is up to you, just as whether you view a given situation in your waking life as a trial or a challenge.

A final pair of contrasting attitudes is the mindfulness that distinguishes lucidity from its contrary. Mindless habit is not necessarily an undesirable condition, although habitual mindlessness undoubtedly is. The main advantage that conscious behavior offers over habitual behavior is increased flexibility. However, if the situation is one of relatively constant circumstances that demand unchanging responses, habit is a more economical approach. Mindless responses are fine, as long as they fit the situation. However, if the situation is one of relative unpredictability or novelty, being mindful—knowing what you are doing—will more likely be advantageous.

Life presents us all with a mixture of the expected and the unexpected; whichever you get, it is obviously important for you to be able to respond with your most adaptive form of behavior. Since mindlessness and habit are easy, while mindfulness and consciousness require effort, you are far more likely to fall short in the areas demanding consciousness than you are likely to be *too* mindful when you should be automatic, although this also can happen. It is therefore likely that you would benefit from an improvement in your capacity to be conscious. Because mindfulness or lucidity seems harder to attain in the dream than in the waking state, practice in lucid dreaming should be especially effective in improving your waking capacity for mindfulness.

Idries Shah, the foremost contemporary exponent of Sufism, was once asked to name "a fundamental mistake" that most people make. He replied: "To think that [we are] alive, when [we have] merely fallen asleep in life's waiting room."[2]

It is a traditional doctrine of esoteric psychologies that the ordinary state or consciousness we call "waking" is so far from seeing things as they are in "objective reality" that it could be more accurately called "sleep" or "dreaming." Bertrand Russell comes to much the same conclusion by a very different path: "If modern physics is to be believed," the philosopher writes, "the dreams we call waking perceptions have only a very little more resemblance to objective reality than the fantastic dreams of sleep."[3]

Philosophers aside, if you were asked, "Are you awake *now?*" you would probably reply, "Certainly!" Unfortunately, feeling certain that we are awake provides no guarantee that we *are* awake. When Samuel Johnson kicked a stone as if to say, "We *know* what's real," he was expressing this sense of certainty. Yet Dr. Johnson could have *dreamed* he kicked a stone and felt the same. The illusory sense of certainty about the completeness and coherence of our lives leads us to what William James described as a "premature closing of our accounts with reality."[4]

How do you know that you are awake right now? You may say you remember waking up from your last night's sleep. But that may merely have been a "false awakening," and you may fool yourself now by dreaming that you are not dreaming anymore. Perhaps what we take to be "true awakenings" are really just another degree of partial or false awakenings. A novelist has similarly argued:

> Why, my friend, should these successive degrees not exist? I have often dreamt that I was awakening from a dream, and in a dream I have reflected on the preceding dream: on waking, I was then able to reflect on my two dreams. Owing to its greater clearness, the second one was a sort of waking in relation of the first. And as for this real waking, who is to say that it will not appear to me as a dream one day in its turn in relation to an even clearer view of the sequence of things? . . . So many things here below remain confused and obscure to us; it is impossible that the true waking state lies here.[5]

Once more, let us try to really ask ourselves, "Are we awake?" You will note how difficult it is to genuinely raise the question. To ask sincerely whether we are really awake requires honest doubt—however slight. And this is no easy matter for most of us. But doubting the indubitable is the business of philosophers. As Nietzsche put it, " . . . the man of philosophic turn has foreboding that underneath this reality in which we live and have our being, another and altogether different reality lies concealed, and that therefore it is also an appearance."[6] Indeed, Schopenhauer considered his own propensity at times to regard both people and things "as mere phantoms and dream-pictures" as the very criterion of philosophic ability.[7]

How might we not be fully awake? It may be that we possess a higher sense (let us say, a form of intuition) that ordinarily remains asleep when our lesser, though better known, senses awake. Thus, as was suggested above, the experience we call "awakening" and consider complete may in fact be only a partial awakening. As Orage has written,

> It may be feared that there is something morbid in the foregoing speculations; and that an effort to see our waking life as merely a special form of sleep must diminish its importance for us and ours for it. But this attitude towards a possible and probable fact is itself morbidly timid. The truth is that just as in night-dreams the first symptom of waking is to suspect that one is dreaming, the first symptom of waking from the waking state—the second awaking of religion—is the suspicion that our present waking state is dreaming likewise. To be aware that we are only partially awake is the first condition of becoming and making ourselves more fully awake.[8]

Given the virtual impotence of mere philosophical reasoning to raise the genuine suspicion that we are only partially awake, it is fortunate that there is another, more effective, means of approaching the question. This other approach, as will by now come as no surprise, is lucid dreaming. Lucid dreams can plainly show us what it is like to think we are awake and then to discover we are not. J. H. M. Whiteman's book, *The Mystical Life*, provides an example of the most extreme form this discovery can take. Professor Whiteman exlained that he thought his nocturnal mystical experience was stimulated by the meditative state in which he listened to the performance of a celebrated string quartet on the previous evening. The concert so moved him that for a few moments, he seemed to be "rapt out of space by the extreme beauty of the music," and for a little while was caught up in "a new state of contemplation and joy." Afterward, Whiteman remembered going to bed "peacefully composed and full of a quiet joy." With day residue like this, we may well imagine he was about to have an interesting night! His first dream of the night appeared, at the beginning, to be rather irrational. "I seemed," he wrote, "to move smoothly through a region of space where, presently, a vivid sense of cold flowed in on me and held my attention with a strange interest. I believe that at that moment the dream had become lucid. Then suddenly, . . . all that up to now had been wrapped in confusion instantly passed away, and a new space burst forth in vivid presence and utter reality, with perception free and pin-pointed as never before; the darkness itself seemed alive. The thought that was then borne in upon me with inescapable conviction was this: 'I have never been awake before.'"[9] It is unusual for lucid dreamers to be driven as far as Whiteman's conviction of never having been awake before. But it is not at all unusual for lucid dreamers to experience similar feelings in reference to their previous dream lives. In fact, this is how the first experience of extended lucidity strikes most people; they are astonished to realize that they have never before been awake in their dreams.

Lucid dreaming can be a point of departure from which to understand how we might not be fully awake—for as ordinary dreaming is to lucid dreaming, so the ordinary waking state might be to the fully awakened state. This capacity of lucid dreams, to prepare us for a fuller awakening, may prove to be lucid dreaming's most significant potential for helping us become more alive in our lives.

At the beginning of this book, I spoke of a treasure of incalculable value: a precious jewel. If you find it, "you come into a permanent endowment and bequest of knowledge . . .": you discover the secret of who you really are. Lucid dreaming may have something to contribute to your finding yourself, as does this ancient traditional tale, which is said to contain all wisdom in its various levels of interpretation:

THE PRECIOUS JEWEL

In a remote realm of perfection, there was a just monarch who had a wife and a wonderful son and daughter. They all lived together in happiness.

One day the father called his children before him and said:

'The time has come, as it does for all. You are to go down, an infinite distance, to another land. You shall seek and find and bring back a precious Jewel.'

The travellers were conducted in disguise to a strange land, whose inhabitants almost all lived a dark existence. Such was the effect of this place that the two lost touch with each other, wandering as if asleep.

From time to time they saw phantoms, similitudes of their country and of the Jewel, but such was their condition that these things only increased the depth of their reveries, which they now began to take as reality.

When news of his children's plight reached the king, he sent word by a trusted servant, a wise man:

'Remember your mission, awaken from your dream, and remain together.'

With this message they roused themselves, and with the help of their rescuing guide they dared the monstrous perils which surrounded the Jewel, and by its magic aid returned to their realm of light, to remain in increased happiness for evermore.[10]

The Future of Lucid Dreaming

The art and science of lucid dreaming, as readers of this book will be aware, is still in its infancy. Although we have learned enough about this extraordinary state of consciousness to be intrigued by its exciting potential, there is much more yet to be discovered. Much of this exploration can be carried out by adventurous individuals, developing and testing techniques for traveling in and using this new world of lucid dreaming. Other work requires modern technology, though there are as yet only a few laboratories engaged in this endeavor. One of these is the Stanford University Sleep Research Center, where we currently have a three part research program in progress with the following major goals:

- To further investigate the phenomenology and physiology of lucid dreaming.
- To develop improved techniques for inducing, stabilizing, and utilizing lucid dreams.
- To continue to map the psychophysiological relationships within REM connecting subjectively experienced dream events and objectively measured physiological processes.

An Invitation

We are seeking financial support for our research and would welcome your fund-raising ideas and inquiries. If you would like to become involved in the exploration of lucid dreaming, there are several ways you can participate. If you contact us at the address below, we will be able to inform you about the various activities in which you may participate, such as correspondence courses, lectures, weekend workshops, and research projects. We look forward to hearing from you. Please write to:

Lucidity Project
P.O. Box 2364
Stanford, CA 94305

~~~~~~~~~~~~~~~~~

Notes

Chapter 1

1. Sparrow, G. S., *Lucid Dreaming: The Dawning of the Clear Light* (Virginia Beach: A.R.E. Press, 1976), pp. 26–27.

2. Tulku, T., *Openness Mind* (Berkeley: Dharma Publishing, 1978), p. 74.

3. Shah, I., *Wisdom of the Idiots* (New York: Dutton, 1971), pp. 122–23.

4. Tulku, op. cit., p. 77.

5. Fabricius, J., "The symbol of the self in the alchemical 'proiectio,' " *Journal of Analytical Psychology*, 18 (1973): 41–58.

Chapter 2

1. Aristotle, *On Dreams*, from Hutchings, R. M., ed., *Great*

Books of the Western World, vol. 8 (Chicago: Encyclopedia Britannica, 1952), pp. 702–06.

2. Kelsey, M. T., *God, Dreams and Revelation* (New York: Augsburg, 1974), p. 264–265.

3. Evans-Wentz, W. Y., *Tibetan Yoga and Secret Doctrines* (London: Oxford University Press, 1935), pp. 221–22.

4. deBecker, R., *The Understanding of Dreams* (London: Allen & Unwin, 1965), p. 153.

5. Shah, I., *The Sufis* (London: Octagon Press, 1964), p. 141.

6. Aquinas, St. Thomas, *Summa Theologica,* vol. 1 (New York: Benziger Brothers, 1947), p. 430.

7. Freud, S., *The Interpretation of Dreams* (New York: Avon Books, 1965), p. 93.

8. Saint-Denys, H., *Dreams and How to Guide Them* (London: Duckworth, 1982).

9. Freud, op. cit., p. 93.

10. McCreery, C., *Psychical Phenomena and the Physical World* (Oxford: Institute of Psychophysical Research, 1973), p. 88.

11. Myers, F. W. H., "Automatic Writing—3," *Proceedings of the Society for Psychical Research* 4, part II (1887): 241–42.

12. Mach, E., *The Analysis of the Sensations,* 2nd ed. (Jena: Fisher, 1900), pp. 114–15.

13. deBecker, op. cit., p. 139.

14. Freud, op cit., p. 611.

15. Ibid.

16. Ibid.

17. van Eeden, F., "A study of dreams," *Proceedings of the Society for Psychical Research* 26 (1913): 431–61.

18. Ibid.

19. Ibid.

20. Ibid.

21. Green, C., *Lucid Dreams* (Oxford: Institute for Psychophysical Research, 1968), pp. 142–43.

22. Arnold-Forster, M., *Studies in Dreams* (London: Allen & Unwin, 1921), p. x.

23. Fox, O., *Astral Projection* (New Hyde Park, N.Y.: University Books, 1962), pp. 32–33.

24. Ibid., p. 34.

25. Ouspensky, P., *A New Model of the Universe* (London: Routledge & Kegan Paul, 1931, 1960), p. 272.

26. Ibid., p. 274.

27. Ibid., p. 279–80.

28. Moers-Messmer, H. von, "Traume mit der gleichzeitigen Erkenntnis des Traumzustandes," *Archiv für Psychologie*, 102 (1938): 291–318. (Translated by Beth Mügge.)

29. Ibid.

30. Ibid.

31. Rapport, N., "Pleasant Dreams!" *Psychiatric Quarterly* 22 (1948): 309–17.

Chapter 3

1. Loomis, A. L.; Harvey, E. N.; and Hobart, G., "Cerebral states during sleep as studied by human brain potentials," *Journal of Experiential Psychology*, 21 (1937): 127–44.

2. Blake, H; Gerard, R. W.; and Kleitman, N., "Factors influencing brain potentials during sleep," *Journal of Neurophysiology* 2 (1939): 48–60.

3. Aserinsky, E. and Kleitman, N., "Regularly occurring periods of eye motility and concomitant phenomena during sleep," *Science*, 118 (1953): 273–74.

4. Vogel, G.; Foulkes, D.; and Trosman, H., "Ego functions and dreaming during sleep onset," *Archives of General Psychiatry* 14 (1966): 238–48.

5. Named in honor of radio pioneer Heinrich R. Hertz, the Hertz is today the internationally accepted unit of frequency equivalent to cycles per second.

6. Green, C., *The Decline and Fall of Science* (London: Hamish Hamilton, 1976), p. 109.

7. Ibid., p. 110–11.

8. Faraday, A., *The Dream Game* (New York: Harper & Row, 1976), p. 263.

9. DeMille, R. E., *Castaneda's Journey: The Power and the Allegory* (Santa Barbara: Capra Press, 1976).

10. Tact usually prevents me from giving expression to these latter reflections publicly. However, fictional characters have no need to mince words, and several years ago, when I asked "don Juan" what he thought of the latest Carlos Castaneda book, *The Eagle's Gift,* he laughed uncontrollably and bluntly replied: "Bird droppings." I hope Dr. Castaneda, the author, appreciates the sense of humor he gave his creation. But then, as the saying goes, "None learned the art of archery from me who did not make me, in the end, their target."

11. Malcolm, N., *Dreaming* (London: Routledge & Kegan Paul, 1959).

12. Ibid., p. 48–50

13. Ibid., p. 50.

14. Hartmann, E., "Dreams and other hallucinations: an approach to the underlying mechanism," from Siegal, R. K. and West, L. J., eds., *Hallucinations* (New York: John Wiley & Sons, 1975), p. 74.

15. Berger, R., *Psychosis: The Circularity of Experience* (San Francisco: W. H. Freeman & Co., 1977), p. 121.

16. Rechtschaffen, A., "The single-mindedness and isolation of dreams," *Sleep* 1 (1978): 97–109.

17. Dement, W., "Report IV(B): Comments to Report IV" from Lairy, G. C., and Salzarilo, P., eds., *The Experimental Study of Human Sleep: Methodological Problems* (Amsterdam: Elsevier, 1975), p. 290.

18. Schwartz, B. A. and Lefebvre, A., "Contacts veille/ P.M.O. II. Les P.M.O. morceleés." *Revue d'Electroencephalographie et de Neurophysiologie Clinique* 1 (1973): 165–76.

19. The APSS changed its name to the SRS (Sleep Research Society) in 1983, and back to the APSS in 1986.

20. Foulkes, D. and Griffen, M., "An experimental study of 'creative dreaming,' " *Sleep Research*, 5 (1976): 129; Griffen, M. and Foulkes, D., "Deliberate presleep control of dream content: An experimental study," *Perceptual and Motor Skills*, 45 (1977): 660–62.

21. Ogilvie, R.; Hunt, H.; Sawicki, C.; and McGowan, K., "Searching for lucid dreams," *Sleep Research*, 7 (1978): 165.

22. Tart had not thought of using lucid dreamers as on-the-scene reporters from the dream world. This addition was in fact proposed by Celia Green, in *Lucid Dreams* (Oxford: Institute for Psychophysical Research, 1968), p. 130.

23. Roffwarg, H.; Dement, W.; Muzio, J.; and Fisher, C., "Dream imagery: Relationship to rapid eye movements of sleep," *Archives of General Psychology*, 7 (1962): 235–58.

24. LaBerge, S., "Lucid dreaming: some personal observations," *Sleep Research*, 8 (1979): 158.

25. Worsley, A., Personal communication, 1981.

26. Worsley, A., "Personal experiences of lucid dreaming," from Gackenbach, J. I. and LaBerge, S. P., eds., *Lucid Dreaming: New Research on Consciousness During Sleep* (New York: Plenum, in press.)

Chapter 4

1. Hall, C., "Do we dream during sleep? Evidence for the Goblot hypothesis," *Perceptual and Motor Skills*, 53 (1981): 239—46.

2. LaBerge, S. P. "Psychological parallelism in lucid dreams," from Ahsen, A.; Dolan, A. T.; and Jordan C. S., eds., *Handbook of Imagery Research and Practice* (New York: Brandon House, in press).

3. LaBerge, S. P. and Dement, W. C., "Voluntary control of respiration during REM sleep," *Sleep Research*, 11 (1982): 107.

4. LaBerge, S. P. and Dement, W. C., "Lateralization of

alpha activity for dreamed singing and counting during REM sleep,'' *Psychophysiology,* 19 (1982): 331–32.

5. LaBerge, S. P.; Greenleaf, W.; and Kedzierski, B., ''Physiological responses to dreamed sexual activity during lucid REM sleep,'' *Psychophysiology,* 20 (1983): 454–55.

Chapter 5

1. Faraday, A., *The Dream Game* (New York: Harper & Row, 1976), pp. 39–40.

2. Fox, O., *Astral Projection* (New Hyde Park, N.Y.: University Books, 1962), p. 90.

3. Gillespie, G., ''Lucidity language: A personal observation,'' *Lucidity Letter* 1(4) (1982): 5.

4. Ouspensky, P., *A New Model of the Universe* (London: Routledge & Kegan Paul, 1931, 1960) p. 281.

5. Green, C., *Lucid Dreams* (Oxford: Institute for Psychophysical Research, 1968), p. 85.

6. Garfield, P., *Creative Dreaming* (New York: Ballantine Books, 1974), p. 143.

7. McCreery, C., *Psychical Phenomena and the Physical World* (London: Hamish Hamilton, 1973), p. 114.

8. Garfield, P., *Pathway to Ecstasy* (New York: Holt, Rinehart & Winston, 1979), pp. 134–35.

9. McCreery, op. cit., p. 91.

10. Rapport, N., ''Pleasant Dreams!'' *Psychiatric Quarterly* 22 (1948): 309–17.

11. Faraday, A., *The Dream Game* (New York: Harper & Row, 1976), p. 334.

12. Yram, *Practical Astral Projection* (New York: Samuel Weiser, 1967), p. 113.

13. Fox, op. cit., p. 32–33.

14. Green, op. cit., p. 99.

15. Ibid., p. 100.

16. Fox, op. cit., p. 43–44.

17. Garfield, op. cit., p. 45.

18. Gackenbach, J. and Schillig, B., "Lucid dreams: the content of waking consciousness occurring during the dream," unpublished paper.

19. Fox, op. cit., p. 35–6.

20. Sparrow, G. S., *Lucid dreaming: the dawning of the clear light* (Virginia Beach: A.R.E. Press, 1976), p. 13.

21. Yram. op. cit., p. 113.

22. Ouspensky, op. cit., p. 282.

23. McCreery, op. cit., pp. 118–19.

24. Pompeiano, O. and Morrison, A. R., "Vestibular influences during sleep, I. Abolition of the rapid eye movements of desynchronized sleep following vestibular lesions," *Archives Italiennes de Biologie,* 103 (1965): 564–95.

25. Lerner, B., "Dream function reconsidered," *Journal of Abnormal Psychology,* 72 (1967): 85–100.

26. Tart, C., *Altered States of Consciousness* (New York: E. P. Dutton, 1975), p. 63.

27. Ghose, Sri Auribindo, *The Life Divine*, vol. 18 (Pondicherry, India: Sri Aurobindo Press, 1970), p. 425.

Chapter 6

1. Evans-Wentz, W. Y., ed., *The Yoga of the Dream State* (New York: Julian Press, 1964), p. 216.

2. Rajneesh, B. S., *The Book of the Secrets—I* (New York: Harper & Row), 1974, p. 118.

3. Ibid., p. 144–45.

4. DeRopp, R., *The Master Game* (New York: Dell, 1968), p. 61.

5. Rajneesh, op. cit., p. 142.

6. Tholey, P., "Techniques for inducing and maintaining lucid dreams," *Perceptual and Motor Skills* 57 (1983): 79–90.

7. Tulku, T., *Openness Mind* (Berkeley: Dharma Publishing, 1978), p. 136.

8. Tholey, op. cit.

9. McCreery, C., *Psychical Phenomena and the Physical World* (London: Hamish Hamilton, 1973), p. 86.

10. Garfield, P., "Psychological concomitants of the lucid dream state," *Sleep Research,* 4 (1975) 184.

11. Tart, C., "From spontaneous event to lucidity: A review of attempts to consciously control nocturnal dreaming," from Wolman, B. B., ed., *Handbook of Dreams* (New York: Van Nostrand Reinhold, 1979), p. 261.

12. Castaldo, V. and Holtzman, P., "The effect of hearing one's voice on sleep mentation," *The Journal of Nervous and Mental Disease* 144 (1967): 2–13.

13. Dement, W. and Wolpert, E., "The relation of eye movements, body motility, and external stimuli to dream content," *Journal of Experimental Psychology* 55 (1958): 543—53.

Chapter 7

1. Green, E.; Green, A.; and Walters, D., "Biofeedback for mind-body self-regulation: Healing and creativity," from *Fields Within Fields . . . Within Fields* (New York: Stulman, 1972), p. 144.

2. Ibid.

3. MacKenzie, N., *Dreams and Dreaming* (New York: Vanguard, 1965), p. 83.

4. Jaffe, D. T. and Bresler, D. E., "The use of guided imagery as an adjunct to medical diagnosis and treatment," *Journal of Humanistic Psychology,* 20 (1980): 45–59.

5. Levitan, H., "Failure of the defensive functions of the ego in dreams of psychosomatic patients," *Psychotherapy and Psychosomatics* 36 (1981) 1–7.

6. Van Eeden, F., "A study of dreams," *Proceedings of the Society for Psychical Research* 26 (1913): 431–61.

7. Ibid.

8. McCreery, C., *Psychic Phenomena and the Physical World* (London: Hamish Hamilton, 1973), pp. 102–04.

9. Freud, S., "Fragment of an analysis of a case of hysteria," from *Standard Edition of the Complete Psychological Works of Sigmund Freud* (London: Hogarth Press, 1953), p. 68.

10. Freud, S., "Introductory lectures on psychoanalysis," from *Standard Edition of the Complete Psychological Works of Sigmund Freud,* vol. 15 (London: Hogarth Press, 1916–17), p. 222.

11. Kedrov, B. M., "On the question of scientific creativity," *Voprosy Psikologii,* 3 (1957): 91–113.

12. Kaempffert, W., *A Popular History of American Invention,* vol. II (New York: Charles Scribner's Sons, 1924), p. 385.

13. Dement, W., *Some Must Watch While Some Must Sleep* (San Francisco: W. H. Freeman, 1972), p. 101.

14. Faraday, A., *Dream Power* (New York: Coward, McCann & Geoghegan, 1972), p. 303.

15. Dement, op. cit., p. 102.

16. Steiner, S. S. and Ellman, S. J., "Relation between REM sleep and intracranial self-stimulation," *Science* 177 (1972): 1122–24.

17. Rhinegold, H., "Tapping into Your Dream Power," *Oui Magazine* (1981): 80–125.

Chapter 8

1. Hobson, J. A. and McCarley, R. W., "The brain as a dream-state generator: An activation-synthesis hypothesis of the dream process," *American Journal of Psychiatry* 134 (1977): 1335–48.

2. Freud, S., "Introductory lectures on psychoanalysis," from *Standard Edition of the Complete Psychological Works of Sigmund Freud,* vol. 15 (London: Hogarth Press, 1916–17), p. 153.

3. Hobson & McCarley, op. cit.

4. Goleman, D., "Do dreams really contain important secret meaning?" *New York Times,* July 10, 1984.

5. Ibid.

6. Kiesler, E., "Images of the night," *Science,* 80 (1980): 1436–43.

7. Hobson, J. A., "The reciprocal interaction model of sleep cycle control: A discussion in the light of Giuseppe Moruzzi's concepts," from Pompeiano, O. and Marsan, C. Ajmone, eds., *Brain Mechanisms and Perceptual Awareness* (New York: Raven Press, 1981), p. 398.

8. Durgnat, R. and Hobson, J. A., "Dream dialogue," *Dreamworks* 2 (Fall 1981): 76–87.

9. Crick, F. and Mitchison, G., "The function of dream sleep," *Nature* 304 (1983): 111–14.

10. Melnechuck, T., "The dream machine," *Psychology Today* 17 (1983): 22–34.

11. Roffwarg, H. P.; Muzio, J. N.; and Dement, W. C., "Ontogenic development of the human sleep-dream cycle," *Science* 152 (1966): 604–19.

12. Greenberg, R. and Pearlman, C., "Cutting the REM nerve: An approach to the adaptive role of REM sleep," *Perspectives in Biology and Medicine* 17 (1974): 513–21.

13. Cohen, H. and Dement, W. C., "Sleep: Changes in threshold to electroconvulsive shock in rats after deprivation of 'paradoxical' phase," *Science* 150 (1965): 1318–19.

14. Hartmann, E., *The Function of Sleep* (New Haven: Yale University Press, 1973).

15. Dallet, J., "Theories of dream function," *Psychological Bulletin* 6 (1973): 408–16.

16. Rossi, E. L., *Dreams and the Growth of Personality* (New York: Pergamon, 1972), p. 142.

Chapter 9

1. Nietzsche, F., "Misunderstanding of the dream," Aphorism #5, *Human All Too Human* from Kaufman, W. ed., *The Portable Nietzsche* (New York: Viking Press, 1954), p. 52.

2. Celia Green (1967) asked two samples of undergraduates from two British universities whether they had ever had an "experience in which you felt you were 'out of your body.' "

She received 19 percent positive responses out of 115 subjects in the first sample, and 34 percent positive responses out of 380 in the second. Hornell Hart (1954) received 27 percent positive replies from 155 Duke University sociology students, while Charles Tart (1971) received 44 percent positive responses from 150 experienced marijuana users. From D. S. Rogo, ed., *Mind Beyond the Body* (New York: Penguin, 1978) p. 36.

3. Rhine, L. E., "Psychological processes in ESP experiences. Part II, Dreams," *Journal of Parapsychology* 26 (1962): 172–99.

4. Sheils, D., "A cross-cultural study of beliefs in out-of-the-body experiences, waking and sleeping," *Journal of the Society for Psychical Research,* 49 (1978): 691–741.

5. Priestley, J. B., *Man and Time* (London: Aldous Books, 1964), p. 225–26.

6. Ullman, M. and Krippner, S., *Dream Telepathy* (New York: MacMillan, 1973), p. 111.

7. Of the 13 experimental studies carried out, 9 yielded statistically significant results. Replications in laboratories elsewhere yielded less consistent results: two were positive, three negative, and one equivocal.

8. Rogo, D. S., "Introduction: Autobiographical Accounts," from Rogo, D. S., ed., *Mind Beyond the Body* (New York: Penguin, 1978), pp. 248–49.

9. Harary, S. B., "A personal perspective of out-of-body experiences," from Rogo, op. cit., pp. 248–49.

10. Ibid., pp. 356–57.

11. deBecker, R., *The Understanding of Dreams* (London: Allen & Unwin, 1965), p. 249.

12. Rowland, E., "A case of visual sensations during sleep," *The Journal of Philosophy* 6 (1909): 353–57.

13 Osis, K., "Perspectives for out-of-body research," *Parapsychology Research,* 3 (1973), 110–13.

14. deBecker, op. cit., pp. 394–95.

15. Fox, O., *Astral Travel* (New York: University Books, 1962), p. 47.

16. deBecker, op. cit., pp. 76–78.

Chapter 10

1. Freud, S., *Metapsychological Supplement to the Theory of Dreams*. Collected Papers, vol. IV (London: Hogarth, 1946) p. 137.

2. Faraday, A., *The Dream Game* (New York: Harper & Row, 1976), p. 267.

3. Mann, T., *The Magic Mountain* (New York: Vintage, 1969), p. 726.

4. Ibid., p. 495.

5. Ibid., p. 497.

6. Ibid., p. 727.

7. Moody, R., *Life After Life* (Atlanta: Mockingbird Books, 1977), pp. 23—24.

8. Gabbard, G. O.; Twenlow, S. T.; and Jones, F. C., "Do 'near-death experiences' occur only near death?" *Journal of Nervous and Mental Disorders* 169/(6),(1981): 374–77.

9. Noyes, R., "Attitude changes following near-death experiences," *Psychiatry* 43 (1980): 234–41.

10. Bucke, R., quoted in James, W., *Varieties of Religious Experience* (New York: Collier Books, 1961), p. 314.

11. Ring, K., "The nature of personal identity in the near-death experience; Paul Brunton and the ancient tradition," *Anabiosis* 4(1) (1984): 3–20.

12. Evans-Wentz, W. Y., *Tibetan Yoga and Secret Doctrines* (London: Oxford University Press, 1935), p. 167.

13. Ibid., p. 166.

14. Ibid., p. 222.

15. Narayana, R., ed., *The Dream Problem and Its Many Solutions in Search After Truth*, vol. 1 (Delhi, India: Practical Medicine, 1922), p. 301–5.

16. Shah, I., *Wisdom of the Idiots* (London: Octagon Press, 1969), p. 122–23.

Epilogue

1. Dr. Judith Malamud has pursued a similar approach to "lucid living." See her chapter in Gackenbach, J. and LaBerge, S., eds., *Lucid Dreaming: New Research on Consciousness During Sleep.* (New York: Plenum, in press).

2. Shah, I., *Seekers After Truth* (London: Octagon Press, 1982), p. 33.

3. LaBerge, S., "Lucid dreaming: Directing the action as it happens," *Psychology Today* 15 (1981): 48–57.

4. James, W., *The Varieties of Religious Experience* (New York: Modern Library, 1929), p. 378–79.

5. Moritz, K. P., quoted in deBecker, R. *The Understanding of Dreams* (London: Allen & Unwin, 1965), p. 406.

6. Nietzsche, F., Quoted in deBecker, p. 138.

7. Ibid.

8. Orage, A. R., *Psychological Exercises* (New York: Samuel Weiser, 1930), p. 92.

9. Whiteman, J. H. M., *The Mystical Life* (London: Faber & Faber, 1961), p. 57.

10. Shah, I., *Thinkers of the East* (London: Octagon Press, 1971), p. 123.

Index

Actions, control of, 115–17
Activation-Synthesis model of
 dream process, 203–10
Active sleep. *See* REM sleep
Adaptive functions, 220–21
Alpha rhythm, 45–46, 51, 88,
 173–74
Altered States of Consciousness
 (Tart), 56–57
Anomaly, 121–22, 123, 233
Anxiety dreams, 181–84
Anxiety reduction, 180–85, 191
Application(s) of lucid dreaming,
 3–6, 8–19, 167–96
 to anxiety reduction, 180–185
 to athletic performance, 189–
 190
 to creative problem solving,
 186–191
 to decision making, 185
 to health and healing, 169–79
Aquinas, Saint Thomas, 25
Archetypal images, 52

Aristotle, 20, 25
Arnold-Forster, Mary, 35, 182
Aserinsky, Eugene, 48
Association for the
 Psychophysiological Study of
 Sleep (APSS), 64–67, 70–74
Assumptions, effects of, 112–14
Astral projection. *See* Out-of-body
 experiences
Attention, focus of, 152
Attitudes, 273–76
Automatic behaviors, 220
Awakening, 118–20, 131–35,
 183–84, 276–78
Awareness, levels of, 107–108,
 120–28

Baudelaire, Charles, 19
Beethoven, Ludwig van, 5
Benefits of lucid dreaming, 8–18
Berger, Hans, 45–46
Bergman, Ingmar, 6
Bergmann, Ralph, 63

Bible, quoted, 105–106
Bioelectrical potentials of brain,
    42–47, 49–50
Biofeedback, 165
Bizarreness. *See* Anomaly
Black-and-white dreams, 9
Blake, William, 5, 194
Blavatsky, Helena Petrovna, 241
Body image, 241–42, 244
Brain. *See also* Brain activity
    brain stem dream state
        generator hypothesis, 203–
        209
    "reward" system of, 195
    sleep-inducing centers of, 46–
        47
Brain activity
    of cerebral cortex, 47, 88–89,
        207, 220
    cerebral hemisphere
        specialization, 79–81, 87–88
    electrical potentials and, 42–45,
        46–47
    during REM sleep, 14, 48–50
    of reticular formation, 46
Brain Information Service,
    UCLA, 50
Brain waves, 45, 51. *See also*
    Alpha rhythm; Delta waves;
    Electroencephalogram
    recordings; K-complexes;
    Sleep spindles
Breathing, 85–87
Brown, Alward Embury, 38
Browne, R. T., 153
Bruner, Jerome, 110–11
Bucke, Richard M., 260
Buddhism, 15, 17, 147–48, 201,
    261–72
Burton, Richard, 198

Calloway, Hugh (pseud. Fox,
    Oliver), 35–36, 101, 118,
    119, 122, 147, 248–49
Castaneda, Carlos, 58–59, 135
Caton, Richard, 43–44
Characters in dreams, 104–108,
    117

Childhood. *See* Development of
    concept of dreaming
Circadian rhythm, 214
Cognitive functioning, 108–10,
    217–18
Coleridge, Samuel Taylor, 5
Color in dreams, 9
Communication by lucid
    dreamers, 70–71, 77, 81–82,
    207
Compensation, 175
Conflict, 199–202, 204
Conscious action, 115–16
Consciousness, 2, 26, 103–104,
    121
    of dreaming, 7–8, 12–14 (*see
        also* Lucid dreaming)
    function of, 221
    memory and, 109
Control, 8
    of dreams, 27, 116–117
    of physiological functions, 173–
        174
Cook, Laurie, 71
Counting in lucid dreams, 81, 82,
    87–89, 149–150
Creative Dreaming (Garfield), 58,
    65–66
Creativity, lucid dreaming applied
    to, 5–6, 167–96, 225–26
Crick, Francis, 210–13, 224

Dallet, Janet, 219
Dane, Joe, 159–60
Darwin, Charles, 74–75, 214
Davidson, Julian, 69
Daydreaming, 38–39
Death, 258–66, 272
Decision making, 5, 185–86
Déjà rêvè, 124
Delage, Yves, 34, 130
Deliberate actions, 115
Delta waves, 53, 170, 174
Dement, William C., 48–49, 50,
    64, 68–69, 165, 192–93
Demon-dreams, 175–78
Deprivation of REM sleep, 213,
    217–18

deRopp Robert, 146

Detachment, 12, 107, 119, 121–28, 146

Developmental function, 219

Development of concept of dreaming, 139–140, 224, 236

Dream actor, 104–108

Dream characters, 102–108, 117

Dream duration, 81–84

Dream ego, 104–108

Dream journals 142

Dream recall, 141–143

Dream yoga. *See* Tibetan dream yoga

Dreaming (Malcolm), 60

Dreamlets, 150–51, 160

Dreams and How to Guide Them (Saint-Denys), 26–27

Dreamscape (film), 193

Drives, 110. *See also* Motivation

Drowsiness, brain waves during, 52

Dylan, Bob, 252

EEG, 45–46

Ego of dreamer, 264–69, 270–71

Electrical potentials of brain, 42–47, 49–50

Electro-oculogram (EOG) recordings, 48

Electroencephalogram (EEG) recordings, 45–46

Electromyogram (EMG) recordings, 50–54

Ellis, Havelock, 30

EMG, 50–54

Emotion, and lucidity, 121

Emotional adjustment, 218–19

conflict, 119–20

involvement, 119, 120–28

quality of lucid dreams, 118–20

Environmental stimuli, 160–64

Erotic dreams *See* Orgasms; Sexual activity

Erwin, William, 231

Evans, Christopher, 218

Evolution, and sleep, 214–16, 218

Exercise, physical, 170

Existential meaning of dreams, 222–23

Expectations, 110–14, 132–33

Experience of lucid dreaming, 9–13, 100–37

Experimental research. *See* Scientific research

Extrasensory perception, 228

Eye movements during dreaming, 48–49. *See also* REM sleep

as communication, 68–71, 75–77, 79–80, 207

sleep stages and, 50–54

unusual patterns of, 78–79

False awakenings, 129–31, 239, 277–78

Faraday, Ann, 57–58, 100–101, 255

Feedback, positive, 135

First experiences of lucidity, 9–11

Flexibility of behavior, 186, 218, 220–21, 276

Flying dreams, 90–92, 123, 223, 235

Foulkes, David, 66, 80

Fox, Oliver. *See* Calloway, Hugh

Freedom, sense of, 10, 36, 115–16, 118

Freud, Sigmund, 4, 18, 62, 180, 183–84, 220, 254

on lucid dreaming, 31–32

on meaning of dreams, 91–92, 198–203, 224

Functions of dreaming, 197–226

Gackenbach, Jayne, 120

Galvani, Luigi, 43

Garfield, Patricia, 65, 89, 113–14, 153, 156, 157, 195

Genital responses, 89–95

Gennadius, 21–22

Ghose, Sri Aurobindo, 136

Gleason, Adele, 247–48

Goethe, Johann von, 169
Green, Alyce, 168–69
Green, Celia, 55–56, 67, 113, 119
Green, Elmer, 168–69
Greenberg, Ramon, 217–18
Greenleaf, Walter, 89
Guest, Judith, 6

Habitual actions, 8, 115, 220–21, 276
Handel, George Frederick, 195
Harary, Keith, 233–34
Hartmann, Ernest, 63, 218–19
Healing. See also Health
  dream content and, 174–79
  hypnosis applied to, 172
  self-, 169–75
Health, 169–75, 218–19
Hearne, Keith, 75–77, 112, 165
Heraclitus, 50
History of lucid dreaming, 21–41
Hobson, Allan, 203–209
Howe, Elias, 5, 187–88
Hypnagogic state, 52, 127, 148, 168–69, 171
Hypnosis, 159, 172

Ibn El-Arabi, 25
Illumination level in dreams, 112–13
Illumination stage of creative process, 188–89
Image technique, 148
Imagery, 147–49, 155–56, 171
Imagination, 15, 23, 38–39, 96–97
Incubation stage of creative process, 188
Induction of lucid dreaming, 138–61
  MILD technique for, 155–58
Initiation of lucidity, 121–28
Instability of dreams, 122–23
Instinctive actions, 115
Institute of Psychophysical Research, 55
Intention, 152, 155, 156

Interpretation of dreams, 179
Interpretation of Dreams, The (Freud), 31
Intuition, 186

James, William, 277
Johnson, Samuel, 277
Jouvet, Michel, 216–17
Jung, Carl, 18, 174, 264

K-complexes, 52
Kamiya, Joe, 49
Kedzierski, Beverly, 71
Kekulé, Friedrich August, 5
Klee, Paul, 5
Kleitman, Nathaniel, 48–49, 50
Knowledge, types of, 185–86
Kramer, Milton, 208–209
Krippner, Stanley, 230
Kuhn, Thomas, 74

Laboratory research. See Scientific research
Landscapes of the Night: How and Why We Dream (Evans), 218
LaPlace, Pierre Simon, 65
Latent content of dreams, 201
Learning, 218–21
  of lucid dreaming, 2–3, 19, 28, 138–66
Lefebvre, A., 64
Lerner, B., 134
Levitan, Harold, 174
Life After Life (Moody), 256–57
Light in dreams, 112, 125
"Light-Switch" phenomenon, 112
"Limiting stabilization," 135
Loewi, Otto, 5
Lucid dreamers, 9–12, 129
  attitudes of, 273–76
  and dream characters, 104–108
  levels of awareness of, 107–108, 120–28
Lucid dreaming
  defined, 2–3
  developing interest in, 54–77

scientific researchers and, 61–77
Lucid Dreams (Green), 55–56
Lucidity, degrees of, 9

McCarley, Robert, 203–209
McCreery, Charles, 123
Mach, Ernst, 30, 33
Malcolm, Norman, 60–61
Mammals, 213–21
Manifest content of dream, 201
Mann, Thomas, 255–56
Manual of Standardized Terminology Techniques and Scoring System for Sleep Stages of Human Subjects, A (Rechtschaffen and Kales), 50–51
Maury, Alfred, 29–30, 62
Meaning of dreams, 197–98, 221–24
Meditation, 157, 263
Memory, 4, 109, 154, 204–205, 217–18. *See also* Recall of dreams and lucid dream initiation, 124, 154
Mendeleev, Dmitri, 187–88
Mental imagery, 147–48, 155–56, 171
Merton, Robert K., 74
Method of induction. *See* MILD
Meyers, Frederic W. H., 35
Microawakenings, defined, 64
MILD (Mnemonic Induction of Lucid Dreams), 71, 89, 126–27, 155–58
Milton, John, 244
Mind-body relationships, 5, 13, 98
Mindfulness, 276
Misconceptions, 14–15
Mitchison, Graeme, 210–13, 224
Mnemonic Induction of Lucid Dreams. *See* MILD
Moers-Messmer, Harold von, 38–40, 112, 134
Monsters in dreams, 175–178
Moody, Raymond, 256–257

Morning, REM sleep in, 155–56
Motivation, 110, 127, 141, 142, 144, 154, 157–58, 191–93
Motor skills, 189–90
Movement sensations, 131–34
Mozart, Wolfgang Amadeus, 5
Muscle paralysis in REM sleep, 68, 86–87, 216, 217, 238
Muscle tension, 51, 131–32
Mutual dreams, 228, 247–52
Myers, Frederic W. H., 28–29, 55
Mystical experiences, 260–61
Mystical Life, The (Whiteman), 278–79

Nagel, Lynn, 69–73, 161
Narayana, Ram, 265–67
Near-death experiences, 256–61, 271
Nicklaus, Jack, 6, 189–90
Nietzsche, Friedrich, 30–31, 175, 227, 237–38, 278
Nightmares, 121, 175–78, 180–85
Non-lucid dreaming, 3, 11, 194, 274–75
Noyes, R., 259
NREM (non-rapid eye movement) sleep, 14, 53–54, 157, 213–15
    lucid dreams during, 151, 160

OBES. *See* Out-of-body experiences
Orage, A. R., 138, 278
Orgasms, 89–95, 114, 195
Origin of Species (Darwin), 74–75
Osis, Karlis, 245–46
Ouspensky, Piotr D., 36–38, 40, 113, 127–28, 147, 148
Out-of-body experiences, 140, 228–29, 231–247, 257–58

Paradoxical sleep. *See* REM sleep
Parapsychology, 55–56, 227–52
Pathway to Ecstasy (Garfield), 89

Pearlman, Chester, 217–18
Perception
  expectations and, 110–12
  versus imagination, 15–16, 22–
    23, 94–97
  subjectivity of, 274–75, 276–77
  vividness of, 96, 120 (see also
    Vividness)
Personal growth, 3–5
Personality factors, 120
Physical health, 4–5
Physiological determinants of
    dreams, 197, 203–206, 209–
    10
Physiological reactions to dreams,
    5, 16, 49–50
Piaget, Jean, 139–40, 224
Pleasure, 194–95
Post-hypnotic suggestion, 159–61
Postman, L., 110–11
Practice, 143
Pre-lucid dreams, defined, 122
Precognitive dreams, 229–30
Premature awakening, 118–19
Preparation stage of creative
    process, 188
Pribram, Karl, 69
Problem solving, creative, 186–91
Psychological determinants of
    dreams, 197, 199–203, 206–
    209
Psychophysiological research, 49–
    50
Psychosomatic syndromes, 5, 174
Psychotherapeutic use of dreams,
    169–79

Rajneesh, Bhagwan Shree, 145,
    146
Rapid eye movement (REM)
    stage of sleep. See REM
    sleep
Rapport, Nathan, 40–41, 118,
    127, 147, 148
Reality, 15, 16, 227–28, 263–64,
    276–77
Rebirth, 9, 254–55

Recall of dreams, 3, 8, 205, 211–
    13, 224. See also Memory
Rechtschaffen, Allan, 63, 67
Reciprocal dreams, 228, 247–52
Rehearsal function, 191–94
Reiser, Morton, 205–206
Relaxation, 45, 71, 131–32
REM (rapid eye movement)
    sleep, 14, 46, 53–54, 151,
      157, 216, 217–19
  deprivation of, 213, 217–18
  dreams after varying periods of,
    82–83
  functions in mammals, 213–21
  lucid dreaming during, 70–71,
    156
  muscle paralysis during, 68,
    86–87, 216, 217, 238
  periods per night, 14
  scientific research on, 14, 78–
    99
  time between periods of, 53–54
  vestibular system and, 134
Repressed impulses, 202
Resnais, Alain, 6
Respiration in dreams, 85–87
Restorative function of sleep, 202
Reticular formation, 47
Reverse-learning theory, 210–13
Rhine, L. E., 231
Ring, Kenneth, 257, 259–60
Role-playing, 264–65
Rossi, Ernest, 219
Rowland, Eleanor, 238–39
Russell, Bertrand, 276–77

St. Augustine, 21, 23
Saint-Denys, Hervey de, 26–27,
    32, 33, 34, 38, 108–109,
    112, 115–16, 117, 152–53,
    176–78, 193–94
Saint-Saens, Charles Camille, 5
Scherner, Karl, 125
Schopenhauer, Arthur, 278
Schwartz, B. A., 64
Scientific research
  on dreaming, 48–77

Index

03

on lucid dreaming, 6, 13, 25–26, 78–99
on sleep, 42–49
Scientific researchers, attitudes of, 59–60, 62–67, 72–74
Self-
control, 115–17, 173–74
development, 3–5
discovery, 279–80
reflection, 102–103, 124–25
remembering, 145–46
Sensations of movement, 131–34
Sexual activity, 16, 81, 89–95, 114, 157
"Shadow element," 174–75
Shah, Idries, 276
Shared dreams, 228, 247–52
Shepard, Roger, 69
Shiels, Dean, 229
Simonton, Carl, 172
Singing in lucid dreams, 79, 80, 87–88
Sleep
functions of, 170, 215
onset of, 45, 47, 51, 149–52
stages of, 50–54
Sleep (journal), 67
Sleep spindles, 52
Smith, Roy, 71
Smoking reduction, 192–93
Society for Psychical Research, 28, 55
Sparrow, Scott, 10, 125, 134, 157
Spinning technique, 131–35
Stanford University Sleep Laboratory, 5, 13, 14, 69–72, 89–99
Stabilizing lucid dreams, 135
Stevenson, Robert Louis, 5
Stoyva, Johan, 49
Stress, and REM sleep, 170
Subjective experiences, 49–50, 249
Sufis, 25, 126, 249–51, 268, 276
Suggestion, 153–54, 159–62
post-hypnotic, 159–60
Sun, 215
Symbolic conflict resolution, 179

Symbolic interpretation, 205, 222, 223
Tantra, 24–25
Tariqavi, 268
Tart, Charles, 56–57, 68, 134–35
Tartini, Giuseppe, 5
Telepathic experiences, 229–31, 251. *See also* Mutual dreams
Termination of lucid dreams, 128–31
Tholey, Paul, 146–47, 148–49
Tibetan dream yoga, 23–25, 67, 117, 127, 144–45, 194, 261–64
Time in dreams, 79–84
Timing of lucid dreams, 151
Transcendence, 2, 272
Transcendental experiences, 268–72
Transformation of dream content, 262–63
Transpersonal identity, 270–72
Tulku, Tarthang, 15, 17, 147–48

UCLA Brain Information Service, 50
Ullman, Montague, 230
Unconscious, 4, 26, 199–203
"Unlearning" hypothesis, 210, 212–13

Validation of lucid dreaming, 70–71, 75–77
Van Eeden, Frederik Willems, 32–34, 57, 67, 156, 175
Verification stage of creative process, 188
Vestibular system of inner ear, 134
Visualization, 147–48, 155–56, 171
Vividness, 96–97, 103, 120, 172
Volta, Alessandro, 43
Voluntary action, 115–16

Wagner, Richard, 5, 17–18, 26
Wakefulness, 157
Waking. *See* Awakening

Waking life, 3–4, 11, 273, 276–
    77
Wallace, Alfred Russel, 74–75
Whiteman, J. H. M., 278–79
Whitman, Walt, 252–53
Wish fulfillment, 194–96
Wolpert, E., 165
Worsley, Alan, 75–77

Yoga. *See* Tibetan
    dream yoga *Yoga of the
    Dream State,
    The,* 144, 194
Yram, 118

Zarcone, Vincent, Jr., 69

About the Author

Psychophysiologist Stephen LaBerge, Ph.D., is a world-renowned pioneer in dream research and is currently engaged in lucid dreaming research at Stanford University.

GETTING HELP FROM YOUR DREAMS